D0849204

STRATEGIC POWER AND NATIONAL SECURITY

Strategic Power and National Security

J. I. Coffey

UNIVERSITY OF PITTSBURGH PRESS

TO MY FATHER

Library of Congress Catalog Card Number 75-158188
ISBN 0-8229-3229-6
Copyright © 1971, J. I. Coffey
Henry M. Snyder & Co., Inc., London
Manufactured in the United States of America

Contents

Tables

Preface

With the possible exception of the war in Vietnam, no subject has been so hotly debated in recent years as that of the relative priority to be accorded programs for "the common defense" as against those for "the general welfare." Many highly placed and well-informed Americans have argued that the growth of Soviet military capabilities, the advent of Communist China as a nuclear power, and the rapid changes in many parts of the globe pose threats to U.S. interests which necessitate powerful (and expensive) armed forces. Others, equally well qualified, maintain that the threats are exaggerated, that smaller (and less costly) forces would suffice to insure American security, and that valid domestic requirements have too long been sacrificed to marginal military ones.

This book represents an effort to address one part of that issue: the requirements for strategic nuclear forces. It has focused on these forces for three reasons: (1) the United States has recently begun several new weapons programs and is planning others, such as a new bomber and an underwater missile launch system, which would affect both the composition and the costs of strategic offensive and defensive forces for years to come; (2) there are still opportunities for making meaningful adjustments in those programs, either unilaterally or through the Strategic Arms Limitation Talks in which the United States and the USSR are now engaged; and (3) strategic nuclear forces play so important a role that any inquiry into American defense policy, any examination of American military requirements, must begin by looking at the implications for national security of various levels and types of strategic weapons systems.

As is true in most cases, this assessment of the relationship between strategic power and national security represents the culmination of years of work, the results of which have from time to time appeared in print. Although no section of the book consists merely of reprints, several have drawn heavily upon material published elsewhere. I should, therefore, like to make special mention of an article on "Strategic Superiority, Deterrence and Arms Control," which appeared in *Orbis*, XIII, no. 4 (Winter 1970) and formed the genesis of chapter 3; and of the paper "Threat, Reassurance, and Nuclear Proliferation" in Bennett Boskey and Mason Willrich, eds., *Nuclear Proliferation: Prospects for Control* (New York: Dunellen Publishing Co., 1970), which appears in part in chapter 5.

I should also like to acknowledge the assistance I have received on this book. Dr. Morton Halperin, currently with the Brookings Institution; Dr. Johann J. Holst of the Norwegian Institute of International Affairs; Captain Donald A. Mahley, United States Army; and Professor Frederick C. Thayer of the University of Pittsburgh all read the manuscript in draft, with varying degrees of pleasure. Captain Mahley, Mr. Jean Abinader, and Mr. Kenneth C. Thompson, all students in the Graduate School of Public and International Affairs of the University of Pittsburgh, helped with the research. Julianna Mahley was largely instrumental in producing seemingly innumerable drafts, and my wife, Rosemary K. Coffey, was responsible for editing the last of them. Finally, the LaSalle-Adams Fund paid for some of the research and typing. To all those contributors named—and others unnamed who also helped in one way or another—my thanks.

J. I. COFFEY

May 1971

STRATEGIC POWER AND NATIONAL SECURITY

1
Introduction

      As the Bible says, "There is a time for everything under the heavens," and this is a time for change. Although most calls for change have sounded on the domestic stage, they have also echoed in the foreign arena. Prominent Senators have demanded cuts in U.S. forces stationed overseas and have sought to impose new constraints on economic and military aid to American allies. Leading Congressmen have questioned the need for additional weapons systems; powerful mayors, the rationale for ongoing defense programs; and people from all fields and all walks of life, the balance between expenditures for national security and those for domestic well-being. Nor has the clamor gone unheard in the executive branch: President Nixon has cut down troop strength in Vietnam, has reduced the military budget, has announced changes in the defense policy formulated by the previous administration, and has initiated comprehensive studies which could induce further alterations in U.S. strategic concepts, force postures, and defense expenditures.

      The impetus to the revisions already made and to the reexamination still under way came not only from awareness of a shift in public attitudes, not only from the natural tendency of an incoming President to assert his own views on military matters, but also from new factors in the politico-military environment. One such factor is a significant increase in Soviet strategic forces, with the USSR for the first time surpassing the United States in numbers of intercontinental ballistic missiles (ICBMs).[1] A related factor is that innovations in weaponry make it theoretically possible for the USSR to destroy in place large numbers of American bombers and ICBMs, even as they enable the United States to multiply its own retaliatory capabilities through the introduction of MIRVs (multiple independently-targetable reentry vehicles) or to defend them through the deployment of antiballistic missiles (ABMs). Thus the recent—and continuing—changes in U.S. and Soviet strategic nuclear forces alone would make desirable a reassessment of programs for the future.

These are not, however, the only factors contributing to such a reassessment; the United States must also bear in mind that Communist China will develop a significant nuclear capability within the next decade. Even comparatively small forces might enhance China's prestige, increase its freedom of action, and pose problems for the United States should there be another confrontation in the Far East. And while the Chinese, beset by internal difficulties and embroiled with the USSR in both doctrinal and territorial disputes, are unlikely to challenge directly American interests or to threaten American allies, this does not rule out the necessity for considering the effectiveness—and the desirability—of measures to cope with Communist China's strategic strike forces.

This is even more true with respect to measures aimed at the USSR, which is at one and the same time a threat to and a partner of the United States. Even as it has built up its strategic strike forces, the Soviet Union has expressed willingness to consider limitations on such forces; even as it has introduced naval vessels into the eastern Mediterranean, it has cooperated with the United States in avoiding confrontations between its ships and those of the American Sixth Fleet. The desire of the Soviet leaders to avoid nuclear war, or conflicts likely to lead to war, has induced both caution in the exercise of their own military power and collaboration in efforts to restrain the use of force by others—as in the guarantees against nuclear aggression issued by the United States, the USSR, and the United Kingdom. Thus any review of strategic programs must take into account the impact on U.S.-Soviet relations of doing too much as well as the possible consequences of doing too little.

Another factor affecting the review is that of relations with America's allies, which have been thrown into some disarray by the growth and extension of Soviet power, by U.S. efforts to deal with the USSR, and by the political and military consequences of the war in Vietnam. To the extent that the allies are still fearful of Communist pressures, the United States must consider how to offer reassurance and support—hopefully without stimulating counteractions on the part of the USSR and Communist China. To the extent that the allies are worried over the potential consequences of a U.S.-Soviet *détente*, the United States must recognize that this limits the range and nature of agreements with the USSR on the reduction of armaments. And to the extent that Vietnam has absorbed American attention and resources, the United States is constrained in what it can do, either politically or militarily, to implement measures acceptable to the allies—if indeed any set of measures could gain universal allied acceptance.

This is equally a problem at home, where there is increasing opposition to the extent and scope of American commitments, to the forces and programs required to uphold them, and to the massive expenditures needed to support those forces. Partly because this is "the winter of our discontent," the Congress and the public have been participating in the review of military policies and programs to a far greater extent than on previous occasions. For this reason, among others, it is believed that a timely analysis of defense policies may be helpful in fixing the pattern for the next decade.

Obviously, any thorough analysis should cover the whole spectrum of U.S. defense policy, from that governing limited nuclear war in NATO to that dealing with assisting threatened allies to build more stable—and more responsive—governments. But such an analysis, which would involve consideration not only of military but of foreign policy, and not only of policy but of complex and costly programs, is perhaps too much for a single work. Moreover, many aspects of overall defense policy depend on decisions with respect to the size and the composition of strategic nuclear forces, that is, with respect to levels of strategic power. Just as the concept of massive retaliation shaped the force postures and the programs of the fifties, so concepts adopted today may shape those of the seventies—perhaps to an even greater extent. Hence, this study will focus primarily on the contributions of U.S. strategic nuclear forces to the achievement of relevant U.S. objectives —in other words, on strategic power and national security.

Even within this restricted context, however, a number of important and difficult questions must be answered:

1. Are strategic forces in the seventies to have uses other than that of deterring a nuclear attack on the United States? Should they, for example, be designed to *fight* nuclear wars? And should they also be relied upon to deter local aggression, or is their task simply to prevent the escalation of any conflicts involving the United States and another nuclear power?

2. What is likely to be the impact on Communist behavior of a shift in the strategic balance?* Is it true, as one eminent Sovietologist has suggested, that, if the USSR achieved even strategic parity, it might "be tempted to undertake a more extensive, more acute, and more dangerous range of risks in order to pursue its declared, long range ambition to reshape the world according to its own dogma"?[2] And are U.S. ballistic missile defenses necessary to preclude an "irrational" Communist China from initiating nuclear war during a crisis or a local confrontation with American troops?

3. To what extent can U.S. strategic nuclear forces instill a sense of security in America's allies? Does this depend on the size, the nature, and the capabilities of these forces or on other factors, such as the extent to which the allies have a voice in decisions on their use? Is even this enough, or will more and more countries attempt to safeguard their interests by building their own nuclear forces?

---

* Even though the Communists are not the only ones who cause problems for the United States, and even though in the long run the United States may face new and different opponents, the emphasis on *Communist* behavior in this question, and in the book as a whole, is warranted on two bases: (1) at the moment, U.S. defense policies and programs are oriented primarily toward coping with the threats to American interests posed by the Communist countries; and (2) two of these, the USSR and Communist China, possess nuclear weapons, and hence must be given "top billing" in any analysis of the requirements for, and the uses of, American strategic power.

4. To what extent may American procurement of new weapons systems—which Indian Ambassador V. C. Trivedi characterized as "vertical [nuclear] proliferation"—make control over nuclear weapons more difficult?[3] To what extent does this stimulate similar procurement by other countries? And if the United States wishes, in agreement with the USSR, to stop the arms race, what kinds of arrangements would both achieve this aim and enable this country to maintain adequate and effective strategic nuclear forces?

The answers to these questions—if they are in fact answerable —depend in part upon an evaluation of military and technical factors, such as the thrust and the accuracy of intercontinental ballistic missiles or the effectiveness of the over-the-horizon radar. But they depend in even larger measure upon an assessment of less tangible and more subjective elements. For instance, Secretary of Defense Melvin R. Laird has argued that the Chinese Communists, because of their predominantly rural society and their willingness to take great losses of life, might not be deterred by American strategic offensive forces.[4] If correct, this estimate could warrant the deployment of BMDs (ballistic missile defenses), but if erroneous it could have serious adverse consequences, among them that of stimulating the arms race. Thus views concerning the nature of deterrence, opinions as to probable Communist behavior, assessments of allied interest, and estimates of responses to shifts in American defense programs must all be considered, along with more largely military factors, in attempting to answer the questions posed earlier.

In subsequent chapters, I will first discuss the military-technical factors which affect the size and the composition of U.S. strategic nuclear forces; next I will talk about the political and psychological impacts of different levels of strategic power; and, finally, I will try to assess their implications for national security and national well-being. Admittedly, the coverage will be partial rather than complete and broad rather than detailed; not even the Pentagon, in a multivolume series, could do justice to every aspect of the problem. Hopefully, however, what is written here will suffice to illuminate alternatives and to provoke discussion of the issues, which is all that any author can ask.

2
The Backdrop

The Threat

For the past twenty years the United States has maintained strategic nuclear forces superior in size, in delivery capabilities, and in flexibility of response to those of the USSR; indeed, the rapid U.S. buildup of land- and sea-based missiles in the early 1960s gave it long-range strategic strike forces three or four times as large as those of the Soviet Union. Any hope, however, that the USSR might rest content with powerful but inferior strategic nuclear forces seems shattered by the events of the last few years. Between 1965 and 1970 the Soviet Union quintupled the number of ICBMs deployed and almost tripled its force of submarine-launched ballistic missiles (SLBMs), many of the additions being longer-range missiles on larger and quieter submarines. It has improved its antisubmarine warfare capabilities by building specialized escort vessels, by launching new attack submarines, and by commissioning two helicopter carriers—the first the USSR has ever had. It has strengthened its air defenses by the installation of both long-range, high-altitude surface-to-air missiles (SAMs) and the shorter-range but more flexible SAM-3, of which so much has been heard from the Middle East. Moreover, the Soviets not only have emplaced antiballistic missiles around Moscow but have pushed the development of advanced interceptors and of improved radar for ballistic missile defenses; in consequence, they could, as Secretary of Defense Laird testified, deploy "a

8

more extensive and effective ABM defense" around their cities, their weapons sites, or both.[1]

Although these measures have not, so far, affected the ability of the United States to maintain what its leaders consider an adequate deterrent, they have caused shifts in the strategic balance (see table 1). As President Nixon put it, "From 1950 to 1966, we [Americans] possessed an overwhelming superiority in strategic weapons. From 1967 to 1969, we retained a significant superiority. Today, the Soviet Union possesses a powerful and sophisticated strategic force approaching our own."[2]

More important than past shifts in the strategic balance is the prospect of future ones. If Soviet weapons programs continue at the rate estimated by the Department of Defense, by 1975 the USSR could not only double its 1970 ICBM forces but also equip its heavier missiles with MIRVs; even a so-called "low force-low technology" approach would give the Soviets almost 2,000 reentry vehicles in their ICBM force by the mid-70s.[3] Moreover, the USSR could also build by this time thirty-five to fifty new nuclear submarines carrying sixteen missiles each (see table 2).[4] Unless the United States took appropriate countermeasures, it is conceivable that the Soviet Union, through a coordinated strike against missile sites and air bases, could drastically reduce the land-based components of the U.S. strategic deterrent. It is also possible that the USSR, by improvements in antisubmarine warfare operations or by the deployment of ballistic missile defenses or both, could substantially degrade retaliatory strikes by U.S. missile-submarines. And while it is questionable whether even a successful Soviet first strike could reduce damage from an American retaliatory attack to "acceptable" levels, the mere possibility has stirred American decision makers to action.

A further stimulus is the projected growth of Chinese Communist nuclear power. As of early 1970, China probably possessed fewer than a hundred nuclear weapons of all types, and its available delivery systems were limited to one diesel-powered missile-submarine and a handful of obsolescent medium bombers which lacked the range to attack the United States. However, the Chinese have pushed ahead with testing and development of both medium-range ballistic missiles (MRBMs) and intermediate-

TABLE 1: United States and Soviet Intercontinental Strategic Strike Forces

Type	1965 U.S.	1965 USSR	1970 U.S.	1970 USSR
ICBMs				
Small (SS-11, Minuteman)	(880)[a]	—	(1,000)	(960)
Medium (SS-8, Titan II)	(54)	(220)	(54)	(200)
Large (SS-9)	—	—	—	(280)
Subtotal	934	220	1,054	1,440
SLBMs	464	105[b]	656	350[b]
Bombers	780	150+	550	145
Total	2,178	475+	2,260	1,935
Number of warheads carried (approximate)	6,078	775+	5,300[c]	2,225[c]
Deliverable megatonnage (approximate)	6,400	1,650	5,600	9,700

SOURCES: The figures for 1965 are taken from a presentation by Secretary of Defense Laird in U.S. Congress, Senate, Committee on Foreign Relations, Subcommittee on Arms Control, International Law and Organization, *Hearings, ABM, MIRV, SALT, and the Nuclear Arms Race*, 91st Cong., 2d sess., 1970, pp. 306–07. The overall figures for 1970 are derived from the *Statement of Secretary of Defense Melvin R. Laird Before the House Armed Services Committee on the FY 1972–1976 Defense Program and the 1972 Defense Budget*, 9 March 1971, mimeographed, pp. 45–47 and table 2, p. 165 (hereafter cited as *Laird Statement, 1971*). The breakout of Soviet ICBMs comes from the *Washington Post*, 10 March 1971, p. 1, and the information concerning the U.S. deployment of MIRVs on fifty Minuteman III missiles (which is reflected in the warhead totals) from the *Pittsburgh Press*, 1 April 1971, p. 16. The calculations of force loadings and deliverable megatonnage were based on information given in *The Military Balance, 1970–1971* (London: Institute for Strategic Studies, 1970), table 2, pp. 107–08, except that: (1) all U.S. heavy bombers were assumed to carry four 1.1 MT bombs and two 1 MT air-to-surface missiles (ASMs), and (2) all Soviet heavy bombers were assumed to carry two 1 MT bombs and one 1 MT ASM. This slightly overstates the capability of both bomber forces to carry ASMs.

a. Assumed to include 500 Minuteman Is with a 1 MT warhead and 330 Minuteman IIs with a 2 MT warhead.

b. Including those SLBMs carried by Soviet nonnuclear submarines. In addition the Soviets currently have some 350 SLCMs (submarine-launched cruise missiles) which could be employed against targets in the United States (see appendix table 3).

c. The *Laird Statement, 1971*, table 2, p, 165, arrives at different totals by counting only four weapons per American bomber and one per Soviet plane. In addition, Mr. Laird may have made an arithmetical error, since the total number of Soviet weapons cannot be less than 1,935, a figure which is consonant with the projections for mid-1971.

range ballistic missiles (IRBMs) and could by the mid-70s have eighty to a hundred such missiles operational. Conceivably, they could by that time also deploy ten to twenty-five ICBMs which could reach targets in the United States. And if the Chinese fired these ICBMs, they could inflict upward of seven million fatalities on an undefended America (see table 3).[5]

Whatever the likelihood of a Chinese (or a Soviet) nuclear attack, the mere possibility may, some have argued, inhibit the United States from employing its own strategic strike forces, except as a last resort, or from engaging in combat with Chinese or

TABLE 2: Soviet Intercontinental Strategic Strike Forces, Circa 1975

Type	Number of Launch Vehicles	Number of Warheads	Deliverable Megatonnage
ICBMs			
SS-8s	200	200	1,000
SS-9s	500+	1,500+	7,500+
SS-11s, SS-13s, etc.	1,800	1,800	1,800
SLMs			
SS-N-6 SLBM (comparable to			
Polaris A-1)	800	800	800
Sark SLBM[a]	45	45	45
Bombers			
Bear, Bison, etc.	145	435	435
Total	3,490+	4,780+	11,600[b]

SOURCES: *Statement of Secretary of Defense Melvin R. Laird Before a Joint Session of the Senate Armed Services Committee and the Senate Subcommittee on Department of Defense Appropriations on the Fiscal Year 1971 Defense Program and Budget,* 20 February 1970, mimeographed, pp. 103–05 (hereafter cited as *Laird Statement, 1970);* and *Laird Statement, 1971,* p. 169. Deliverable megatonnage is calculated on the basis of information given in *The Military Balance, 1970–1971* (London: Institute for Strategic Studies, 1970), table 2, pp. 107–08, with the following exceptions and additions: (1) Instead of one 25 MT warhead, the SS-9 was assumed to have three 5 MT warheads, as estimated by Mr. Laird in U.S. Congress, House, Subcommittees of the Committee on Appropriations, *Hearings, SAFEGUARD Antiballistic Missile System,* 91st Cong., 1st sess., 1969, pp. 8–10 (hereafter cited as *Hearings, SAFEGUARD Antiballistic Missile System),* and (2) All bombs and ASMs were given an assumed yield of 1 MT.

a. Assumes all nonnuclear missile-submarines phased out by 1975 (see appendix table 2).

b. Approximate total.

TABLE 3: Chinese Communist Strategic Strike Forces, Circa 1975

Type	Number of Launch Vehicles	Number of Warheads	Deliverable Megatonnage
ICBMs	10 – 25	10 – 25	30 – 75
MRBMs/IRBMs	80 – 100	80 – 100	16 – 20
SLMs[a]	3	3	3
Medium bombers[b]	5 – 10	10 – 20	30 – 60
Total	98 – 138	103 – 148	79 – 158
Deliverable against the United States	10 – 25	10 – 25	30 – 75

Source: *Hearings, SAFEGUARD Antiballistic Missile System*, pp. 12–13.

a. Even if the Chinese should develop missiles for their one G-class diesel-powered submarine, such submarines do not, in Mr. Laird's words "pose a large threat against the continental United States" *(Laird Statement, 1970, p. 109)*.

b. These are not capable of reaching the continental United States even on one-way missions.

Soviet troops. Under these circumstances, it is suggested, the USSR and Communist China may feel freer to mount local offensives against vulnerable areas such as Iran or Thailand, or to press nonnuclear powers such as Japan and India for political concessions. At the very least they may be more willing to initiate or to support revolutionary movements abroad and to stand up to the United States should the latter attempt to intervene. Thus growing Soviet and Chinese nuclear power could induce American counteractions well beyond those needed simply to safeguard U.S. retaliatory forces.

And the Response

In point of fact they have. For example, the Safeguard antiballistic missile system sponsored by the Nixon administration is intended not only to defend U.S. bombers and ICBMs from Soviet missile strikes but also to protect American cities from Chinese nuclear attacks.[6] In addition, the United States plans to install three MIRVs on each of some 500 Minuteman III ICBMs and ten on each of 496 Poseidon SLBMs; together with the development of lighter air-to-surface missiles for strategic bombers this could boost the total number of strategic warheads to approximately

12,000 (see table 4). The forces programmed for 1975 would not only hedge against any further Soviet deployment of ABMs but would multiply the destructive power of any American missiles surviving a Soviet assault. Furthermore, they would enable the United States to retaliate simultaneously against the USSR and Communist China or to strike at the latter without worrying that

TABLE 4: United States Intercontinental Strategic Strike Forces, Circa 1975

Type	Number of Launch Vehicles	Number of Warheads	Deliverable Megatonnage
ICBMs			
Titan II	27	27	135
Minuteman II	500	500	1,000
Minuteman III	500	1,500	300
SLBMs			
Polaris A-3	160	480	196
Poseidon	496	4,960	248
Bombers			
B-52 G/H[a]	255	4,080[b]	1,734[b]
FB-111	71	426[b]	213[b]
Total	2,009	11,953	3,800[c]

SOURCES: Information concerning the size of the U.S. bomber force is from the *Statement of Secretary of Defense Clark M. Clifford on the Fiscal Year 1970–74 Defense Program and 1970 Defense Budget*, 15 January 1969, mimeographed, pp. 58–59 (hereafter cited as *Clifford Statement*), as modified by the *Laird Statement*, *1970*, pp. 111–12. Force loadings for B-52s are estimated at four 1.1 MT bombs and twelve 200 KT SRAMs (short-range attack missiles), for FB-111s at two bombs and four SRAMs. It is reported that the B-52 could carry up to twenty SRAMs; hence these figures are conservative. See *Aviation Week and Space Technology*, 91, no. 22 (December 1969), pp. 47–48.

Information about the program for installing three 200 KT MIRVs on each of 500 Minuteman III ICBMs and ten 50 KT MIRVs on each of 496 Poseidon missiles comes from the *New York Times*, 9 June 1969, p. 3, data on the warheads from the *Washington Post*, 27 May 1970, p. A-3, and 22 June 1969, p. A-1.

Information on the planned phasedown of the Titan II after fiscal year 1973 comes from the *Clifford Statement*, p. 60, on the warhead size from *The Military Balance, 1970–1971* (London: Institute for Strategic Studies, 1970), table 2, pp. 107–08.

a. This assumes that all of the B-52 C/F bombers are placed on active reserve, as currently envisaged by the Department of Defense.

b. Based on B-52s carrying only twelve SRAMs rather than the twenty which represent maximum load and the FB-111s carrying four SRAMs rather than six.

c. Approximate total.

this would weaken the deterrent to Soviet attack. Thus even if the United States does not procure other weapons now under development (such as a larger ICBM, a longer-range submarine-launched missile, and a new intercontinental bomber), it should have strategic strike forces comparable to those of the USSR and in some respects superior.

Even though some of these responses were initiated by former President Lyndon B. Johnson, the Nixon administration seems to have adopted and endorsed them. In the process various spokesmen have stressed that the overall aim was peace through strength. Thus Mr. Nixon defined the "overriding purpose" of the U.S. strategic posture as "political and defensive: to deny to other countries the ability to impose their will on the United States and its allies under the weight of strategic military superiority. We must insure that all potential aggressors see unacceptable risks in contemplating a nuclear attack or nuclear blackmail or acts which could escalate to strategic nuclear war, such as a Soviet conventional attack in Europe."[7] Mr. Laird stated that the maintenance of peace required that the United States be in a position to "absorb a first strike from any potential enemy and still be able to deliver a devastating retaliatory blow"; should U.S. forces not be sufficient for this purpose "our deterrent would be lost and the chances of a global nuclear war greatly increased."[8]

Although few Americans would quarrel with Mr. Nixon's declaration of intent or Mr. Laird's emphasis on peace through deterrence, they might well differ over the strategic postures needed to support these policies; hence, it is important to understand the premises upon which these postures are based. The first such premise seems to be that the Soviets (and presumably the Chinese Communists) can be deterred from attacking the United States only by the absolute certainty that any such attempt would result in their virtual destruction. Thus Deputy Secretary of Defense David Packard testified, "There is general agreement on what is needed to deter a deliberate attack. We need to assure the potential aggressor [that] if he strikes us he will receive a retaliatory blow which will destroy him as a nation."[9] Former Secretary of Defense Robert S. McNamara insisted that the United States must have "an ability to inflict at all times and under all foreseeable conditions an unacceptable degree of damage* upon any single aggressor, or combination of aggressors."[10] Secretary of Defense Laird not only quoted approvingly his predecessor's definition of the requirements for deterrence but argued elsewhere that to deter a Soviet first strike "we must always be in a position where we can inflict unacceptable damage on the Soviet Union, even after absorbing the first blow."[11]

Coupled with the belief that only high levels of damage will be "unacceptable" to the USSR, and that even comparable numbers of fatalities might not deter Communist China,[12] is the belief that the damage inflicted should be greater than the damage received. As former Chairman of the Joint Chiefs of Staff General Earle G. Wheeler, Jr., put it, "[we should] insure that the United States and its allies emerge [from any nuclear war] with relative advantage irrespective of the circumstances of initiation, response and termination."[13] Although the Nixon administration has not endorsed this view, it has decided to prevent the Soviet Union "from gaining the ability to cause considerably greater destruction than the United States could inflict in a nuclear war."[14] To insure that growing Soviet strategic strike forces would not enable the USSR to achieve a favorable war outcome, Mr. Nixon reportedly doubled the number of fatalities which the United States should inflict in a strategic nuclear exchange[15]—thereby adding a new dimension to the concept of unacceptable damage and increasing the requirements for "assured destruction forces."†

Ideally U.S. officials would like to see not only a relative American advantage but a situation wherein the United States would receive little or no damage from a Chinese nuclear strike and only limited damage from one by the USSR. For this reason the Joint Chiefs of Staff have continued to urge the "development of an effective ballistic missile defense against the Soviet threat."[16] And successive Secretaries of Defense have rejected this approach only because they considered it infeasible; for example, Mr.

---

* Mr. McNamara defined *unacceptable damage* as the deaths of one-fifth to one-fourth of the Soviet population (44 to 55 million) and the destruction of one-half of Soviet industry. This figure has not been officially changed by the Nixon administration. and the only report of any alteration suggests that it has been raised.

† *Assured destruction forces* are those needed to inflict *unacceptable damage*, however that may be defined, under the worst of circumstances.

McNamara stated, "If we could actually build and deploy a generally impenetrable shield over the United States, we would be willing to spend $40 billion,"[17] and Mr. Laird said that the United States relied on the deterrent to protect its cities against Soviet attack only "because we have no better alternative."[18]

This lack of a better alternative has aroused considerable concern about the utility of American strategic strike forces in protecting U.S. allies and interests. In the words of former Secretary of Defense McNamara, the fact that both sides would suffer mutual destruction from a nuclear exchange "narrows the range of Soviet aggression which can be effectively deterred by our nuclear forces."[19] For this reason the Kennedy and Johnson administrations adopted a policy (so far unchanged) of building up conventional forces as barriers to aggression, of deploying tactical nuclear weapons to back up and supplement resistance by these forces, and of relying on the threat of escalation to deter large-scale invasion or the use of nuclear weapons. Thus for purposes of extended deterrence the United States apparently counts on the difficulty of, and the risks attendant on, Communist incursions rather than on the strength of U.S. strategic strike forces.

This approach seems, however, to be reversed when the United States considers ways of handling crises and confrontations. Instead of depending on local forces to deter or to cope with Soviet or Chinese Communist pressures, the tendency is to regard strategic power as the key to success. For instance, Mr. Nixon, in defending his decision to deploy ABMs, stated, "I do not want to see an American President in the future, in the event of any crisis, have his diplomatic credibility be so impaired because the United States was in a second-class or inferior position. We saw what it meant to the Soviets [during the Cuban missile crisis] when they were second."[20] And Mr. Laird added that as far as the Chinese Communists were concerned even overwhelming superiority might not suffice; in the absence of an ability to drastically limit damage from a Chinese attack, "Our cities would be hostage to the Chinese ICBM force, and the President would have no other alternative but to back down [from a confrontation with Communist China] or risk the destruction of several major U.S. cities and the death of millions of Americans."[21]

In brief, current American policy calls for strategic strike forces capable under the worst of circumstances of inflicting on the USSR very heavy losses, losses at least comparable to those the USSR could inflict on the United States. The Nixon administration has ostensibly settled for forces "sufficient" to achieve these goals rather than insisting on strategic superiority—although it should be noted that the present interpretation of sufficiency would still give the United States over twice as many deliverable warheads as the USSR five years hence (see tables 2 and 4). It has programmed ABMs capable of protecting American ICBM sites and of degrading or nullifying a Chinese missile launch but has eschewed as infeasible the installation of "heavy" defenses against Soviet attacks on centers of population. And it has continued to rely primarily on conventional forces to meet a conventional attack, holding back tactical nuclear weapons until these are needed to give warning of American intentions or, on a large scale, to check an enemy assault, and reserving strategic strike forces to inhibit an opponent from escalating the conflict or to retaliate if he does escalate.

Criticisms of the Response

Not surprisingly this policy has been criticized on a number of grounds, one of them being that it does not provide for continued American superiority not only in deliverable warheads but also in launch vehicles, in deliverable megatonnage, and in the ability to inflict damage. According to its proponents, strategic superiority, however defined, is needed both to preclude the USSR from escalating any conflict and to lend credibility to the American deterrent. If the United States does not have nuclear superiority, the Soviet Union may, it is argued, be freer to encourage and support "wars of national liberation," to practice "nuclear blackmail," and even to engage in limited wars; as Senator Henry M. Jackson once said, "International peace and stability depend not on a parity of power but on a preponderance of power in the peace-keepers over the peace-upsetters."[22] Furthermore, superiority could nerve an American President to stand up to the USSR in a confrontation and might induce a Soviet leader to back down, as many believe it did in the Cuban missile crisis. For these reasons a number of thoughtful and influential Americans have at one time or another called for American strategic strike forces more powerful than those of the Soviet Union.

Some individuals who share the same views about the erosion of the U.S. deterrent and the consequent impact on Communist behavior have chosen to call for strong strategic defenses instead of—or along with—superiority in strategic strike forces. The argument here is that the prospective loss of even a few million lives may dissuade American officials from ordering a nuclear strike, and that the far higher losses which the USSR (or the China of 1990) could inflict would virtually rule out any such action. Knowing this, an aggressive opponent might be tempted to assail vulnerable outposts, such as Berlin or Taiwan, and an overconfident one to press the United States too hard. Since strategic defenses could guard against this possibility, could preclude damage from an inadvertent launch, and, above all, would be essential to the survival of the United States in any general nuclear war, they have been supported by a number of American leaders; for example, Senator Richard Russell, former Chairman of the Senate Armed Services Committee, strongly urged the construction of comprehensive ballistic missile defenses, on the ground that "if we have to start over again with another Adam and Eve, . . . then I want them to be Americans and not Russians—and I want them on this continent and not in Europe."[23]

Conversely, a good many people have criticized the Defense Department not for doing too little but for attempting too much. They maintain that defenses against a Soviet nuclear strike are infeasible and those against a Chinese attack unnecessary. Like Senator J. William Fulbright, Chairman of the Senate Committee on Foreign Relations, they consider the projections of Soviet capabilities made by the Department of Defense to be unrealistic and the premise that the USSR could, even then, destroy all three components of the U.S. strategic deterrent to be unfounded.[24] They note that the USSR may respond to American procurement of new weapons—just as the United States has reacted to Soviet moves—and that even limited measures may simply stimulate the production of strategic armaments by both sides. They may also decry the consequent costs, the resultant increase in the influence and power of the military, and the probable increase in international tensions. And they may, as did Representative John B. Anderson, ask instead for a "halt to this insane nuclear version of keeping up with the Joneses"—in short, for limitations on strategic armaments which, in their judgment, could stabilize both the strategic balance and the international environment.[25]

Alternatives for the Future

The preceding discussion suggests that current U.S. policy for the maintenance of a strategic deterrent and its supporting weapons programs has been criticized on a number of counts:

1. that it does not clearly and unequivocally insure strategic superiority, which is useful in safeguarding retaliatory forces; essential in waging nuclear war; and critical in deterring local aggression, in resisting Communist pressures, and in managing crises;

2. that it will not reduce damage and casualties from a nuclear exchange to tolerable levels, thus imperiling the continued existence of the nation, reducing the credibility of the deterrent, and leaving the United States open to nuclear blackmail; and, conversely,

3. that it may stimulate the arms race, increase tensions, and multiply costs without enhancing national security—and may actually diminish that security by prompting other nations to upgrade and/or increase their strategic weapons systems.*

* A fourth criticism might be that it does not take sufficiently into account the impact of mutual strategic deterrence on Communist behavior and on allied opinion and hence does not generate local defense forces of the quantity or the type needed to cope with possible Soviet and Chinese Communist assaults on, and pressures against, friends and allies of the United States. So far, however, this criticism has not been voiced, partly because the Nixon administration has not made any significant changes in the doctrine and the force postures bequeathed by the Johnson administration. If and as the "Nixon Doctrine" of reducing commitments and cutting back on the forces earmarked to uphold them is implemented, then more may be heard about U.S. conventional capabilities. That, however, is the subject for another book—not this one!

Obviously, these brief outlines of official statements on the criteria for assessing U.S. strategic power and of three sets of views held by dissenters from those criteria cannot do justice to the complexity of the problem—nor are they intended to do so. Rather, they are intended to introduce some broad alternatives which should be considered in determining future levels of strategic power and which, therefore, will be analyzed in this book. The next chapter will examine the usefulness of strategic nuclear forces in waging war, with particular reference to the potential capabilities of those forces now programmed, of still more powerful strategic strike forces, and of stronger strategic defenses. Chapter 4 will assess the implications for deterrence of alternative force postures, chapter 5 their possible impact on Communist political behavior, and chapter 6 their significance for relations between the United States and its allies. Chapter 7 will consider the effect on U.S. strategic power of possible arms control measures and the consequent implications for deterrence, for Communist behavior, and for alliance relationships. A final chapter will attempt to summarize the results of these analyses, to reexamine the validity of the current criteria, and to suggest changes in strategic force postures and in U.S. defense policies which could—hopefully—enhance both national security and national well-being over the next decade.

3
Strategic Power and Nuclear War

As previously noted, American policy calls for the maintenance of strategic nuclear forces capable under the worst of circumstances of destroying the Soviet Union as a viable society and of crippling China through attacks on key political and industrial centers. It calls also for the United States to inflict on the USSR damage at least comparable to that which it would receive and to emerge from any nuclear exchange with only limited damage from Chinese nuclear strikes, if not from those launched by the Soviets. Some might question such objectives on the grounds that they are too costly economically, too likely to increase international tensions, or too reflective of the belief that America has a right to be "first" in everything. While these are all points which should be given consideration, it might be helpful before considering them to ask three preliminary questions:

1. Does the safety of the United States and the protection of its vital interests require that it be capable of implementing these objectives?
2. Is it feasible to achieve such capabilities?
3. If so, what types and levels of strategic power may be required to achieve them?

This chapter will focus primarily on questions 2 and 3, beginning with a definition of strategic power and continuing with an assessment of the advantages and limitations of three different strategic postures. Question 1 will be dealt with in the next two chapters, which will attempt to assess the validity of the objectives summarized here and hence the necessity for implementing them.

What Is Strategic Power?

Although power is commonly viewed as a crucial factor in relations among states, it is a factor which is difficult to define since it can encompass virtually everything from the strength of a country's armed forces to the skill and stamina of its leaders. While *strategic power* has generally been defined more narrowly as the capability to deliver nuclear weapons upon the homeland of an adversary, even this definition includes technical factors such as the ranges and payloads of delivery vehicles, political ones such as the willingness of allies to provide facilities for nuclear weapons, and economic ones such as the industrial capacity, skilled manpower, and financial resources needed to build the weapons.

Moreover, even if one follows the example of the Department of Defense in categorizing as *strategic* only delivery vehicles of intercontinental range (bombers, ICBMs, and missile-submarines)* and those systems designed to defend against similar weapons, this does not automatically equate strategic power with numbers of (or ratios between) the launch vehicles possessed by two countries. For one thing, these vehicles differ with respect to the number of warheads which they can carry, the megatonnage which they can deliver, and other technical characteristics; for some purposes the quick-firing and versatile Minuteman II may be superior to the Soviet SS-9, despite the latter's higher thrust and greater payload. For another, there may be differences in the abilities of weapons systems to survive an attack or to penetrate enemy defenses—on both of which counts bombers have been rated as less effective than missiles. For a third, asymmetries in the geographic locations of two countries or in the distribution of their populations may mean that different numbers of weapons

---

* Theoretically, aircraft carriers should also be included under this heading, as at one time they were; however, neither they nor submarines equipped with short-range missiles (such as the Soviet W-class boats) are normally listed as strategic weapons systems. Neither are Soviet medium bombers and medium- and intermediate-range ballistic missiles, although these are certainly "strategic" in the eyes of Western Europeans. (See appendix table 3.)

will be needed to inflict comparable damage. (For example, as many people live in the 50 largest U.S. cities as in the 400 largest Soviet cities; hence, while two hundred 1 MT Soviet warheads could kill 120 million Americans, over twelve hundred comparable U.S. weapons would be required to kill the same number of Russians.)[1]

Rather than calculating strategic power in terms of launch vehicles, the Department of Defense has preferred to employ another standard, that of "the number of separate warheads that are capable of being *delivered* with accuracy on individual high-priority targets with sufficient power to destroy them."[2] This takes into account the technical characteristics of weapons systems as well as their ability to survive a first strike and to penetrate enemy defenses. However, it does not allow for differences in warhead yields, which may be significant; for instance, multi-megaton warheads may be more effective in attacking some types of targets or may create effects, such as fire storms or tidal waves, which cannot be generated by smaller warheads. Nor does it take into account differences in the number of targets to be attacked, either because the population of one side may be more largely dispersed or because that side may possess other weapons not normally entered in the strategic balance, such as medium-range ballistic missiles or extensive air defense systems. Thus the number of deliverable warheads, while a more reliable indicator than the number of launch vehicles, is not a definitive one.

Neither is deliverable megatonnage—which is a composite of the number of launchers, the yield of the warheads which they can carry, and, in more sophisticated analyses, their survivability and penetrability. For one thing, superiority in deliverable mega-tonnage is essentially meaningless when a relatively small number of weapons can inflict heavy damage. For another, it may be misleading if the launch vehicles are vulnerable to attack or have difficulty penetrating enemy defenses; as former Deputy Secretary of Defense Paul Nitze pointed out in 1968, the then current U.S. strategic strike forces could inflict heavier damage on the USSR than would have been possible using the forces of a decade earlier, despite a reduction of some ten thousand megatons in U.S. delivery capabilities.[3] Finally, deliverable megatonnage provides no guide to the ability to limit damage, which can be ascertained only by a more detailed examination of the force postures of both sides. Thus whatever its intrinsic appeal and psychological impact, deliverable megatonnage does not necessarily measure strategic power and must be rejected in favor of another criterion.

The preferred measure—and the one which will be used throughout this book—is the ability to inflict damage in a nuclear exchange. This takes into account all the asymmetries mentioned earlier and all the technical characteristics of weapons systems to which reference has been made. In addition, it includes the ability of each side to launch counterforce attacks or to build effective strategic defenses. It comes closest to equating strategic capabilities with the absolute or relative ability to "punish" an opponent, which is one (although decidedly not the only) component of deterrence. It is the standard most commonly employed in estimating the consequences of changes in force postures or advances in weapons technology. Moreover, since the ability to inflict and to limit damage is prominent among the criteria utilized by the Nixon administration in determining the adequacy of U.S. strategic nuclear forces,[4] strategic power must be measured on this basis and not in terms of launch vehicles, deliverable warheads, deliverable megatonnage, or other indicators sometimes used.

This complicates the task of estimating strategic power, which can be ascertained only after extensive analyses involving various scenarios which postulate a possible nuclear exchange and which set reasonable values for factors such as systems reliability, missile accuracy, warhead yield, and penetrability that will affect the outcome of that exchange. Fortunately, much work of this nature has been done, and enough of the results have been released to enable broad judgments about strategic nuclear capabilities. It is therefore possible, without engaging in—or having to read about—exhaustive quantitative analyses, to put into context arguments about the potential utility of new or additional weapons and to evaluate various strategic postures. This approach will be followed here in examining both the forces programmed by the Nixon administration and alternatives which would markedly alter the size or the composition of those forces.

Strategic Forces and Nuclear War

Strategic Sufficiency

As indicated previously, the Soviet Union has embarked on a buildup of its strategic strike forces which, if it continues at the rate estimated by the Department of Defense, could by 1975 give the USSR more than twice as many launch vehicles as it now has.* By that date the USSR could also deploy advanced exoatmospheric ballistic missile defenses either around its weapons sites or its key cities—probably the latter.[5] These forces would enable the USSR to launch attacks of unparallelled magnitude against the United States, to decrease drastically the current ability of the United States to limit damage from such attacks through counterforce strikes, and to degrade U.S. retaliatory strikes against Soviet cities.

At first glance it would seem that these improvements in the Soviet force posture would give it a meaningful and exploitable strategic advantage. Unfortunately for the Soviet Union, present American forces are so powerful and so versatile that it is questionable whether it could achieve a significant edge in the ability to inflict damage even if U.S. capabilities remained constant.† It is, however, possible that the USSR could induce a shift in the strategic balance sufficiently great to preclude the United States from achieving its objective of inflicting comparable damage in a nuclear exchange. To obviate this, the Nixon administration, under the concept of "strategic sufficiency," proposes to more than double the number of deliverable warheads by installing MIRVs on many U.S. missiles. It also plans to deploy antiballistic missiles which could safeguard some of the American ICBMs against Soviet counterforce strikes (and most of the American people against small-scale attacks on cities), to modernize U.S. air defenses, and to improve further U.S. capabilities to wage antisubmarine warfare. If its programs are all adopted, and if Soviet programs go forward at the rate earlier estimated by Mr.

---

* See chapter 2, pp. 8–11, and especially table 2.
† See the section in this chapter on "Strategic Power and Strategic Stability," and especially table 5.

TABLE 5: Comparison of U.S. and Soviet Strategic Nuclear Capabilities, Circa 1975

	U.S.	USSR
Numbers of launch vehicles[a]	2,009	3,490
Number of warheads (approximate)	11,953	4,780[b]
Megatonnage deliverable in a first strike (approximate)	3,800	11,600
Ballistic missile interceptors[c]	400–500(?)	600(?)

SOURCE: Figures for the USSR come from table 2 and those for the United States from table 4.

a. Soviet IRBMs, MRBMs, medium bombers, and SLCMs are excluded from these totals, as they were from earlier tables, in order to enable a direct comparison of intercontinental delivery capabilities.

b. Although it is conceivable that by 1975 the USSR could install MRVs or MIRVs on missiles other than the SS-9 or more than three MIRVs on the SS-9 itself, the Department of Defense did not, as of late 1970, include these possibilities in its estimates of Soviet strength.

c. The U.S. figure, which includes Spartan, but not the shorter-range Sprint, is based on incremental implementation of the Safeguard program, the Soviet figure on potential capabilities.

Laird, the situation in the mid-70s would look something like that in table 5.

With forces of this size the United States would be able, at the very least, to inflict unacceptable damage upon the USSR, that is, to kill one-fifth to one-fourth of the Soviet people in a retaliatory strike and to destroy one-half of the Soviet industrial capacity.[6] For example, the reentry vehicles from the 250 to 300 Minuteman ICBMs which Mr. Laird estimates would survive a Soviet disarming strike[7] could kill upward of 50 million Russians;* even if these reentry vehicles were degraded or completely destroyed by Soviet ballistic missile defenses, the USSR would still have to cope with the more than five thousand smaller warheads carried

* According to the *Statement of Secretary of Defense Robert S. McNamara Before the Senate Armed Services Committee on the Fiscal Year 1969–1973 Defense Program and 1969 Defense Budget,* 22 January 1968, mimeographed, p. 57, two hundred 1 MT warheads could kill 52 million Soviets and destroy 72 percent of Soviet industry. The surviving Minutemen could carry either one 2 MT warhead or three 200 KT warheads, which together could inflict on soft targets damage almost equal to that created by a 1 MT bomb.

by Polaris and Poseidon SLBMs, as well as with the surviving intercontinental bombers. It is conceivable that the USSR could suffer greater damage from an American second strike in 1975 than it would today, as the larger number of survivable warheads would enable the United States to launch attacks against small Soviet cities which previously were unprofitable targets.

However, it is unlikely that the United States, despite its superiority of approximately two to one in deliverable warheads and its Safeguard ABM system, would fare much better than the Soviet Union in a nuclear exchange. Presumably, the United States could muster for a first strike some five to six thousand low-yield but reasonably accurate warheads without cutting into the forces needed to deter Communist China or to destroy the USSR, should this prove necessary. However, even if these were all aimed at Soviet intercontinental delivery vehicles (leaving untouched the shorter-range missiles and bombers targeted against NATO Europe, Japan, and other allies), many Soviet bombers and missiles would probably survive.* Furthermore, even the sea-based component of Soviet nuclear forces could deliver up to 1,000 megatons on undefended targets. Although U.S. ballistic missile defenses could knock down some of the incoming warheads, the Safeguard system is not intended to protect centers of population (with the exception of Washington, D.C.) against attacks of the magnitude which the USSR could deliver. Hence not even the sizeable augmentation of its strategic nuclear forces described earlier would give the United States a meaningful capability to limit damage from a Soviet retaliatory strike—not when two hundred 1 MT warheads can kill 80 million Americans.

* Assuming that 5,000 reentry vehicles were actually launched (which ignores readiness, reliability, and in-flight performance), that they were accurate to within 0.2 of a mile and that they each carried one 100 KT warhead, they could knock out all but 100 of the 2,500 Soviet missiles, even if these were in hardened sites which could withstand blast pressures of 100 pounds per square inch (psi). If, however, these weapons sites could withstand 200 psi (which is less than U.S. missile silos can resist), the United States would have only about an 85 percent probability of destroying them, which means that, on the average, 375 Soviet missiles could survive. And if Soviet ballistic missile defenses intercepted as few as 10 percent of the incoming American RVs, at least 125 Soviet ICBMs (and perhaps as many as 500) could survive, depending on the resistance to blast of Soviet missile silos.

This is not surprising, since the United States apparently relies more on the possibility of precluding damage through successful deterrence of a Soviet strike than on drastically reducing it through war-fighting capabilities. Moreover, Soviet defense postures are presumably tailored to preclude this, just as American ones are designed to prevent the USSR from eroding U.S. capabilities for assured destruction. What it does suggest, however, is that even sizable and costly weapons programs such as those upon which both the United States and the USSR are now embarked are not likely to upset the strategic balance. And if they threatened to do so, either country could take measures to restore it, by alerting and redeploying existing forces, by ordering some of its ICBMs to fire on warning of an attack, or—if the threat were a long-term one—by initiating new programs.*

In the case of Communist China the situation will be very different. In absolute terms China's strategic delivery capabilities could rise dramatically over the next five or six years, from almost zero to ten to twenty-five ICBMs and eighty to one hundred MRBMs (see table 3). However, although the intercontinental missiles could inflict 7 to 11 million casualties on an undefended America,[8] and while the shorter-range ones could devastate U.S. bases and allied cities in the Pacific island chain, these capabilities could be significantly degraded. For one thing, U.S. disarming strikes could knock out a number of soft missiles, unless the Chinese had both adequate radar and a doctrine of firing on warning. For another, planned ballistic missile defenses will supposedly reduce American fatalities to less than 1 million.[9] And for a third, a relatively small number of U.S. warheads (perhaps fewer than one hundred) could kill over 50 million Chinese and destroy more than half of China's industrial capacity.[10] Although the Chinese could probably cause some American casualties and could certainly hold America's Asian allies in hostage for U.S. behavior, they cannot hope to pose a major threat to the United States.

This does not mean that the situation is a happy one; as President Nixon said, "Any nuclear attack—no matter how small; whether accidental, unauthorized, or by design, by a superpower

---

* See the next section, "Strategic Superiority."

or by a country with only a primitive nuclear capability—would be a catastrophe for the U.S., no matter how devastating our ability to retaliate."[11] Furthermore, it is conceivable that the Chinese could, by the end of the decade, appreciably increase the number of casualties they could inflict on the United States—ballistic missile defenses or no. And if present trends in Soviet strategic programs continue, the USSR will maintain in 1975–1980 the same ability it now has to destroy the United States—if it is willing to commit suicide in the process.

Strategic Superiority

It is precisely this prospect—that the outcome of nuclear exchange would entail mutual destruction—which has caused some defense analysts and officials to call for building new bombers, for deploying more missiles, and for taking other steps to insure that the United States leads the USSR in numbers of launch vehicles and/or in the megatonnage which these can carry, as well as in deliverable warheads. Admittedly, larger and more powerful strategic nuclear forces do offer numerous benefits, militarily as well as psychologically. For example, superiority in numbers of launch vehicles or in numbers of deliverable warheads could guard against uncertainties in missile reliability, survivability, penetrability, and so on, and thus insure that one could always inflict unacceptable damage on an adversary. Moreover, numerical superiority could serve as a hedge against greater-than-anticipated improvements in an opponent's counterforce capabilities. For instance, Congressman Craig Hosmer calculated that the USSR, with missiles equal in number to those of the United States, could destroy 92 percent of the 1,054 land-based ICBMs in a first strike counterforce attack, whereas former Deputy Secretary of Defense Paul Nitze estimated that they could knock out fewer than 40 percent;[12] superiority would guard against the possibility that the Soviets could achieve reliability rates, accuracies, and warhead yields nearer those employed by Mr. Hosmer than those used by Mr. Nitze.

Furthermore, superiority in launch vehicles or in deliverable warheads could allow greater resources to be devoted to damage limitation in either a first or a second strike. It could enable attacks on a large number of nonstrategic targets (such as tactical air bases, marshaling yards, and supply centers) without unduly depleting forces which might be needed for intrawar deterrence or to stave off attacks by another nuclear power. And it could facilitate the saturation or exhaustion of Soviet ballistic missile defenses, thereby assuring that residual American forces could inflict unacceptable damage.

Whether strategic superiority is essential to all of these tasks is perhaps questionable; for instance, decoys, chaff, and other penetration aids could also degrade the effectiveness of ballistic missile defenses. And whether superiority in launch vehicles, warheads, or megatonnage could increase the ability of the United States to limit damage from a Soviet attack remains to be seen.

One way of attempting this would be to build more ICBMs or SLBMs, with the aim of destroying a very high percentage of Soviet bombers, land-based missiles, and those missile-submarines still in port. While the number of warheads required for this will depend to some extent on their accuracy, range, and yield, and to some extent on the dispersion and hardening of weapons sites, one could assume that an attacker cannot succeed without employing at least as many reentry vehicles as there are targets. In practice, moreover, considering faulty intelligence; uncertainties about weapons effects; and malfunctions, aborts, and inaccuracies in delivery systems, more warheads than targets will certainly be required (e.g., Dr. John S. Foster, Jr., Director of Defense Research and Engineering, estimated that 500 Soviet SS-9s, with an 80 percent reliability rate, each carrying three 5 MT separately guided warheads with quarter-mile accuracy, would be needed to destroy some 950 U.S. Minuteman missiles, a ratio of about three to two between available reentry vehicles and targets).[13] Even in 1962, when Soviet strategic nuclear forces were more vulnerable than they are today, the United States would have suffered 50 million fatalities from a Soviet retaliatory strike, despite an advantage of three or four to one in numbers.[14] To achieve the degree of superiority needed for a successful counterforce attack against even current Soviet strategic strike forces—much less against those projected for 1975—would be extremely difficult; the Chairman of the Joint Chiefs of Staff testified in 1968, when Soviet capabilities were significantly less than they are now, that "it is literally impossible to buy sufficient forces . . . to destroy the enemy strike capability before it is launched against the United States."[15]

An alternative (or complementary) way of achieving superiority would be to push for qualitative improvements in existing or programmed weapons systems. For example, multiple warheads launched by a single missile can substitute for larger numbers of missiles, the consequent loss in deliverable megatons perhaps being offset by the lower cost per warhead. Greater accuracy in the delivery of either individual or multiple warheads may reduce the number of reentry vehicles that have to be directed against a missile site or air base in order to insure its destruction; so far as counterforce attacks against undefended targets are concerned, it is immaterial whether this accuracy is achieved through better guidance systems for unpowered reentry vehicles, or through maneuverable warheads, or both. Increased yields from nuclear warheads may also reduce the number of reentry vehicles that have to be dispatched against a single target, as higher blast pressures and greater radii of destruction can partly offset inaccuracies.* Thus there are a number of ways in which the United States could enhance the effectiveness of its counterforce attacks, ways whose attractiveness depends in part on the state of the art, in part on their relative cost, and in part on their comparative usefulness against Soviet strategic nuclear forces.

Equally, however, there are numerous actions that the USSR could take to increase the survivability of these forces. For example, it could build superhardened missile sites, whose destruction would require either more or larger-yield warheads. It could make land-based missiles mobile or semimobile and change locations frequently enough to insure that many of them could not be targeted by a potential enemy. It could shift from land-based to sea-launched missiles, carried either on submarines or in more vulnerable but considerably cheaper surface ships, as proposed for the NATO Multilateral Nuclear Force. It could place larger

---

* Multimegaton warheads may also have secondary effects, such as blacking out radar and inducing electron flows in communications equipment, which could enhance their disruptive impact on an opponent's offensive and defensive systems.

numbers of bombers on air alert, build long-endurance platforms such as nuclear-powered aircraft or cruise-type missiles, or orbit weapons of mass destruction, which, whatever their accuracy and their cost/effectiveness, could almost certainly insure the destruction of a few cities. If all else failed, it could (as Soviet officials have hinted they might do) program fixed missiles to fire on warning, thereby increasing the certitude of retaliation—admittedly at the expense of enhancing the possibility of inadvertent war.*

While the specific results of these interactions cannot be spelled out in detail, the broad pattern of efforts to achieve meaningful strategic superiority is quite clear. As General Wheeler said in 1968, "The Joint Chiefs of Staff have examined all types of pre-emptive attacks and first strikes and things of that kind, and we can find none that is attractive [to the United States]."[16] Or, as former Assistant Secretary of Defense Alain C. Enthoven put it, "If you talk about politically exploitable superiority—the threat to attack and destroy their forces—I think they [the Soviets] have been getting survivable forces independently of what we do. I don't think that we could have bought our way out of that development at any reasonable cost."[17] Only if the possible Soviet responses are deliberately forsworn, are limited by lack of resources, or are constrained by formal or tacit arms control agreements, is the United States likely to obtain a significant advantage through improving its strategic strike forces—and even that is not likely to reduce damage to a level that the United States will find tolerable.

Strategic Defenses

This immediately raises the question whether passive defenses (fallout or blast shelters) or active ones (air defenses, antisubmarine warfare forces, and ballistic missile defenses) might not be more effective than new missiles or more warheads in limiting damage from a nuclear strike—and hence should be expanded, in lieu of or along with stronger strategic strike forces. Certainly, defenses could increase the likelihood that centers of government, command and control systems, and other facilities needed for directing and terminating a nuclear war would survive and that

---

* Even vastly inferior opponents, such as Communist China, can adopt some of these techniques, such as deploying semimobile missiles or firing on warning; it is this latter possibility that has stimulated calls for American ballistic missile defenses.

resources absolutely essential to the continued functioning of the country would remain intact. They could also reduce overall damage, both by knocking out enemy launch vehicles before they reach their targets and by minimizing the effects of the nuclear weapons they deliver. Moreover, they can require an opponent to devote disproportionate resources to the destruction of the most lucrative (and presumably the best defended) targets. They may also make it necessary for him to employ some of his weapons against air defense direction centers or missile site radars, thereby further reducing the number available for other uses.

Furthermore, the mere existence of defensive systems complicates the planning and conduct of a nuclear strike and creates uncertainties about its outcome. For one thing, they necessitate careful consideration of trade offs between probable losses from unimpaired defenses and the costs of degrading those defenses. For another, attacks against key components of defensive systems must be coordinated with strikes against the targets they are defending and a slipup in one means decreased effectiveness in the other. And for a third, defensive systems may inhibit the use of some weapons systems in a surprise attack; for instance, the USSR probably could not position missile-submarines for a strike against U.S. air bases without such a move being detected and offset.

The double utility of defensive systems—in complicating the process of launching a nuclear strike and in reducing the damage from it—has served to justify their existence despite great expense and admitted imperfections. Moreover, the cost to an opponent of offsetting defensive systems may be about equal to the costs of those systems, and their effectiveness in limiting damage is probably greater than that of other methods, such as building more missiles. Accordingly, there have been pressures, both in the government and outside it, to construct comprehensive and extensive defenses, active and passive: in short, to follow a policy of building strategic defenses.*

---

* See chapter 2, p. 18. Additional arguments in favor of such a course may be found in William R. Kintner, ed., *Safeguard: Why the ABM Makes Sense* (New York: Hawthorn Books, 1969), and in Johan J. Holst and William Schneider, Jr., eds., *Why ABM?: Policy Issues in the Missile Defense Controversy* (New York: Pergamon Press, 1969).

If, however, the objective is to reduce damage from a Soviet nuclear attack to low levels, as against complicating such an attack or making it somewhat more costly, other problems arise. There is, for example, little doubt that a relatively small investment in fallout shelters could save millions of lives in the event of nuclear war. However, to expect that civil defense programs could, even if they included comprehensive—and very expensive—blast shelters, so reduce damage as to render a nuclear strike relatively harmless seems unreasonable; the USSR could, if necessary, increase the number of megatons delivered on target, change the composition of its warheads to make fallout more lethal and longer lasting, or redesign reentry vehicles to penetrate deeply before exploding near blast shelters. To illustrate the magnitude of the problem, one study by the RAND Corporation indicated that even a $600 billion program to protect people, production facilities, and essential supplies could not guarantee American survival against large-scale Soviet attacks.[18]

Nor do active defenses offer much more promise of reducing damage from a nuclear strike to tolerable levels. It is true that U.S. air defense forces have in some exercises "destroyed" 90 percent or more of attacking planes before these reached the lines where they could release their bombs or launch their air-to-surface missiles; however, in others they have intercepted almost none of the "attackers." Even a 90 percent "kill probability" is not comforting, since only 10 percent of Soviet heavy bombers could kill millions of Americans. In actual combat the prospects of precluding high levels of damage are not very good, since the Soviets may employ unanticipated tactics, use novel penetration aids, or disrupt the air defense system by missile strikes against key components. Officials have testified that both U.S. and Soviet bombers could successfully penetrate each other's air defenses and that not even the improved system now programmed could prevent the Soviets from killing some 8 million Americans.[19]

As for antisubmarine warfare forces, their effectiveness is even more problematical. Since it is deemed impracticable to maintain over long periods of time the combination of hunter-killer submarines and patrol planes required to establish effective barriers to Soviet (or Chinese Communist) submarines, heavy reliance is placed on coastal surveillance systems to detect incoming subs and to vector the destroyers, helicopters, and patrol planes that conduct the actual attack. While these surveillance systems are reasonably effective out to several hundred miles (thanks in part to the fact that most Soviet-built submarines are comparatively noisy), it is possible for the Soviets to stand outside their range and strike at coastal targets. Theoretically, improved methods of detection (such as satellite-borne infrared sensors) could enhance the ability of the United States to locate and track enemy submarines, but in practice there are severe limitations to the potential effectiveness of all types of sensors.[20] Given these limitations, the problem of delivering weapons on those submarines which are located, and their ability to take advantage of "blind spots" in the defenses, it is understandable that former Chief of Naval Operations Admiral Thomas H. Moorer deemed it very difficult to limit damage from sea-mobile systems.[21] Moreover, the newer Soviet nuclear-powered submarines, armed with a Polaris-type missile, may prove almost as invulnerable as U.S. missile-submarines, which both Admiral Moorer and Rear Admiral Levering Smith, Project Manager of the Fleet Ballistic Missile System, consider largely immune to Soviet antisubmarine warfare forces.[22]

Furthermore, whatever their theoretical effectiveness, both air defenses and antisubmarine warfare forces are vulnerable to missile strikes against air bases, operations centers, and communications facilities and hence dependent on a successful defense against ballistic missiles. And in the absence of antimissile missiles, there is no sense in trying to build up other components of strategic defense forces to the point where they could blunt attacks by bombers and submarines, since even if these were significantly degraded Soviet ICBMs could kill over 100 million Americans. Thus efforts to reduce fatalities from a nuclear strike depend heavily upon the effectiveness of antiballistic missile systems.

At first sight the potential utility of antimissile missiles in limiting damage—and hence, in conjunction with powerful strategic offensive forces, of altering the strategic balance—seems great indeed. Without question they could safeguard against accidental weapons launchings, drastically reduce damage from attacks by small nuclear powers, introduce uncertainties into calculations of strategic capabilities, and degrade a retaliatory strike by another superpower; whether they could so reduce the damage from such a strike as to upset the strategic balance is more problematical. In the first place, even comprehensive ballistic missile defenses, costing as much as $40 billion, could not preclude the USSR from killing 10 to 20 million Americans—a number which might be high enough to deter the United States from initiating nuclear war in all save the most desperate of situations.[23] In the second place, the Soviets could penetrate or saturate U.S. ballistic missile defenses; for instance, simply by introducing penetration aids and multiple warheads the USSR could then kill 40 to 70 million Americans, while if it also added 550 mobile ICBMs, the figure would rise to 90 to 100 million.[24] And finally, the Soviet Union could bypass U.S. antiballistic missiles by employing circumglobal rockets, or evade them by building up its bomber force or by introducing supersonic cruise-type missiles. As President Nixon stated, "The heaviest [ballistic missile] defense system we considered, one designed to protect our major cities, still could not prevent a catastrophic level of U.S. fatalities from a deliberate all-out Soviet attack."[25]

Soviet reactions to any American attempt to build extensive missile defenses might leave the United States in a worse position than before. If the Soviets increased or upgraded their own strategic strike forces, in an effort to maintain their assured destruction capability at a high level, they could, as Mr. NcNamara has pointed out, largely nullify the advantages of American antimissile missiles and leave each side in the same relative position as before, after the expenditure of additional billions of dollars. If they chose instead to extend their embryonic ballistic missile defenses,* this could (if carried far enough) begin to erode American assured destruction capabilities; indeed anticipation of this has prompted the decision to deploy Minuteman III and Poseidon missiles capable of carrying MIRVs and the emphasis which has been given for some years to decoys and other penetration aids. Finally, should the Soviets choose to improve their strategic strike

---

* As of mid-1970 the Soviets had deployed around Moscow some sixty-four Galosh antimissile missiles, similar to the American Spartan exoatmospheric interceptor but of shorter range.

forces *and* to deploy more antiballistic missiles, they might cut so deeply into American retaliatory capabilities as to require offsetting increases in U.S. strategic nuclear forces. Thus American defensive systems can significantly affect the strategic balance only if the USSR can be persuaded to limit its responses to any improvements which the United States may make.

This is, of course, not true so far as Communist China is concerned. According to Defense Department estimates, the Chinese in 1975 will have no long-range bombers, only one or two obsolete missile submarines, and a handful of ICBMs (see table 3). Against such a force projected American strategic defenses should be highly effective: U.S. hunter-killer submarines could report departures from Chinese naval bases; U.S. sonar stations should be able to track Chinese submarines; U.S. radar should detect launches by either submarine-based or land-based missiles; and Spartan and Sprint interceptors should be able to knock down most—if not all—of the incoming missiles.

This does not mean that the United States could wholly preclude damage from a Chinese nuclear strike. For one thing, the U.S. ABM system might not work as planned. For another, the Chinese could concentrate their missiles against one or two targets, thereby increasing the likelihood of saturating or exhausting the defenses. For a third, they could (admittedly at some expense and with some difficulty) equip their ICBMs with penetration aids, which could be designed to deal specifically with the Safeguard system. And for a fourth, they could employ other and more exotic means of penetrating U.S. defenses, such as launching low-level cruise-type missiles from submarines or using cargo ships to bring nuclear-armed seaplanes within range of coastal cities.[26]

Moreover, in time the Chinese could certainly build more—and more sophisticated—delivery systems which could significantly enhance their ability to inflict damage on the United States. Although American defenses could be upgraded in parallel with increases in Chinese capabilities, improvements in defenses could ultimately reach a point of diminishing returns—by 1985, if not by 1980. (It is also possible that such improvements might be barred by agreements between the United States and the USSR on the limitation of strategic armaments.) Hence, while a posture emphasizing strategic defenses as a means of limiting damage from a Chinese attack may be useful in the short run, its long-term utility may be questionable.* And whether it is either necessary or helpful to the protection of broader U.S. interests is perhaps even more questionable.†

Strategic Forces and Damage Limitation

To recapitulate, it would seem that even a posture of strategic sufficiency would enable the United States to achieve its primary objective: that of being able to launch crippling retaliatory strikes upon the USSR and Communist China; thus 1 percent of the warheads which will be carried by American missiles and bombers in 1975 could inflict 20 million casualties on the USSR or Communist China. Furthermore, this posture would enable the United States both to emerge from any nuclear exchange in a position far more advantageous than that of Communist China and to reduce damage from a Chinese attack to very low levels—at least in the short run. However, it would not preclude the Soviet Union from inflicting on the United States damage at least equal to that which the United States could cause, in part because higher percentages of the American people are concentrated in large cities, in part because the equally numerous Soviet missiles would carry larger (if fewer) warheads, and in part because it would be difficult to destroy Soviet reentry vehicles before they could reach their targets.

Unfortunately for its proponents, superiority in numbers of launch vehicles or of deliverable warheads, or in deliverable megatonnage, offers little promise of bettering the situation. Even though the United States supposedly will have twice as many

* For arguments to the contrary, see the testimony of Secretary of Defense Melvin R. Laird in U.S. Congress, House, Subcommittees of the Committee on Appropriations, *Hearings, SAFEGUARD Antiballistic Missile System*, 91st Cong., 1st sess., 1969, pp. 26–29. A fuller official statement of the role which ABMs could play in an integrated defense program will be found in U.S. Congress, Senate, Committee on Foreign Relations, Subcommittee on Arms Control, International Law and Organization, *Hearings, ABM, MIRV, SALT and the Nuclear Arms Race*, 91st Cong., 2d sess., 1970, esp. pp. 286–89.

† See chapter 5, pp. 102–03.

reentry vehicles in 1975 as will the USSR (and could have more), and even though multiple warhead missiles may be lucrative targets, the United States could not hope to knock out enough Soviet launch vehicles to preclude heavy damage from a retaliatory strike; for example, 1 percent of the projected Soviet warheads could kill up to 50 million Americans. While increases in launch vehicles could add to American counterforce capabilities, and higher-thrust missiles with larger-yield warheads could enhance the ability of the United States to destroy both hard and soft targets, there is no reason to suppose that such augmentations could significantly alter the situation: Soviet forces are too powerful. Furthermore, there is no necessity for the USSR to restrict its 1975 forces to the levels now estimated—nor any reason to believe that it would do so, should the United States significantly increase its own strategic nuclear capabilities.

The same is true of strategic defenses, which otherwise might offer promise. For one thing, the United States would find it very difficult to cope with the sizable and versatile Soviet forces projected for 1975. For another, the installation of ballistic missile defenses around American cities might, as the Nixon administration pointed out in rejecting the Sentinel system, provoke the USSR into further increasing its strategic strike forces, in order to maintain its own deterrent posture. And even if it chose not to do this, it could take other measures (such as targeting low-level, cruise-type, submarine-launched missiles against coastal cities) which could add markedly to its ability to inflict damage on even a well-defended America.

To sum up, it would appear that the United States and the Soviet Union now have strategic nuclear forces of such size, diversity, and complexity that each country can destroy the other. Furthermore, both countries have the technical skills, the industrial bases, and the economic resources needed to maintain this capability, despite anything the other can do. Although either can cause perturbations in the strategic balance, neither can upset it if the other takes prudent countermeasures. In fact, the great lesson of the current debate over American defense policy should be that efforts to achieve militarily significant advantages are likely to have more impact on levels of armament and on defense expenditures than on the strategic balance between the United States and the USSR.

Strategic Power and Strategic Stability

This immediately raises the question whether different (and perhaps smaller) force postures might not better serve U.S. interests, at least over the next few years. By way of illustration, the Safeguard ABM system has been justified on the ground that it is essential to cope with projected Soviet capabilities resulting from an increase in the number of launch vehicles, accurate multiple warheads (or MIRVs) for high-thrust Soviet ICBMs, quieter nuclear submarines carrying longer-range missiles, and perhaps improved ballistic missile defenses. As envisioned by Mr. Laird, Soviet submarines would strike at U.S. air bases (possibly launching their missiles on a depressed trajectory which would make them more difficult to detect) while the SS-9 missiles would attack U.S. ICBM sites; in conjunction, these could destroy 95 percent of the Minuteman and Titan missiles and "most" of the 200-odd U.S. bombers on ground alert. And while two-thirds of the Polaris and Poseidon missiles would be on submarines at sea, these could, according to Mr. Laird, be threatened by new Soviet antisubmarine warfare measures or knocked down by Soviet ballistic missile defenses, should these be built.[27]

Although threats of this nature cannot be ignored, it is necessary that they be put in perspective. In the first place, not all of them are currently realizable; the erosion of U.S. retaliatory capabilities depends in part on the ability of the USSR to develop a system for retargeting ICBMs against missile sites which were not struck initially and in part on its devising "some weapon, technique or tactic which might increase the vulnerability of our POLARIS/POSEIDON submarines."[28] In the second place, some of these threats could be offset by comparatively simple countermeasures, such as improving the radar coverage of the seaward approaches to the United States (to give earlier warning of SLBM launchings), relocating additional bombers on overseas bases (in order to complicate the timing of counterforce attacks and to force the redeployment of Soviet surface-to-air missiles and fighter-interceptors), and putting some bombers on air alert. (Ten B-52s can carry enough nuclear weapons to kill 20 million Soviet citizens; three times that many on air alert should insure that these ten reach their targets.) In the third place, Soviet success depends on the United States *not* launching its ICBMs on warning, that is, on the continuance of a firing doctrine rather than on alterations in strategic postures. While firing at first warning may increase the likelihood of an inadvertent launch, and hence be undesirable, it may make sense to retaliate with those Minutemen which survive the initial Soviet salvo and not await their destruction by the second wave of SS-9s postulated in Mr. Laird's scenario.

Moreover, the USSR could not in fact be certain that its new weapons or its supposedly advantageous strategic posture could enable it to reduce damage from U.S. retaliatory strikes to low levels, since peacetime operational data concerning the reliability, accuracy, and effectiveness of weapons systems may not hold up under combat conditions. (For example, the German antiaircraft defenses in World War II were about one-tenth as effective as they had been in prewar tests.) In addition, it is always possible that the process of readying forces for a first strike may be detected or that the difficulty of coordinating an attack by dissimilar weapons systems may give warning of that attack, in either case enabling the United States to launch some elements of its retaliatory forces. And finally, American countermeasures might begin to erode Soviet capabilities, thereby forcing the USSR either to initiate nuclear war before it had secured maximum advantage from its new weapons or to watch that advantage disappear.

This is particularly true since the time required for the USSR to develop and deploy even those new weapons now feasible is on the order of five years. During this same period the United States could take further measures to safeguard its retaliatory forces, such as pouring additional concrete around its missile silos, making some of its ICBMs land-mobile, or even shifting many of them to ships, as previously discussed. Although some of these measures (such as hardening silos) are both costly and of short-term utility, others (such as the movement of missiles to sea or their emplacement on the bottoms of the Great Lakes) could offset even maneuverable reentry vehicles, warheads guided by telemetry or equipped with homing sensors, and other technological innovations of the post-1975 period. And they do indicate what could be done to make current U.S. forces less vulnerable, even to strenuous and far-reaching efforts by the Soviets to improve their counterforce capabilities.*

Equally, other choices in U.S. weapons programs could further U.S. objectives, possibly at less cost and certainly with fewer complications. For example, MIRVs offer peculiar and significant advantages in coping with Soviet ABMs, in that warheads from several missiles could be directed against the same target or several warheads from the same launch vehicle could be sent in on different trajectories, so as to arrive at different times, thereby complicating the task of directing and controlling interceptors.[29] However, they also make launch vehicles more lucrative targets for counterforce strikes and, by multiplying the number of warheads available, make such strikes more feasible—and more threatening. Although the United States has reportedly decided not to develop highly accurate MIRVs, the Soviets can never be sure of this; moreover, they may recall the testimony of former Secretary of the Air Force Harold R. Brown that "the MIRV is designed to have a higher kill probability [against hardened targets] than our present missiles" and that even if it failed to achieve the desired CEP† it would be "as good as what we have now."[30] In consequence, the USSR may enlarge its own ICBM force beyond the level which would otherwise be deemed necessary.

Fortunately, MIRVs are not the only means of penetrating ballistic missile defenses. One alternative would be to develop a

---

* Even unforeseeable—and as yet unattainable—innovations, such as laser missile defenses, or magnetic fields capable of deflecting or destroying incoming bombers, could be bypassed by means of multimegaton underwater mines or the detonation in outer space of high-yield nuclear weapons. While any or all such innovations might require alterations in force postures or strategic concepts, there is no reason to believe that they could prevent either side from killing millions of people, should it wish to do so.

† Circular error probable—the zone within which, on the average, 50 percent of the missiles fired at a target should hit.

powered reentry vehicle, whose changes of course could increase the amount of time which would have to be spent in tracking incoming warheads or could confuse a launch control radar guiding an interceptor to its target. If this seems too much like a super-MIRV, the United States could rely more heavily on chaff to obscure the reentry vehicle or on decoys and on the deliberate fragmentation of tankage to multiply the number of objects which must be attacked. Or it could employ electronic jamming and nuclear blackout to degrade tracking and missile control radar.[31] Admittedly, none of these methods is as certain as the present plan for exhausting an opponent's ABM system by sending over more warheads than he has interceptors, but the latter calls for large numbers of reentry vehicles which, in the present context, means MIRVs.[32] If, however, the Soviets likewise install MIRVs, they may have a potential advantage in that their higher-thrust rockets can carry more and/or larger multiple warheads than any American ICBMs now operational.

Admittedly, foregoing the increases in U.S. strategic nuclear forces planned for the early seventies would to some extent affect the prospects for meeting the criteria devised by the Nixon administration. The major shortfall would be in the ability to "defend against major damage from small attacks or accidental launches" through deploying ballistic missile defenses;[33] however, this option could be precluded by agreements on the limitation of strategic armaments, may be of dubious value, and is in any case of short-term utility. Measures such as those described previously should rule out a rational Soviet decision to launch a surprise attack or to "strike the United States first in a crisis," other criteria by which the administration evaluates U.S. forces; even if the United States gave up both ABMs and MIRVs, its forces would not be inferior to those which the USSR might develop under the "low force-low technology" parameter mentioned by Mr. Laird (see table 6). Although a "high force-high technology" approach could give the USSR numerical superiority—and possibly enable it to inflict more damage than it would receive—it is by no means certain that Soviet strategic nuclear forces would be all that effective against an altered American posture. In any case there is no basis for supposing that this high force-high technology posture will be the Soviet choice,* since there is some possibility of precluding it through arms control agreements, and there are many ways of offsetting it, of which the U.S. altered posture shown in table 6 is but a particular and incomplete example.

TABLE 6: Hypothetical U.S. and Soviet Force Postures, Circa 1975

Type	U.S. Basic Posture[a]	Soviet Low Force–Low Technology Posture[b]	U.S. Altered Posture[c]	Soviet High Force–High Technology Posture[d]
ICBMs	1,027	1,440	527	2,500
SLBMs	656	605	656	845
Ship-borne or bottom-based missiles	–	–	500	–
Bombers	326	145	326	145
Total launchers	2,009	2,190	2,009	3,490
Total warheads	6,509	3,040	6,509	4,780
Deliverable megatonnage (approximate)	4,025	7,200	4,025	11,600
Ballistic missile interceptors	–	200–400(?)	–	600(?)

a. Assumes 1975 bomber force, hardened missile silos, etc., but not ABMs or MIRVs.

b. Assumes no further deployment of Soviet ICBMs, beyond those in place at the end of 1970, MRVs but no MIRVs for the SS-9, and the lower level of projected Soviet SLBM capabilities. See *Statement of Secretary of Defense Melvin R. Laird Before a Joint Session of the Senate Armed Services Committee and the Senate Subcommittee on Department of Defense Appropriations on the Fiscal Year 1971 Defense Program and Budget*, 20 February 1970, mimeographed, p. 48, para. 3a, and the more detailed discussion on pp. 102–05.

c. Assumes 1975 bomber force, hardened missile silos, some transfer of ICBMs to ships, barges, etc., but no ABMs or MIRVs.

d. From table 2.

* Secretary of Defense Laird testified in 1970 that "there are no clear indications at this time concerning the long-term Soviet objectives for their ICBM force, either in quantity or in quality." *Statement of Secretary of Defense Melvin R. Laird Before a Joint Session of the Senate Armed Services Committee and the Senate Subcommittee on Department of Defense Appropriations on the Fiscal Year 1971 Defense Program and Budget*, 20 February 1970, mimeographed, p. 104.

The point here is not that all previous choices have been wrong but rather that there are many ways of stabilizing the strategic balance, not all of which necessitate increases in current U.S. forces. Since stability (in the sense of a mutual Soviet-American ability to inflict heavy damage on one another) seems the best one can hope for, prudence suggests that it be sought without multiplying costs, without intensifying the arms race, and without generating new fears and tensions, internally or externally. Whether it can be achieved through restraint, or whether it must be pursued through a continuing arms buildup, depends upon Soviet as well as upon American decisions.

Obviously, these decisions (as well as those by the Chinese Communists) will not be based solely upon the utility of strategic forces in waging war. As noted earlier, President Nixon has indicated that "the overriding purpose of our strategic posture is political and defensive: to deny other countries the ability to impose their will on the United States and its allies under the weight of strategic military superiorty. We must insure that all potential aggressors see unacceptable risks in contemplating a nuclear attack or nuclear blackmail or acts which could escalate to strategic nuclear war, such as a Soviet conventional attack on Europe."[34] The next two chapters will consider whether and to what extent achievement of this broader objective depends on the maintenance of particular levels and types of American strategic power.

4
Strategic Power and Deterrence

If the analysis just completed is correct, it indicates that by taking prudent precautions the United States should be able to destroy scores of Soviet and/or Chinese cities, even under the worst of circumstances. Since deterrence* is based on the theory that the potential aggressor will act only when the predicted benefits exceed the probable costs, this finding should be comforting, as few conceivable gains would be worth such staggering losses. However, as noted earlier, the Nixon administration has not been satisfied with this and has maintained that the United States should be able to inflict on the USSR casualties at least equivalent to those it would suffer itself, even if this means going above the levels of unacceptable damage set previously by Mr. McNamara.[1] And some American officials and analysts have argued that even this is not enough, that the United States should emerge from any nuclear exchange with a relative advantage over its adversary and with only comparatively small losses of life and property.†

Although many of the arguments for maintaining a strategic advantage are based on beliefs that Soviet and Chinese leaders are less mindful of human values than their American counterparts, are more motivated to pursue expansionist policies, and are more inclined to take risks in the pursuit of their objectives,

---

* As used here *deterrence* means the ability "to hinder or to prevent action by fear of consequences, or by difficulty, risk, unpleasantness, etc." *Webster's Third New International Dictionary of the English Language*, 2d ed, unabridged, p. 711.

† See chapter 2, pp. 15–16.

these arguments also derive from some of the problems and paradoxes of deterrence.[2] One such problem is that the ability of a nuclear-armed aggressor to inflict damage on the deterrer may inhibit the latter from actually launching a strategic strike, thereby reducing the punishment for aggression from a certainty to a possibility. Another is that if the damage ratios are favorable to the aggressor, he may be even more inclined to act, since now his benefits would exceed his costs—at least in a material sense—even if the deterrer *did* initiate nuclear war. And a third is that the presumed reluctance of the deterrer to suffer heavy losses and/or to accept a disadvantageous war outcome may so weaken the credibility of the deterrent as to make aggression (and perhaps nuclear war) more likely. Thus it is understandable that many Americans have insisted that the United States be at least "first among equals" insofar as strategic power is concerned.

However, as any student of the subject will admit, prospective levels of damage (or "consequences") are only one factor in deterrence, along with the determination actually to inflict that damage under certain prescribed circumstances, communication to an opponent of one's intent to do this, his perceptions of both intent and resolve, and his subsequent analysis of the potential costs, the possible risks, and the probable benefits of taking (or not taking) the proscribed action. In many instances these subjective elements may be more significant than the actual ability to cause casualties; when the United States, despite its overwhelming strategic superiority, refused to intervene in the Hungarian Revolution of 1956, this decision sprang in part from a belief that the USSR would fight in order to preserve its control over the states of Eastern Europe. But even if one accepts the premise that levels of damage are all-important, as many Americans apparently do, it does not follow that shifts in the strategic balance will necessarily weaken the deterrent to aggression against the United States, its allies, or its interests—a thesis which will be discussed next.

Strategic Power and Military Operations

For one thing, current U.S. strategic retaliatory forces should, despite the Soviet buildup of the last few years, be able to inflict on the USSR more than 120 million fatalities—enough, in Mr. McNamara's words, to "destroy the Soviet Union as a viable 20th Century society."[3] Even if the United States did nothing to offset the estimated growth of Soviet nuclear power during the next five years, its forces should be able to kill 40 to 50 million people; in fact, those elements of the missile-submarine fleet normally at sea could probably deliver at least one nuclear weapon on every Soviet city of over 100,000 population within their range.* And, as previously noted, planned measures to protect, defend, and disperse other elements of the strategic strike forces, and to install MIRVs, will enable the United States to kill over 100 million Soviets under the worst of circumstances—without employing the weapons targeted against Communist China.†

Whatever moral judgments one may pass on such a high capacity for assured destruction, it offers several advantages with respect to deterrence. First of all, it virtually eliminates uncertainties about the level of damage which would suffice to deter an aggressor from taking a proscribed action. Secondly, it may well diminish the willingness to run risks; psychological studies indicate that even inveterate gamblers hesitate to bet when the potential losses are large, even if the odds appear to be favorable. Thirdly, it may, as Herman Kahn suggests, "impress even the irrational and irresponsible with the degree of their irrationality, and therefore with the need for caution."[4] Fourthly, the ability to inflict heavy casualties includes the ability to inflict lighter ones without prejudicing the ultimate utility of the strategic strike forces for intrawar deterrence or for bargaining about war termination. Thus there is much to be said for being able to inflict heavy damage.

However, this leaves unanswered the question: How heavy need heavy be? Even the lowest of the figures cited previously is equal to the population of Britain or France and higher than the losses suffered by all the combatants in World War II. To assume

---

* Two-thirds (27) of the 41 submarines are usually on station; these carry 432 missiles with approximately 650 warheads which could be equipped with penetration aids. Even after allowing for possible losses to Soviet antisubmarine warfare forces, attrition by any Soviet ballistic missile defenses, etc., it is reasonable to assume that at least a third of these could reach their targets. The USSR has only 221 cities of over 100,000 people.

† See chapter 2, pp. 12–13.

that the drive for power or the search for security would motivate a state to accept such losses is to make a mockery of all the theories of interstate relations and all the practices of statecraft; indeed, it would represent a negation of the basic purpose of a state: to preserve the lives and to enlarge the well-being of its citizens. As McGeorge Bundy, former Special Assistant to the President for National Security Affairs, says, "A decision that would bring even one hydrogen bomb on one city of one's own country would be recognized in advance as a catastrophic blunder; ten bombs on ten cities would be a disaster beyond history; and a hundred bombs on a hundred cities are unthinkable."[5] And if a national leader himself did not recognize this, there are presumably those among his associates who would.

Admittedly, no one can say with assurance what levels of prospective damage would be unacceptable to an opponent, since this will depend in large measure upon the importance he attaches to the accretion of power, to the preservation of human lives, and to the maintenance of peace as an end in itself. Since his values differ from our own, it is obvious that what may deter us may not deter him—or vice versa. Moreover, we cannot be sure that his views tomorrow will be the same as those he holds today, inasmuch as levels of damage which are deemed unacceptable when considering whether to launch a nuclear strike may change with perceptions of threat or "evidence" of hostility. What one can say, with some reason, is that the potential consequences of a nuclear war, even between unequals, are so dire that no nation will lightly start one.

If this judgment is correct (and all the nuclear powers seemingly behave as if it were), it casts doubt on the validity of the American belief that only very high levels of prospective damage can deter various forms of aggression. It also calls into question another American idea: that deterrence hinges on the ability to inflict at least as much damage as an adversary can—and hopefully more. True, some individuals seek accretions of power (for themselves or for the institutions of which they are members), are more inclined than others to take risks in the drive for power, and may attach less importance to the costs attendant on any such drive. This does not mean that such individuals necessarily occupy positions of leadership only in the Communist world;

those who so claim might well take another look at the psychological profiles of some American officials. Nor does it mean that these individuals are deterred from action only by outcomes potentially less advantageous for their countries than for the United States; the enormous destruction attendant on even a small-scale nuclear exchange may well suffice. (In fact, to judge by the extraordinary measures taken by the United States to preclude even minimal casualties from a Chinese Communist attack, not even very favorable exchange ratios are likely to persuade one nuclear power to strike at another.)

Moreover, the attacker can never be sure that his advantages will hold up or that the damage from any retaliatory strike will fall within acceptable limits, whatever these might be. Despite the attractive simplicity of most calculations, there are dozens of variables (such as the effectiveness of warning systems, the reliability of missiles, and the effects of nuclear detonations in outer space) whose potential impact on the ability of one's own forces to inflict or to limit damage can be assessed only within wide ranges of probability. This is even more true in the case of enemy capabilities, where technical information may be lacking and where gross errors may occur; for example, the United States tended to overestimate Soviet forces in the late 1950s, partly because the USSR was deliberately "puffing up" its claims, partly because the United States lacked adequate means of verifying the rate of deployment of Soviet weapons. Although this can be guarded against by estimating capabilities to inflict damage on the assumption that everything works optimally for the enemy and minimally for oneself, even such "worst case" assessments are valid only within limits—especially since the other side may be operating on the same assumptions and on the basis of different figures for weapons systems characteristics.

This may not, however, reassure the deterrer, who is presumably conscious of his own reluctance to engage in nuclear war and worried lest his adversary, sensing this, be emboldened; accordingly, he may, by building more powerful strategic nuclear forces, seek both to buttress his own determination and to communicate his intent to respond to aggression. To him, low levels of damage to his homeland are meaningful not only in and of themselves but because they may nerve him to retaliate—and thus reduce the possibility that he may have to do so. Even marginal advantages may be valued out of all proportion to their worth, because they can be construed as giving evidence of determination, and hence as enhancing the credibility of the deterrent. Thus it is not surprising that the United States has sought to maintain some sort of lead over the USSR nor that Mr. Nixon has refused to define his concept of strategic sufficiency solely in terms of the levels of damage which would be unacceptable to a potential aggressor; as Margaret Mead points out, deterrent forces "have to be convincing . . . to the group of people to whom we have delegated the task of thinking about them,"[6] as well as to prospective enemies.

However, determination is not measured solely by relative ability to inflict damage; in fact, there are many other useful ways. For one thing, the willingness to launch a strategic strike may vary with the importance of the interests threatened, which suggests that those areas treasured most highly are least likely to be attacked. Thus, interests must be evaluated on the basis of their symbolic as well as of their actual importance; deterrence of an attack on West Berlin may work largely because the United States, by its presence, its commitments, and its demonstrated willingness to risk war in defense of its position, has indicated the importance it attaches to that city. The degree of interest must, of course, be looked at from both sides, since other countries obviously have interests differing from those of the United States. However, this still implies that decisions to employ military power would depend upon the relative value of the stakes at issue, the degree of commitment by both parties, and the local situation, as well as upon the balance of strategic power. If so, this would tend to favor the defender, who might (simply by virtue of his position) have a preponderance of interests and hence be willing to run greater risks to achieve his aims.

Furthermore, willingness to retaliate may well rise with the level of the provocation or the nature of the threat; a nuclear riposte to a sizable assault is more likely (and hence deterrence of such an assault is more credible) than in the case of a minor incursion. This indeed is the basis of U.S. policy for the defense of Western Europe, which rests on the assumption that the Soviets would not pursue any attack to the point where the allies would be forced to employ nuclear weapons. And while one may argue about where that point is, or should be, it seems under the circumstances a reasonable premise.

Finally, determination to retaliate may be affected by other factors having little to do with the strategic balance: a feeling of desperation, a determination to draw the line, or a desire to demonstrate that one cannot be pushed around. It may also be influenced by assessments of the aggressor's political cohesion and strength of will which could justify beliefs that *he* would cave in rather than continue a nuclear exchange. Even though such emotions and beliefs are not likely to prevail in calmer moments, they could in time of stress override more rational calculations, a point which any potential aggressor must bear in mind.

All this does not mean that the deterrer must rely solely on a display of irrational behavior and unpredictability to impress an opponent with his determination; there are many other ways of communicating his intention to resist aggression. He can (as the United States has done) repeatedly declare that any use of atomic weapons against his homeland will precipitate a nuclear response. He can enter into alliance arrangements which provide for automatic involvement in the event of any conventional thrust. He can issue broad guarantees to nonaligned nations, or commit himself to take action in the event of specific threats to their security, as President Nixon did in pledging that the United States would shield nonnuclear states against aggression by a nuclear power.[7] He can, in short, both buttress his own determination and express his intent by his declaratory policies and by his commitments.

He can also do this by his actions, which still speak more loudly than words: hence the U.S. garrison in West Berlin, the Seventh Army in West Germany, the Sixth Fleet in the Mediterranean, and the Fifth Air Force in Japan. True, neither words nor deeds necessarily mean that all forms of aggression will precipitate nuclear war, in part because this is palpably absurd, in part because the deterrer may seek, through deliberate vaguenesses and calculated ambiguities, to achieve effective deterrence without binding himself to start such a war. Equally, a nuclear-armed adversary is not likely to believe that every military operation he undertakes will inevitably induce a nuclear strike. However, as one looks at the nature of such operations, it becomes apparent that certainty may not be all that essential to deterrence.

To begin with, it would seem that any direct attack would almost inevitably precipitate a retaliatory strike. While scenarios have been written in which a trembling President grounds the Strategic Air Command, orders U.S. missile-submarines back to port, and turns political control over to a pro-Communist regime rather than risk the further damage which would result from a continuing nuclear exchange, these scenarios seem rather unconvincing; political pressures, panic, desperation, a desire for revenge or even a breakdown in the command and control system could all induce counterstrikes. If this prospect were not enough to deter attack, the United States (or the Soviet Union) could always program its surviving missiles to fire after the first enemy salvo, or could incorporate an automatic authorization to launch into its bomb alarm system—and announce this. Although such measures might increase the likelihood of inadvertent war there are many ways of insuring that only a sizable—and presumably deliberate—attack would trigger a retaliatory strike. And in the improbable event that worst came to worst, the advantages attached to insuring certainty of response (and increasing the damage inflicted) might warrant greater automaticity.

Obviously, a nuclear power is less likely to launch its strategic strike forces in the event of an attack on one of its allies than of an attack on itself; however, the likelihood can never be set at zero. A Soviet (or an American) decision maker must always consider the possibility that his opponent might initiate nuclear war, since the importance that opponent attaches to maintaining a given position, to upholding a commitment, or simply to preserving his reputation may all induce seemingly irrational actions. Under some circumstances even the recognition that he would suffer heavy damage from retaliatory strikes may not have sufficient impact to alter his decision for war, particularly since it is difficult to feel emotionally all the implications of a nuclear attack. In most cases, awareness that the probability of escaping nuclear retaliation cannot be determined either with accuracy or with certainty will militate against undertaking any operation which could precipitate such a response. As Glenn Snyder points out, when "the outcome of even the smallest border skirmish *might* be utter devastation, the aggressor's uncertainty is an important deterring factor."[8]

The deterrent effect of uncertainty does not depend solely upon the likelihood that the aggrieved party will immediately initiate nuclear war—which may indeed be small—but upon the possibility that he may subsequently do so. As Schelling suggests, credible deterrence need not "depend on a willingness to commit anything like suicide in the face of a challenge. A response that carries some risk of war can be plausible, even reasonable, at a time when a final, ultimate decision to *have* a general war would be implausible or unreasonable."[9]

Once started, conflicts acquire a momentum of their own, and the participants may wind up taking measures and running risks which at the outset they would have deemed unacceptable; had President Lyndon B. Johnson imagined in 1965 the costs and the consequences of U.S. intervention in South Vietnam, it is unlikely that the marines would ever have landed at Danang. Moreover, during the course of a war the participants may perceive threats, recognize interests, or make commitments which could lead them to intensify or to extend military operations rather than to accept defeat. That either these or previous interests will lead to the initiation of nuclear war cannot be ruled out; as General André Beaufre indicates, escalation could take place if the aggressor tries for a political or strategic stake of great importance, seeks an overly large conventional success, or errs in estimating his opponent's determination.[10] Even if none of these suffices to trigger a deliberate first strike, a local conflict may "go nuclear" inadvertently, because of miscalculations of intent, or because an ally, out of desperation, acts independently.

Admittedly, the possibility that a conflict may escalate serves to inhibit the defender from responding to aggression by a nuclear-armed adversary, even as it inhibits the latter from acting in the first place. Here again, however, a defender can take steps to make escalation almost automatic, as by publicly committing himself to prearranged military responses, such as a thrust up the Helmstadt Autobahn in the event Berlin is attacked. Alternatively, he can place units armed with atomic weapons well forward in his defensive system, or so denude those defenses that he (or his allies) would have to take drastic measures to restore the situation, as in the forward strategy advocated by some West Germans during the sixties. In short, there are many ways in which a defender can increase the likelihood of escalation and with it the uncertainty of an aggressor that he can escape punishment for his actions.

Even without efforts by the deterrer to raise the specter of escalation, or, by consciously "irrational" behavior, to create uncertainties as to future responses, a potential aggressor may find it difficult to calculate precisely the probable consequences of his actions. Problems may arise from the sheer inability of human beings to store, analyze, and digest the information required for anything but the simplest choices among alternatives or from the fact that information may be inadequate, variables too numerous to examine, and decision-making techniques simply not advanced enough to assure reasonable certainty in estimating outcomes. Uncertainties may also arise because of the difficulty of putting oneself in the place of the adversary, whose psychological characteristics, personal experiences, and socio-cultural milieu may all incline him to weigh factors differently. Moreover, vested interests, bureaucratic opposition, and even political aspirations may affect an adversary's decisions, thereby adding further to uncertainties. (If he doesn't know in advance what he will do, how can you?) And uncertainties may be resolved in favor of doing nothing; as British defense analyst Michael Howard indicates, "It could be reasonably argued that, even if there were only one chance in a hundred that a political move would really be met by a threatened nuclear response, that chance would be an effective deterrent to any responsible statesman."[11]

Even if the statesman in question is not responsible, or assesses differently the chance of a nuclear response, he must consider both the difficulties and the costs of overt aggression. For one thing, all of the nuclear powers possess sizable conventional forces and allies who add to the total troop strength on both sides.

These troops are generally concentrated at the points of highest value, or on the approaches to those points, so that an attacker must either settle for lesser (if more easily attainable) objectives or be prepared to overcome heavy resistance. In most instances he may not be able to launch an assault without preparatory measures which could tip his hand; for example, the NATO allies knew weeks in advance of the Soviet moves which preceded the occupation of Czechoslovakia in 1968. And in no case can he count upon speedy success; as Adolf Hitler learned in 1941, it is not possible to calculate accurately either the costs or the outcomes of military adventures.

This is particularly true since the nuclear powers and their allies are not restricted to conventional weapons. If invading armies mass to attack, they become vulnerable to tactical nuclear strikes against troop concentrations, artillery positions, and command installations, whereas if they do not mass they may be unable to break through defenses manned by greatly inferior forces. As with Richard III at Bosworth Field, uncertainty as to the enemy's course of action may constrain one to await attack rather than to launch it.* And even should an attack be launched, the possibility of nuclear strikes against supply centers, lines of communication, and air bases will affect both the efficiency of support operations and the depth to which an invader may be willing (or able) to penetrate.

Furthermore, it is not necessary that any nuclear response take a form which is so likely to escalate the conflict, and hence so difficult to decide upon. A defender might "signal" his intent to go nuclear rather than to accept defeat by detonating one or two nuclear weapons, either over unoccupied areas behind enemy lines or over military targets. He might authorize the limited use of short-range weapons such as the Sergeant missile, thereby checking an enemy advance without extending the battle zone or threatening vital rear area installations. Or he could simply

---

* In fairness to Richard, who was an experienced general as well as a valiant fighter, it should be noted that he was also—and with good reason—uncertain of the loyalty of some of his ostensible supporters, whose defection actually cost him battle, crown, and life. Similar uncertainties may affect decisions in today's world.

seal off his borders by employing atomic demolitions to create a lethal radioactive belt, a measure reportedly favored by some in the Bundeswehr. In sum, it is possible to make it difficult and costly for an aggressor to achieve any significant military success without either initiating a nuclear exchange or taking actions which would be likely to escalate into one.

In addition, a prospective aggressor must consider not only the probable costs, the potential risks, and the uncertain benefits directly associated with military operations but many other costs. For one thing, he must consider whether the use of force will adversely affect his ability to secure the same objective by other and less risky means. He must take into account the possibility that his actions will influence the likelihood of attaining other important goals. He must assess the risks to his allies of his actions and their impact on alliance arrangements. He must face the possibility that his moves might fail, with the result that national prestige, as well as the credibility of future threats, would be diminished. And even if he succeeded in achieving his objective, the rewards of success might be as bad as the consequences of failure in that they could induce his opponents to adopt new defense programs, could bolster tottering alliance systems, and otherwise could strengthen the very elements he was trying to weaken. (If the occupation of Czechoslavakia stimulated increases in European defense budgets and brought to a halt the drawdown of U.S forces in Germany, what might be the impact on NATO of even a minor Soviet incursion into Western Europe?)

Nor are external factors the only ones to be considered: internal goals and policies also affect decisions. At the very least, military operations or preparations for them will cost money and divert resources from other and more productive applications. In the process they may force the abandonment or curtailment of cherished programs, cause distortions in the economy, and generate public discontent—as has the war in Vietnam. And a country which, like the USSR, is seeking to promote communism by demonstrating that it insures social and economic progress—in Khrushchev's homey phrase, "by putting goulash on every worker's plate"—may find this incompatible with an expansionist policy, which could not only draw off resources required for domestic programs but alienate those whom the Soviets are seeking to influence.

Finally, individual leaders must take into account the possible impact on their internal political positions; thus Lyndon Johnson's inability to bring the war in Vietnam to a satisfactory conclusion may well have influenced his decision to withdraw as a candidate for the Presidency. And governments riven by dissension or lacking popular support must bear in mind that the strains of war may lead not just to a loss of political power but to the collapse of the whole regime—a point which the Soviet and Chinese Communist leaders are not likely to forget.

On the whole it would seem that strategic power is not the only element affecting the practice of deterrence—a conclusion from which it is difficult to dissent. But, like many conclusions, this one is frequently ignored or slighted; some statements and analyses tend to give the impression that the balance between U.S. and Soviet strategic strike forces (or the relative rates of deployment of Chinese ICBMs and American ABMs) are the most significant factors making for peace or war.[12] In consequence too much attention may be paid to shifts in the strategic balance and not enough to the risks, the difficulties, and the costs associated with attempts to alter forcibly the political balance.

Strategic Power and Political Pressures

These "risks, difficulties, and costs" carry over into attempts to employ strategic power for political purposes. Even where the purpose is defensive, as in backing up American resistance to the erosion of allied rights in West Berlin or assuring the Cubans of Soviet support in their struggle against "American imperialism," it is hard to achieve credibility, since this derives ultimately from the willingness to use nuclear weapons. A decision to do this is difficult enough in the case of overt aggression, even though this constitutes a palpable breach of the peace, a fact which justifies politically and sanctions legally a forceful rejoinder. When the aggressive act is a nonmilitary one, such as the imposition of an economic boycott, a nuclear response would be so markedly disproportionate as to virtually rule it out, even as a last resort. When the aim is not merely to deter a nation from taking political actions which threaten another country's interests but to compel it to take actions which further them, the inhibitions against the use of nuclear weapons may be even stronger and the validity of threats to do so even more doubtful.

Despite all this, superior strategic nuclear forces have been deemed politically advantageous in that they do pose the possibility of disadvantageous war outcomes and hence make threats of war more meaningful; thus former Secretary of Defense McNamara testified that the only reason Khrushchev withdrew Soviet missiles from Cuba was that "he faced the full military power of the United States, including its [then superior] nuclear weapons."[13] Perhaps more importantly, they have been viewed as increasing the willingness of the state possessing them to exploit its presumed advantage. That either of these propositions is so valid as to warrant efforts to achieve strategic superiority is, however, questionable.

Admittedly, differences in strategic capabilities can have an effect on the willingness of one nuclear power to pressure another or its allies. Even an embryonic strategic strike force may add confidence to the country possessing it and lead that country to believe that it can inhibit a stronger adversary from initiating nuclear war. As its capabilities increase, confidence in its ability to limit responses may also grow, and it may therefore be more willing to cut off supplies to isolated enemy garrisons; to stop the flow of oil and other vital commodities; to provide money, munitions, and even men to dissident elements in other countries; and to threaten military action if countermeasures are taken. And if a nuclear power should achieve strategic superiority, it might then feel freer to maneuver against vulnerable positions, to support third parties in armed conflict, and even to intervene against similar efforts by its opponent, relying on the threat of escalation to preclude further action on his part.

All this, however, presumes that there are vulnerable positions against which to maneuver and that the means of applying pressure exist, so that strategic nuclear forces serve as a counterdeterrent rather than as an instrument of policy. In such a case even disproportionately small forces may suffice. However, as Schelling notes, a threat intended to compel an adversary to take a desired action, unlike a threat aimed at deterring him from taking an undesired one, "often requires that punishment be initiated *until* the other acts, . . . which means that the action initiated has to be tolerable to the initiator."[14] Since not even strategic superiority can insure against an intolerable response to any nuclear punishment, the threat to initiate such punishment may simply not be credible.

True, there are a number of ways in which strategic nuclear forces can be used to exert political pressures and to shape political decisions. For example, a national leader can order test firings of missiles or stage air defense exercises, with attendant publicity, thereby reminding one and all of his country's nuclear capabilities. He can point out to potential enemies the damage they would suffer in a nuclear war and hint that they could avoid this only by expelling foreign forces and abrogating alliance arrangements—a practice long followed by former Premier Khrushchev.[15] He (or his subordinates) can outline particular measures which might be taken should the situation worsen, measures such as a limited disarming strike or attacks on facilities for the production of fissionable materials. And he can couple either general or specific threats to use nuclear weapons with requests for changes in the policies or the practices of an obdurate opponent—that is, he can practice nuclear blackmail.

Such threats may unnerve an unarmed neighbor and make it less receptive to the presence of foreign troops or to the use of its territory for military operations; however, they may also inspire it to seek help from another nuclear power rather than to give in. When the threats are directed against a nuclear-armed state or its ally, they may immediately lead to a confrontation, thereby increasing the risk of war. Furthermore, such a confrontation tends to place on the blackmailer the responsibility for being the first to use atomic weapons, in conformance with his threat. And although he may feel that his own deterrent should rule out a nuclear exchange, he can never be completely sure; hence he himself may have to back down.

Moreover, the nuclear power whose interests or whose allies are threatened has many ways of responding other than by issuing counterthreats. It could offset pressures against allies by providing them with economic aid and military assistance, as the United States did when the Chinese Communists shelled Quemoy in 1958. It could minimize the impact of attempts at nuclear blackmail by redeploying its own nuclear-armed units, by installing defensive systems on allied soil, or by loaning its ally nuclear-capable delivery systems, with or without the warheads to arm them. It could exert counterpressures in another area—as the USSR could have against Berlin when the United States imposed its blockade of Cuba in 1962. Thus even an inferior nuclear power may have ways of coping with pressures by a superior one.

This is particularly true since the costs of intensifying pressures may be disproportionate to the potential gains. They may induce the threatened country to modify its foreign policy and to seek help from others, as India did in 1962 when pressured by the Chinese Communists. They may stimulate greater defense expenditures, as did Soviet pressures on Berlin in 1961. They may inspire new alliance arrangements, as did Soviet threats against Yugoslavia in 1948–1963. Or they may place further strains on existing alliances, as have American sanctions against Cuba.

All these costs might be acceptable were the prospective gains comparable. However, even successful pressures may achieve only marginal advantages, since positions of importance (such as West Berlin) are not likely to be given up and policies of significance (such as that of "a return to the mainland") are not likely to be abandoned. And while even limited success may enhance prestige, extend influence, and enlarge the "image" of a country, such gains may be achieved only at the price of jeopardizing or delaying the attainment of other objectives. By way of illustration, the Chinese Communists could probably regain Hong Kong without employing armed force and without risking a confrontation with the West, simply by fomenting strikes, by ordering their partisans in the city to obstruct governmental activities, and by stopping deliveries of food and water. However, by so doing they would lose an entrepôt of great importance and a major source of badly needed foreign exchange, thereby delaying their program of industrialization. So far, at least, the price seems too high, even though the gains would be substantial and the risks quite low.

Other considerations will affect the willingness of a nuclear power to employ that power, among them concerns about the impact of its actions on public opinion, moral or legal inhibitions to the use of nuclear weapons, reluctance again to employ atomic bombs against nonwhite peoples, or the refusal of key allies to acquiesce in such employment—as happened during the Korean War, when the British government reacted adversely to rumors that the United States was considering such a measure. It must also take into account the domestic political and economic implications of its actions; thus a Communist China which is already arming, stockpiling supplies, and preparing defensive works against the contingency of a clash with the Soviet Union is unlikely to want to assume a similar burden vis-à-vis the United States. And finally, a nuclear power must remember that success in exerting political pressures might adversely affect its long-term interests—as the American success in the Cuban missile crisis may have done by stimulating strenuous Soviet efforts to build up a politically meaningful counterdeterrent to U.S. strategic power.[16]

As for support of revolutionary wars, this means of extending influence has been favored partly because it does *not* risk a nuclear strike, a response which would be so palpably disproportionate to the challenge that its threat is simply not credible. It is, of course, conceivable that the growth of Soviet or Chinese nuclear power would make these states more willing not only to provide money and arms to dissident elements in third world countries, but also to intensify their support by furnishing cadres or "volunteers." However, even "volunteers" are not necessarily decisive and may well be counterproductive, in that they can unite the populace against the "foreigner"; furthermore, such overt actions may increase the likelihood of counterintervention, as they have in Laos. Revolutionary zeal, the ability to employ alternate means, estimates of the nature and effectiveness of possible responses to such challenges—even "the ghost of failures past," such as the abortive Communist efforts in 1948 to take over Burma, India, Indonesia, Malaya, and the Philippines—are all likely to influence decisions. Whether, therefore, external assistance to revolutionary movements will rise in parallel with strategic power is at least problematical.

Admittedly, shifts in levels of strategic power are more likely to affect willingness to risk confrontations by backing opposing parties in a local war, by sending military "technicians" to other countries, and even by practicing "preemptive intervention" in distant areas. Since, however, such activities represent a variant of "extended deterrence," one must again consider all the variables affecting deterrence, such as the level of interest in a particular objective, the degree of commitment to a prescribed outcome, the local balance of forces, the effect of responses on the prospects for achieving other goals, and so on. And there is at least some evidence that under such circumstances the potential outcomes of a strategic exchange have little effect either on willingness to respond to provocations or on readiness to escalate a local conflict.*

More importantly, history suggests that there is scant correlation between levels of strategic power and willingness to back opposing parties in a local conflict. Soviet support for the Chinese Communists in 1945–1946, the Greek rebels in 1947–1948, the North Koreans in 1950–1953, and Lumumba's faction in the Congo in 1960–1961 occurred when the USSR had either no nuclear weapons or palpably fewer than did the United States, and Chinese help was given to the Viet Minh in 1953–1954, a time when the United States was immeasurably superior in nuclear power. Although Soviet aid to Egypt and other Arab states has intensified in recent years, this is probably more a function of the necessity to bolster these states than a concomitant to the growth of Soviet strategic power—just as American restraint

---

* Out of 52 respondents to a questionnaire centered around a hypothetical U.S.-Soviet confrontation in the Middle East, 46 to 49 (as indicated in the table below) deemed it very likely that the United States would respond to a conventional attack on the Sixth Fleet by using conventional weapons against the Soviet Mediterranean Fleet and only 1 or 2 that it would retaliate with strategic nuclear weapons against the USSR—and this despite significant alterations in the stragetic balance.

In the following tables the five situations mentioned are defined as follows: a) *high parity* (both the United States and the USSR are capable of inflicting 100 million deaths in either a first or second strike); b) *low parity* (both the United States and the USSR are capable of inflicting 20 million deaths in either a first or second strike); c) *only the United States has preemptive advantage* (i.e., the United States would save 50 million lives by striking first); d) *only the Soviets have preemptive advantage* (i.e., the USSR would save 50 million lives by striking

in aid to Israel seemingly reflects the desire not to antagonize further the Arabs as much as it does caution in the face of Soviet capabilities.

When it comes to preemptive intervention by mobile troops, or to deployments of ships intended to preclude action by another country, strategic power may loom larger. First of all, the ability to inflict greater damage than an opponent can may nerve a nuclear power to take actions which run a high risk of armed conflict with that opponent. Secondly, it may lead it to engage forces smaller or less effective than those of its opponent, in the belief that the latter will not dare attack them. And thirdly, it may enable it to threaten punitive action against other elements of its opponent's armed forces, his bases, or his allies, without thereby precipitating a first strike.

Essentially, however, this amounts to "playing chicken" in a situation where a Ford is as good as a Cadillac, that is, where the

---

first); and e) *both the United States and the USSR have preemptive advantage.*
Probabilities that the United States would attack the Soviet Mediterranean Fleet with conventional weapons in response to a Soviet conventional attack on the U.S. Sixth Fleet:

Probabilities	High Parity	Low Parity	US Preemptive Advantage	Soviet Preemptive Advantage	Both US and USSR Have Preemptive Advantage
Low	0	1	2	2	3
Medium	2	4	2	2	2
High	49	46	47	47	46
No response	1	1	1	1	1

Probabilities that the United States would respond to a Soviet conventional attack against the U.S. Sixth Fleet with strategic nuclear weapons delivered against the USSR itself:

Probabilities	High Parity	Low Parity	US Preemptive Advantage	Soviet Preemptive Advantage	Both US and USSR Have Preemptive Advantage
Low	50	50	49	50	49
Medium	1	1	1	1	0
High	0	0	1	0	2
No response	1	1	1	1	1

SOURCE: J. I. Coffey and Jerome H. Laulicht, Research Seminar on Deterrence, supported by the University Center for International Studies, University of Pittsburgh, October 1969.

consequences of a crash are likely to be disastrous to both parties. Under such circumstances nuances in levels of damage—if indeed they exist at all—may less meaningfully affect the outcome than qualities of leadership, skill in formulating courses of action, responsiveness to domestic pressures, and other subjective factors. And while national leaders may be so confident of their country's strength and their own purpose as to be willing to risk a showdown, they can scarcely be so certain of their adversary's behavior that they will deliberately provoke one!

The preceding analysis suggests that the relationship between strategic power and political behavior is at best a tenuous one: the degree of interest in a particular issue, the extent of the commitment to a given outcome, the nature of the threat, and a host of other variables ranging from domestic public opinion to the estimated effectiveness of various kinds of pressures may affect the willingness of a nuclear power to take action. Conversely, even a nonnuclear power may have sufficient confidence in these and other constraints to exert severe pressures on a nuclear one— as North Vietnam has on the United States. When the pressuring power also has atomic weapons, it may for this reason believe that there is less likelihood of a strategic nuclear response, in that even the possibility of escalation to a nuclear war between unequals may be a deterrent to the initiation of that war. The same constraints, however, apply to it, and it is not necessarily on this ground any freer to act; in fact, one can say that not even strategic predominance would make the world completely safe for lesser forms of conflict.

In large measure these same judgments apply to the relationship between strategic power and foreign policy. Certainly, the possession of nuclear weapons will buttress even a lesser power against demands for concessions; in that sense the policy of "negotiating from strength" may well be passé. Nuclear weapons may also make a country less willing to compromise (because it sees no necessity to do so) and more persistent in reiterating extreme positions, even if it takes no actions to achieve them. That any level of strategic power will necessarily make it more aggressive in the pursuit of its objectives is another matter entirely; nuclear weapons are not only great defenders of the *status quo* but also persuasive advocates of accepting this rather than risking nuclear war.

Strategic Power and Crisis Management

What, however, if this assessment is wrong, and the Soviets, confident that their improved strategic posture will deter American counterintervention, take actions which pose a significant threat to U.S. interests or prestige, actions such as preemptive intervention in a revolutionary Bahrein, or massive support of Egypt by "volunteers" in a new war against Israel? If this process were long extended and unopposed, Communist "nibbling" might adversely affect U.S. power and allied solidarity, as well as American influence. If, however, it were resisted, then the United States might find itself, as Senator Henry M. Jackson has suggested, in the "most dangerous [type of] confrontation—a showdown between nuclear powers in which Moscow did not feel deterred by our [strategic] forces."[17]

Although such operations by the Communists may seem unlikely and their implied willingness to risk a showdown with the United States may be overstated, the possibilities of a confrontation cannot be ruled out; as illustrated by the "six-day war" between Israel and the Arab states, the nuclear powers could become involved in a crisis for which neither of them was directly responsible. And in future crises, unlike past ones, the United States will have neither strategic strike forces superior to those of the USSR nor an absolute advantage with respect to Communist China. Does this mean, as many argue, that the United States will be more reluctant to stand firm or more hesitant about interfering with Communist moves?*

The answer to this question depends on the validity of two premises: that strategic power is the most important factor in crisis management, if not the decisive one, and that American decision makers require the psychological assurance conferred by strategic superiority in order to stand up to the theoretically more aggressive, more persistent, and stronger-willed leaders of the Communist world. With respect to the latter premise, it is true that crises may cause hesitation, paralysis, even panic; however, they may also focus attention on problems previously ignored or slighted, arouse concern over the consequences of continued inac-

---

* See chapter 2, pp. 17–18.

tion, and inspire a determination to see the matter through to a successful conclusion. The belief that American decision makers will follow the first pattern rather than the second not only does them scant credit but is not borne out by past experience. In major crises such as those resulting from the blockade of Berlin in 1948, the invasion of South Korea in 1950, the shelling of Quemoy in 1958, and the introduction of missiles into Cuba in 1962, American leaders quickly decided to uphold their interests and their allies; debate centered not on what objective to pursue but on how to pursue it.[18] Moreover, to judge by his long, rambling, and obviously distressed communication two days before the end of the Cuban missile crisis, it was Khrushchev rather than Kennedy who lost his nerve in 1962.[19]

Even if U.S. officials should be less iron willed than those of the USSR or Communist China or more concerned about human values, crises are likely to have a pronounced impact on them and on their decisions. For one thing, a direct and immediate threat tends to crystallize values and to polarize opinions, with the result that the undecided and the wavering choose one course of action or another. Secondly, crises may enhance concern with the position of the government, the prestige of the nation, and the future credibility of the deterrent—one reason advanced for the American intervention in July 1965 when it looked as though South Vietnam might come under Communist control was that failure to honor U.S. "commitments" there might lessen their credibility in other areas against different foes. For a third, crises may affect judgment and decisions concerning peace or war by heightening tensions, narrowing the range of alternatives considered, increasing perceptions of hostility, and inducing officials to take actions different from those that they might have taken in calmer moments.[20] Crises may also spur national leaders to adopt extreme policies or to stake out far-ranging declaratory positions, as the leaders of the USSR did in implying that an American attack on Cuba would be dealt with by Soviet rockets, and the late President John F. Kennedy did in announcing that, if a nuclear missile were launched from Cuba against the Western Hemisphere, the United States would initiate "a full retaliatory response upon the Soviet Union."[21]

There are some indications that under these circumstances prospective levels of damage from a nuclear exchange may assume less importance than the successful pursuit of crisis objectives: at the time President Kennedy issued the warning mentioned above, the Soviets could probably have killed 50 million Americans in a retaliatory strike.* Since there are few issues in which the challenger would have a preponderance of interests, and hence be willing to run greater risks to achieve his aims, this concentration on crisis objectives would tend to favor the defender, even when his forces are less powerful. As Beaufre argues, "Mathematically, deterrence should begin to operate when the risk [by which he means the level of damage from a nuclear strike] becomes greater than the stake. Psychologically, however, owing to the various factors of uncertainty . . . the risk exerts a deterrent effect well before it has reached parity with the stake."[22]

If the defender chooses, he may further increase the credibility of *his* deterrent by threats (as illustrated earlier), by unambiguous commitments of support, by pledges to maintain (or to restore) the *status quo*, and by other measures which restrict his freedom of action. He may elevate a particular issue into a test of national will or a pledge of national honor, and mobilize public support for a firm stand. He may calculatedly take seemingly irrational actions which proscribe his future behavior, as Chiang Kai-shek did by placing so much of his army on Quemoy. And while such options are also open to the challenger, they are likely to be less persuasive, if only because the principle of territoriality seems to hold in political life as well as in the animal world.

Finally, crises occur in particular places and cannot be isolated from environmental factors, including the availability of local forces and the possibility of reinforcing them. Local military capabilities may not only significantly affect the outcome of a par-

---

* Schelling evaluates Mr. Kennedy's declaration as "not . . . necessarily either a mistake or a bluff, but . . . a reaction more readily taken on impulse than after reflection, a 'disproportionate' act, one not necessarily serving the national interest if the contingency arose but nevertheless a possibly impressive threat" (Thomas C. Schelling, *Arms and Influence* [New Haven, Conn.: Yale University Press, 1966], p. 41, n. 4).

ticular clash but put the onus of escalating the confrontation on the other party. As the former Chief of Staff of the Air Force testified in 1968, one factor in the favorable resolution of the Cuban missile crisis was that "we [Americans] had a very exploitable superiority in tactical weapons. We could really sink the state of Florida with the tactical aircraft down there."[23] While there may be isolated regions such as northern Iran or upper Burma where U.S. power cannot be applied on equal terms, these are comparatively rare; indeed the United States is capable of a range of activities in distant areas which is unparalleled in military history and is unlikely to be matched in the near future by the Soviet Union, much less by Communist China.

This does not mean that strategic power has no impact on crisis outcomes. At the very least it sets limits to the pressures which can be exerted and the actions which can be taken, lest a confrontation become a conflict and that conflict escalate into nuclear war. Moreover, a crisis raises the question of damage in a nuclear exchange from a variable in a game or a figure in a book to a factor having emotional as well as intellectual impact. It encourages a search for options, political as well as military, and a desire to limit the encounter. Hence, the mere prospect of nuclear war may make for compromise despite the fixed attitudes and rigid positions which are typical of crisis behavior.

In the opinion of most experts this is as true of Soviets and Chinese as it is of Americans. Thus Jan Triska, after studying Soviet behavior in twenty-nine crises, found it "conservative rather than radical, cautious rather than reckless,"[24] while Michael Gehlen, after an independent examination of nine crises, concluded that "the Soviet leadership has been more inclined to use verbal and written ultimatums and warnings than to take a high level of risk in actual policy commitment."[25] And A. Doak Barnett reports a consensus among specialists on Communist China that "in crisis situations, it tends to act with considerable prudence and caution, and repeatedly it has moved to check escalation when there has appeared to be a serious risk of major conflict."[26]

Indeed, as one looks at American and Communist behavior in past crises, it becomes apparent that both sides refrained from taking steps which could have brought their countries into open conflict. For example, in the Quemoy crisis of 1958, U.S. ships prudently stayed at least three miles from Quemoy, and the Chinese, equally prudently, did not fire on them, even though they were within the twelve-mile zone claimed as territorial waters. In the intermittent 1958–1961 Berlin crisis the Soviets were careful not to turn over to their East German allies full control of the access routes to Berlin, as they had threatened to do. For their part the Western allies were both cautious in testing Soviet intentions and willing to compromise with respect to Soviet demands —as in the Solomonic decision not to order troops traversing East Germany to dismount and be counted but to lower the tailgates of trucks so that Soviet officers could more readily count them! Whether this restraint would apply under all circumstances is perhaps questionable, but it may be that nuclear weapons in the hands of an adversary are meaningful in and of themselves; if so, then concerns about the erosion of U.S. strategic superiority may be unwarranted.

Deterrence in the Nuclear Age

As stated at the beginning of the chapter, most official American thinking about deterrence seems to concentrate on one aspect: the level of punishment for a transgression. Such preoccupation with the consequences of a nuclear strike, and with the possible costs resulting from a counterstrike, naturally leads to emphasis upon relative strategic capabilities and to concern about the implications of changes in these capabilities. Thus it is not surprising that the United States has taken steps to offset recent shifts in the strategic balance and to guard against further ones.*

No one would argue that such concerns are unwarranted nor that the United States should not do whatever is necessary to maintain secure and effective strategic retaliatory forces. What may be debatable is whether deterrence of aggression, in all its forms, hinges so largely upon the capacity of these retaliatory forces to match (or to overmatch) the number of Americans that the Soviets or the Chinese could kill in a nuclear exchange. The whole thrust of this chapter has been that it does not.

* See chapter 2, pp. 12–13.

One reason for this judgment is that even a few nuclear weapons can cause so many casualties that the prospect of their employment should tilt any cost-benefit analysis in favor of costs. (Indeed one author suggests that any normal government would be deterred by the prospect of damage so great that neither it nor any successor at all acceptable to it would continue to rule.)[27] Since a retaliatory strike by the United States would involve not just a few nuclear weapons but hundreds and possibly thousands of them, any advantage accruing to the USSR could be considered essentially meaningless.

Even more significant—because less dependent on judgments about the unacceptability of various levels of damage—is that these weapons constitute only one element in the process of deterrence. Determination cannot be measured solely by military strength, or else Belgium would not twice have resisted German invasion. Intent need not be communicated only by stockpiling nuclear bombs but can be manifested in other ways. And perceptions of determination and intent are so dependent on psychological and political analyses, so colored by ambiguities, so clouded by uncertainties, that even significant differences in levels of damage may not weigh heavily in the final decision to commit (or not to commit) aggression.

Furthermore, the prospective aggressor must recognize that the determination and intent of an adversary may alter markedly under pressure: the American decision in 1950 to help South Korea resist invasion from the north could not have been anticipated from its previous policies toward that country. Nor can he rule out the effect on that adversary's decisions of perceptions of threat, of miscalculations of the aggressor's aims, of misinterpretation of data, and of failures of communication. This means that the aggressor's estimates of the likelihood of retaliation must be triply hedged, to account for possible errors in his initial assessment, for the largely unpredictable shifts in behavior which might follow his attack, and for the possibility that even responses short of a strategic strike could, in the long run, escalate into nuclear war. Under these circumstances it is questionable whether even the most foolhardy advisor, even the rashest leader, would rely so heavily on his presumed strategic advantages as to challenge directly a nuclear-armed adversary.

In a larger sense, however, American concerns about Soviet strategic advantages (like the Soviet concerns about American ones) may reflect a view of the world which is no longer valid. For one thing, technology has changed both the nature of military power and the consequences of employing it. Whereas previously a national leader could launch military operations with some expectation that his costs would be minimal, he must now reckon from the beginning with the possibility of losses on a scale never before contemplated. (For example, Hitler apparently estimated that his armies would suffer only nominal losses in defeating the Soviet Union in 1941; no leader today can be so optimistic —or so mistaken.) More importantly, the losses will fall not only upon the military but upon the whole of society, which may collapse under the weight and the speed of a nuclear strike. A nuclear exchange could be so destructive, even to the power which "prevails," that it is difficult to conceive of a gain which to rational men would seem worth the consequences.

Furthermore, the gains from military operations may be of questionable value, even if these operations are successful and nuclear war is avoided. The old adage that new lands, increased population, and added resources automatically result in comparable accretions of strength is no longer true; in the atomic age these components are critical only insofar as they provide the essential base for the development and deployment of a nuclear strike force. As the Soviet experience has shown, the exploitation of domestic resources offers a surer and more positive way to achieve economic-military power than does the acquisition of additional territory. Indeed, it may well be that the costs of organizing and exploiting occupied areas are higher than any benefits derived, as the Japanese found in China, the French recognized in Algeria, and the Russians may be coming to realize in Eastern Europe.

It may, of course, be militarily advantageous to occupy a particular piece of ground or to set up a naval base in distant waters, but only so long as the uses made of these positions do not provoke another nuclear power to strike at them. It may also be psychologically satisfying or politically rewarding to extend one's area of control, but only if this does not involve reprisals. In short, the limited utility of territorial expansion, the uncertainty of success, and the tremendous costs of failure may well combine to dampen the level of conflict and to hold down the scope of interactions among nuclear powers. In the preatomic age, war could be characterized as "the ultimate argument of kings"; today that argument is muted.

But not only military factors affect deterrence in the nuclear age, which differs in many respects from other historical periods. For one thing, people in many countries are pressing for, and in some instances achieving, a louder voice in decisions on foreign policy. For another, most governments are increasingly preoccupied with domestic concerns; the first topic allegedly discussed by Soviet Premier Aleksei Kosygin with West German Chancellor Willy Brandt during the latter's visit to Moscow in 1970 was the state of the corn crop in the USSR! For a third, the political and psychological costs of aggression may be much higher today than in earlier times, partly because the use of force does not have the legitimacy it once enjoyed, partly because many of the ex-colonial countries are fiercely opposed to any moves (by East or West) which might reimpose external controls, partly because the United Nations and various regional associations provide forums for voicing their opposition and bases for organizing it effectively.

These are, of course, tenuous obstacles to aggression by a nuclear power. They are cited not as proof that aggression will never take place but as indications of the nonmilitary factors which will influence decisions on the use of force. Along with the military considerations discussed earlier, they tend both to inhibit the application of military power and to constrain the ways in which it is employed. As Oran R. Young phrases it, in the nuclear age force is used "to affect attitudes, expectations and resolve rather than to engage in violent or even overtly physical contests with an opponent over specific geographical positions."[28]

5
Strategic Power and Communist Behavior

What causes some Americans concern is not the validity of the previously discussed views about the limitations on the use of force in the nuclear age but their applicability to the East-West confrontation. While agreeing that the United States may be inhibited from taking action by fear of the consequences of a nuclear exchange and by uncertainties concerning the eventual outcome of any lesser clash with the USSR or Communist China, they deem the leaders of these two countries more willing than their Western counterparts to engage in armed conflict. And they tend to believe that Communist aggression, or even lesser pressures, can be deterred only if the West possesses superior strategic nuclear forces.[1]

The belief that strategic superiority is necessary to deter the Soviet Union and Communist China is rooted in a number of opinions concerning the behavior of their ruling groups. The first is that the Communists are inherently aggressive and are willing to run great risks and take heavy losses in pursuit of their national and ideological goals; in the words of Secretary of Defense Laird, the Asian Communists are "tenacious opponents and are willing to take great losses of life in achieving their objectives."[2] A second is that the Communists are prepared to use force in the pursuit of these objectives and are inhibited from so doing only by the readiness of the West to respond in kind; as Mr. Laird put it in discussing the likelihood of nuclear war, "The way to maintain peace . . . is to maintain the credibility of that [U.S.] deterrent force."[3]

A corollary to this is the belief that if the Communists obtained

74

an advantage they would be more willing to go to war. Thus some officials and analysts feared, as did Congressman Craig Hosmer, that if the Soviets could drastically reduce the effectiveness of U.S. retaliatory units, they would initiate nuclear war. Others held that, while military uncertainties would probably preclude a deliberate decision to launch a nuclear strike, Soviet strategic superiority could encourage the USSR to employ its conventional troops against members of the Western Alliance. Even a form of strategic parity between the United States and the USSR might, it was suggested, make the latter more willing to undertake military operations which would risk conflict with the former.[4] In fact, it was argued that any shift in the balance of power might increase the readiness of the USSR and Communist China to run greater risks in the pursuit of their objectives and to employ military power for that purpose.[5]

Still stronger has been the fear that the erosion of U.S. strategic superiority might leave the Soviets freer to express their presumed hostility toward the West, to exert pressures against U.S. and allied positions, and to expand their influence, even where this might involve them in a clash with the United States.[6] Along with this went a concern that the Chinese acquisition of a nuclear capability might enable that country to threaten U.S. allies and interests and to practice nuclear blackmail, might encourage it to adopt a more aggressive policy against its non-Communist neighbors, and might lead it to support more openly and more extensively revolutionary activities in other countries. In short, a number of American analysts and officials have been afraid that the loss of U.S. strategic superiority might induce severe alterations in Soviet and Chinese Communist political behavior.

Coupled with these impressions that the erosion of U.S. strategic superiority might induce the Communists to become more aggressive went a concern about the effects of this erosion on the U.S. will to resist such aggression. As the number of fatalities which the United States would suffer from a nuclear exchange rose, so did the doubts about the willingness of this country to initiate such an exchange. Some analysts and officials (in a reversal of the American scenario for a nuclear war circa 1963) went so far as to wonder whether the United States would retaliate to a Soviet disarming strike backed up by the threat to devastate American cities if necessary. More Americans (along with many allied officials) worried about the willingness of the United States to wage nuclear war on behalf of its allies, to sacrifice Chicago in defense of Paris. Still more were dubious about the determination of the United States to resist political pressures and to counter Communist support for "wars of national liberation," partly because such activities might not have the shock action and the unifying effect of overt aggression, partly because they presumably would be directed against points where the U.S. commitment was less firm and U.S. interests less fixed, and partly because they could well involve third parties (as in the Middle East), thereby complicating the situation politically and militarily. More importantly, they doubted whether the United States, increasingly reluctant to take steps which could precipitate a nuclear exchange, could and would stand up to the Communists in a crisis like that of 1962 over Cuba, in the event of another outbreak of war in the Middle East, or in the case of future Chinese Communist operations against India.

In short, a combination of concern about growing Soviet and Chinese Communist nuclear capabilities, belief that these could induce greater bellicosity and a higher propensity to take risks, and worry about one's own responses to aggression (as well as about the confidence of the allies in those responses) generated pressures for American strategic nuclear forces stronger than those which the Nixon administration inherited—or than those which it proposes to build. These pressures took the form not just of calls for more bombers and missiles but of demands that the United States maintain an advantage over the Communist countries in the ability to inflict damage, since only thus could deterrence work.[7] They also sparked proposals for the deployment of ballistic missile defenses which, as initially conceived, not only could protect American cities against Chinese ICBMs but could form the basis for "thicker" defenses aimed at blunting a Soviet attack. As indicated earlier these concerns and beliefs led to the perpetuation of policies and programs which aim at maintaining a marked strategic advantage when one can do so (as in the case of Communist China), and at avoiding a disadvantage when this is the best that one can hope for (as it probably is in the case of the USSR).

There is certainly some validity to these arguments, in that the possession of superior force by one state is an obstacle to its effective employment by others. Moreover, the visible symbols of superiority—bigger bombers, more missiles, newer weapons—may impress friend and foe alike: the launching of Sputnik in 1957 created an image of Soviet strategic power which persisted for almost a decade. However, there are a number of questions which should be answered before deciding that American strategic superiority is essential to the maintenance of peace and the preservation of U.S. interests.

The first such question is whether the linkage between strategic power and deterrence is in fact so close and so direct as to warrant attempts to maintain superior strategic nuclear forces; the burden of chapter 4 was that it was not. The second question is whether the Soviet Union and Communist China are in fact as willing and as able as some Americans believe to employ force against, or to exert pressures against, the United States, its allies, and its interests. And the third is whether this willingness is likely to increase with shifts in the strategic balance. This chapter will attempt to answer these last two questions.

Strategic Power and Soviet Behavior

The conclusion in chapter 4 that levels of strategic power are not necessarily related to political behavior may in one sense be comforting, since it minimizes concern about shifts in the strategic balance, such as have already taken place between the United States and the USSR and will inevitably take place between the United States and Communist China. On the other hand, it can generate new worries, since, if deterrence is not assured even by strategic superiority, how can it be assured at all? The answer, of course, is that it cannot: nothing in human affairs is certain. However, it may well be that official fears of Soviet aggressiveness and Soviet willingness to use force are based on misconceptions both of the situation in the USSR and of the effects on that situation of growing Soviet strategic power.

It cannot, of course, be denied that the transcendent goal of the "triumph of socialism" encourages efforts to erode American influence and to reduce (or offset) American strength. Such efforts also reflect the doctrine that the basic hostility of capitalism poses a constant threat, which can be eliminated only with the transformation of capitalist countries into socialist ones. In addition, they serve the political and security interests of the USSR, which is increasingly assuming the status, the prerogatives, and the concerns of a global power.

However, to argue from this that the Soviets are doctrinally impelled to aggression is going too far; there is nothing in Communist ideology which compels the Soviet Union to engage in military adventures and much which militates against such adventures. Although military power is admittedly an instrument of Soviet policy, it is not the sole instrument. An ideology which requires its followers to think in terms of historical inevitability, which places a premium upon political activism and political achievements, and which looks to the inspiration and the example of communism to undermine the societies and the economies of the capitalist states tends to downgrade the importance of the quicker, but admittedly riskier, military road to success. As Raymond L. Garthoff, one of the ablest writers on Soviet affairs, put it, "The Communist ideology not only does not *require* taking the great risks inevitable to launching a world war in the thermonuclear era; it opposes very strongly any measure smacking of 'adventurism' or taking inadmissible risks."[8]

This ideological predisposition is buttressed by awareness of the consequences of a nuclear war, however started, and by a desire not to trigger one. As Politburo member Mikhail Suslov said in his report of 14 February 1964 to the Central Committee, "One can say frankly that if a world thermonuclear conflict arose, it would be a most terrible tragedy for mankind and would, of course, be a heavy loss to the cause of Communism. . . . For entire nations the question of the victory of Socialism would never arise at all, since they would disappear from the face of the earth."[9] (The Central Committee itself put the matter more simply, saying that "the atomic bomb does not adhere to the class principle: it destroys everybody within range of its destructive action.")[10] Throughout their speeches and writings Soviet leaders have insisted that *they* will never start a nuclear war, which will come (if at all) only as a result of "imperialist aggression." The major consequence of growing Soviet strength has seemingly been to increase the confidence of these leaders that they can avoid a major conflict, not that they can now risk one.

More importantly, significant changes have taken place over the years in Soviet doctrine on the use of force; the last highly placed proponent of the dogma that the success of the Communist movement (and the safety of the Soviet Union) required an "uninterrupted" struggle against the capitalist world was Leon Trotsky, who was exiled in 1927. The view that force is neither a feasible nor a desirable means of promoting the spread of communism was set forth clearly by former Premier Nikita Khrushchev in his speech of 6 January 1961.[11] In that speech Mr. Khrushchev described the disastrous consequences of nuclear war, which made it completely unacceptable as an instrument of policy, and stressed the danger that limited or local wars might escalate into nuclear war. Although he endorsed and promised to support wars of national liberation by oppressed peoples, he stopped short (both then and later) of any commitment to engage Soviet troops in such wars. And while Khrushchev has gone, his policy lingers on.

Fear of the danger and the consequences of nuclear war is not, however, the only factor affecting Soviet policy on the use of force. Pride in past achievements, a desire to preserve and enjoy the fruits of previous efforts, and a belief that "the inevitable victory of socialism" can be promoted through social and economic progress all militate against overt aggression. Moreover, although the insistence of Soviet leaders that the non-Communist world can be gradually and more or less peacefully transformed reflects their confidence in the Communist system, it also reflects a loss of revolutionary *élan*. With the passage of time, the diminution of ideological fervor, and the increased availability of economic-cultural amenities, Soviet society has changed and Soviet dynamism has diminished. As one authority on Soviet affairs phrased it, "Soviet leaders and officials have a viable system which has been created at the cost of great sacrifice, and they are not eager for the risks of adventurous policies."[12] The Chinese Communists put it more graphically: "The Khrushchev revisionists . . . are afflicted with incurable spinelessness. They are scared of revolution, shirk at sacrifice, dare not engage in a retaliatory struggle against U.S. imperialism, and even oppose the revolutionary cause of the people of all countries."[13]

Strategic Power and Soviet Aggression

The foregoing suggests that the Soviets are neither as aggressive as some Americans have feared nor as ready to capitalize upon their alleged conventional superiority as some have judged. This does not mean that strategic power has no impact on Soviet decisions for peace or war, only that this impact may be somewhat different from that commonly assumed—a thesis which will next be examined.

As noted earlier, the United States is currently able to kill over 100 million Soviets, a capability which it could, if necessary, maintain for the foreseeable future. Even if it did nothing for the next five years, and the USSR built the "high-force, high-technology" level described by Mr. Laird, the United States could probably cause the 44 to 55 million fatalities which Mr. McNamara believed would constitute unacceptable damage.[14] Although some analysts maintain that the USSR, which lost 20 to 25 million people during World War II, would be willing to accept proportionately heavy casualties in order to eliminate the United States as a major power, no one has (as far as is known) suggested that they would be willing to suffer twice as many fatalities, even for that objective; others have argued from the same premise that the Soviet Union would be unwilling to suffer again losses on the scale of 1941–1945 and would be deterred by the prospect of many fewer casualties. The Soviets themselves have apparently not changed their view that any nuclear war would result in a degree of devastation which would be unacceptable to them. Indeed, *Pravda* quoted approvingly from the article by McGeorge Bundy cited earlier, "Strategic nuclear clashes can bring no gain whatever, either from the standpoint of national interests or from the standpoint of the ideology or personal political position of any leader in either country."[15]

This suggests that there is no necessary correlation between the growth of the Soviet counterdeterrent and the willingness of the USSR to risk nuclear war: the mere prospect of heavy damage may suffice to deter Soviet aggression.* This prospect would certainly rule out any deliberate attack on the United States, which could only be suicidal. It would probably inhibit not only an all-out assault on NATO Europe but even lower-level military operations, such as a thrust against northern Norway; indeed, the Soviets have tended to discount the possibility of waging limited war in Europe, whose dense population, scant room for maneuver, and great value to both sides imply, in the Soviet view, a rapid and almost inevitable escalation.[16] And while it may be, as Mr. McNamara once said, that this reflects a "doctrinal lag" on the part of the Soviets, it is a lag which should be taken into account in assessing the nature and likelihood of Soviet military action.

Whether the fear of nuclear retaliation or the danger of escalation would deter the Soviets from waging limited wars outside Europe or from undertaking operations such as a "blockade" of Israel is perhaps more questionable; the Soviet view has been that even local wars would so affect the vital interests of the two superpowers that the political results would not be worth the risks involved.[17] Although the growth of Soviet strategic power might reduce the risk that such conflicts would escalate, it might, paradoxically, also make it easier for the Western allies to cope with them; to the extent that deterrence is both mutual and stable the United States would be freer to employ nuclear weapons against attacking forces without precipitating a Soviet first strike. Thus even if the USSR could inflict on the United States high and equivalent levels of damage this would not inevitably weaken the strategic deterrent.

To some extent this would also be true in the interesting but unlikely event that both the United States and the USSR installed ballistic missile defenses and drastically reduced their strategic

---

* Interestingly enough, between 1965 and 1968 Mr. McNamara reduced *his* estimate of what would constitute unacceptable damage by about 25 percent. Since neither level of unacceptable damage had any empirical basis, and since Soviet strategic capabilities actually increased during those three years, this change can only reflect a different perception of Soviet intentions. Thus the question whether a high level of damage is necessary to deter Soviet aggression may have to be answered largely by reference to the attitudes and the images of American leaders, not of Soviet ones.

strike forces, as recommended by Donald Brennan.[18] Although the prospect of lesser damage from a nuclear exchange might make the USSR more inclined to apply force, it could also make the United States more willing to resist it. Furthermore, even 10 to 20 million dead (which is the least one could reasonably expect from such an exchange) might be enough to give pause to the USSR, even if all other circumstances were favorable. And finally, the mere act of arriving at these kinds of controls over strategic armaments would imply such changes in attitudes, such a period of quiescence, and such vested interests in accommodation between the two superpowers that it is difficult to imagine the Soviet Union then shifting to a more aggressive policy.

Even if the Soviets should secure a strategic advantage, a number of factors may predispose them to eschew military moves in favor of alternative means of achieving their objectives. One is that even "low" levels of damage from a nuclear exchange (such as might occur if both the United States and the USSR froze their strategic strike forces and the latter deployed more extensive ballistic missile defenses) would approximate those of World War II, which none of the participants is eager to refight. A second is that even if Soviet leaders find cost-benefit analysis persuasive, their comparative advantage may simply not be meaningful; thus an exchange which killed 90 million Americans and "only" 30 million Soviets might not seem attractive to either side.* And a third is that the associated costs (in terms of damage to friends and allies and of a reduction in the ability to exercise political and military control over the outside world) might themselves be prohibitive. Certainly the Soviets would not want to see Brazil

---

* Early returns of a questionnaire dealing with the levels of damage which the United States and the USSR would accept and demand before launching a nuclear strike during a confrontation over an issue of importance to both showed: (1) for the United States an average level of 10½ million American fatalities to 42 million potentially inflicted on the USSR, and (2) for the USSR an average level of 14 million Soviet fatalities to 40 million potentially inflicted on the United States. Obviously, these results, which reflect the views of Americans rather than of Russians, are suggestive rather than definitive, but they tend to bear out other more intuitive assessments. The statistics are from J. I. Coffey and Jerome H. Laulicht, Research Seminar on Deterrence, supported by the University Center for International Studies, University of Pittsburgh, October 1969.

emerge as the superpower of the twenty-first century—much less Communist China!

Soviet caution in utilizing force to secure national objectives may reflect not only the risks of conducting military operations against the United States and its allies but the difficulties of so doing. To give one illustration, it would be hard for the USSR to launch a successful disarming strike against NATO nuclear forces, either before or during a conventional assault. Although the warning time may be short and the dispersal of tactical aircraft may leave much to be desired, nuclear-armed fighter-bombers are on the alert at scores of airfields from southern Britain to western Turkey. Moreover, semimobile missiles on land, aircraft carriers at sea, and the bombers and missile-submarines under operational control of the Supreme Allied Commander would each require different modes of attack, initiated at different times; in fact, some elements could be dealt with only by Soviet defensive systems. The degree of readiness required for a Soviet disarming strike might be difficult to achieve, the redeployment of units such as missile-submarines hard to conceal, and the coordination of operations essential to tactical surprise almost impossible. And since even one lapse in coordination, one leakage of information, could give away the whole show, it seems unlikely that it would ever be staged. One need not postulate either wholly rational or completely benevolent Soviet leaders to virtually rule out such a "strike from the blue" against NATO Europe (or against the United States). Indeed, one anthropologist characterized the belief that the USSR might launch a first strike as "a projection of our own [American] image of what happens when two opponents face each other," and not as a realistic assessment of Soviet behavior.[19]

Other difficulties would undoubtedly cause the Soviets to think twice before initiating large-scale conventional operations. For one thing, many areas of the world are so remote from the centers of Soviet military power, or access to them is so difficult, as to limit the strength that the USSR can bring to bear. For another, the United States and its allies are reasonably well equipped to defend themselves without recourse to nuclear weapons; thus former Secretary of Defense McNamara testified that NATO troops could "deny the Warsaw Pact any high probability of major success with anything less than a maximum-scale [conventional] attack."[20] And for a third, both American and some allied units possess tactical nuclear weapons, whose mere presence means that an opponent cannot—without grave risk—conduct sizeable conventional campaigns; even a comparatively small-scale tactical nuclear strike could decimate massed troops, destroy supporting weapons, and choke off the flow of reinforcements and supplies required for a continuing advance.[21] Thus even in the absence of a strategic deterrent the conduct of limited war would not necessarily be easy.

The Soviets may, of course, hope that fear of general war, or of the consequences of a tactical nuclear exchange, will inhibit the United States and its allies from employing atomic weapons against invading forces. If so, this is a thin reed upon which to rest: a local conflict may "go nuclear" inadvertently because of miscalculations of intent, because a nuclear-armed ally out of desperation acts independently, or because the United States decides to use nuclear weapons rather than to accept defeat. The higher the stakes and the more massive the assault, the greater the likelihood that strategic as well as tactical nuclear weapons would be employed; in the words of Professor Robert Bowie, former Counselor of the State Department, "The spectre of a Soviet effort to seize Europe, while holding the United States at bay with the threat of a nuclear holocaust, seems wholly fanciful."[22] Whatever the degree of Soviet confidence in the effectiveness of *their* deterrent, it is not likely to approach certainty—and in view of the potentially disastrous consequences of a mistaken estimate, something close to a certainty of success would seem desirable.

Even smaller-scale operations against isolated and vulnerable areas could escalate; as Raymond Aron says, "The recourse to nuclear arms remains an ever-present reality influencing all levels of conflict."[23] Nor would the potential gains from such actions seem worth either the risks or the difficulties involved. Compared to the strength which can be brought to bear in the Mediterranean, the Persian Gulf, and other areas of possible interest to the USSR, Soviet "forces of intervention" are small indeed; according to the

Commander-in-Chief of Allied Forces, Southeastern Europe, the Soviet flotilla in the eastern Mediterranean was (and still is) smaller than the "very modern and very efficient" Italian navy and had not acquired even a fraction of the striking power at the disposal of NATO.[24] Although Soviet forces could in time grow stronger, it will probably be years before they are able to carry out airborne and amphibious landings in distant areas against even light opposition, much less successfully conduct sustained operations in the face of U.S. naval and air power.

All this suggests that shifts in the strategic balance will have only a marginal impact upon the willingness of the Soviet leaders to engage in nuclear war or to take actions which carry significant risks of nuclear war. It also suggests that, even should they be prepared to run such risks, these leaders would find it difficult and costly to achieve meaningful gains through the exercise of military power. While this does not mean that they may not try for such gains, it is a far cry from this to the automatic linkage of Soviet strategic power with a propensity for aggression which characterized many of the statements quoted earlier.

Strategic Power and Soviet Risk-Taking

What, however, about the thesis that growing strategic power will incline the USSR to adopt stronger foreign policies, to push even harder for acceptance of its demands, and to run larger risks in order to secure its objectives? Admittedly, strategic nuclear power may have such an effect, but it is only one among many elements favoring such behavior. This may also be spurred by the Soviet Union's economic strength, by its scientific achievements, and by the creation of more mobile military forces, all of which have made it possible to utilize instruments of foreign policy which Stalin lacked and have made it unnecessary to rely so heavily on external elements. Thus the USSR has, in recent years, changed both its methods of operation and its motives for undertaking operations outside its borders.

Although the Soviet shift from a revolutionary great power to a more traditional one is not an unalloyed blessing, it has had some beneficial side effects. For one, the USSR now has commitments to foreign governments which limit its freedom of action.

For another, the traditional instruments of policy are more vulnerable to counterpressures than the revolutionary ones; the whole Soviet effort in the Mediterranean could collapse if Turkey closed the Dardanelles or the United States blockaded them. For a third, the USSR has developed an interest in limiting perturbations in the political environment, in halting the spread of nuclear weapons, and in solving technical and organizational problems with international ramifications—all of which require American cooperation.

As the Soviets well know, extreme pressures against allied interests could jeopardize all those objectives which depend on American collaboration—including that of keeping "all quiet on the Western front" while Soviet differences with China persist. They may require expenditures of resources and commitments of forces which the USSR can ill afford, as would be the case with any attempt to "take over" the Middle East or to "outflank" NATO by establishing a Soviet presence in North Africa. Above all, they may require a willingness to take drastic measures which neither the present regime nor any foreseeable successor is likely to muster. While the Soviets may, as Dr. Thomas W. Wolfe suggests, "come to accept greater risks in the process of trying to extract political gains from a changed strategic equation . . . possibly to the point of trying to affect political changes [in Europe] by the threat of direct military pressure," the more likely possibility, as he indicates, is that "the Soviet leaders might go no further than attempting to persuade the Europeans that, in the absence of yesterday's nuclear guarantee, they had best work out tomorrow's security arrangements along lines proposed by Moscow."[25]

Soviet reluctance to exert pressures against Western interests, whatever the strategic balance, may stem from past failure to achieve much in this fashion, as evidenced by the five successive postponements or abrogations of former Premier Khrushchev's deadlines for a settlement of the Berlin question. It may also stem from recognition that, save for West Berlin, there are almost no pressure points which are both important and vulnerable; thus the Soviets would either have to settle for small gains in nonvital areas or take drastic and risky actions, such as the occupation of territories in the third world countries, the initiation of a submarine war of attrition at sea, or the practice of nuclear blackmail. And it may stem from the knowledge that any steps taken could immediately bring the USSR into another confrontation with the United States, whose protective shield is extended over most of the countries which are vulnerable to Soviet pressures.

This risk the Soviets are seemingly unwilling to run; as Horelick and Rush point out, not even the self-doubts of American leaders have persuaded the Soviet Union that the United States would not in fact initiate nuclear war, if pressured by the USSR.[26] At any rate the current leaders of the USSR inferentially criticized Khrushchev's actions in Cuba as "rash adventurism," informed the Western allies that their move into Czechoslovakia in no way represented a threat to NATO, and have assured the United States that they will not transgress upon its rights in West Berlin, which they recognize are a matter of "state interest."[27] Although it is possible that Soviet willingness to run risks may increase with a change in regime or with the further growth of Soviet strategic strike forces, concern about war is not the only influence on decisions. For one thing, renewed pressures could solidify the Western Alliance, prompt increased defense expenditures, and cause reconsideration of proposals for a drawdown of U.S. forces in Europe. For another, they could threaten other Soviet objectives, such as the denial of nuclear weapons to West Germany and the legitimization of the German Democratic Republic. And for a third, they could be very costly to the Soviets —especially if they involved embargoes on trade, the stoppage of oil and gas supplies, or other measures designed to affect adversely the West European economy.

Furthermore, the deep divisions within the Communist world do not encourage greater dynamism. The Communist parties of Western Europe have been either opposed to Soviet activism (as have the Italians) or cautiously noncommittal (as have the French). The political malaise in Czechoslovakia is too recent, and the degree of disaffection in Rumania too prominent, to suggest unanimous support even among the countries of Eastern Europe for renewed Soviet efforts to pressure the West. Moreover, the Soviet Union is engaged in an acrimonious quarrel with Communist China, a quarrel which some believe inspired its desire to ease tensions with the West and which might militate against any tendency on its part to heighten those tensions. The differences between the USSR and Communist China not only deprive the former country of political support, but make it hard for it to employ its military and economic power in some areas of the world—as evidenced by the hijacking of Soviet military equipment passing through China on the way to North Vietnam.

These same differences would make Soviet fomentation of "revolutionary war" difficult, since many of the indigenous Communist parties are either pro-Chinese or divided and hence ineffective. The Soviets have not shared the Chinese belief in the efficacy or the desirability of this method of extending communism, but have pragmatically accepted the "national democracies" in the third world countries.[28] And while they have in the past given arms to rebels against colonial control (such as the Algerians), most of their military assistance has gone to factions in a civil war (as in Yemen) or to governments which they hoped thereby to influence, as in the cases of Egypt, India, and Indonesia.

In most instances aid programs have been intended to erode American influence, in some to support elements in opposition to the United States, and in others to buttress one party to a quarrel where the United States was backing the other, directly or indirectly. However, the Soviets have been careful not to press too hard in American "spheres of influence," such as Latin America and the Far East. Moreover, on the occasions when the USSR has introduced military "advisers," these have had limited combat roles; for example, the Soviet pilots in Egypt have so far been employed in ways unlikely to precipitate that confrontation with the United States which is currently of such great concern to American officials.

Despite their high cost and some disenchantment with their results, it is probable that the Soviets will continue economic assistance, arms shipments, and similar means of extending Soviet influence. As part of this effort they may also "show the flag" in more distant ports and perhaps establish new operating bases for their navy and for other components of their mobile forces. Whether they will actually commit Soviet troops against a nation supported by the United States, or will attempt to block American intervention in a third country, is much more problematical. Even if the growth of strategic strike forces should make the Soviets more willing to undertake military adventures, it offers no guarantee of their success; for instance, the United States Marine Corps outnumbers its Soviet counterpart by at least twenty to one. And while the USSR can certainly strengthen its "forces of intervention," it will be years before these can hope to match the powerful and ubiquitous American navy, even in areas close to Soviet borders.

Entirely aside from all the reasons why the USSR may be unwilling or unable to exercise meaningful pressures, there is no apparent congruence between shifts in the strategic balance and Soviet behavior. Thus the Soviet Union was more willing to encroach on Western interests in 1948–1950, when it had virtually nothing in the way of nuclear forces, than in other periods when it was comparatively stronger. Its placatory policy in 1955–1957 was apparently derived not from relative American and Soviet strategic strength but from the desire of former Premier Khrushchev to arrive at a degree of accommodation with the West which would enable him to pursue his domestic objectives.[29] In recent years Moscow has, during the period when its ICBM force was quadrupling in size, come to terms with Washington on the Nuclear Nonproliferation Treaty, joined with the United States and the United Kingdom in issuing guarantees to the signatories of that treaty, helped arrange the Paris Peace Conference for the settlement of the Vietnam war, and engaged in negotiations on the limitation of strategic armaments.

This does not mean that the USSR will be wholly quiescent in the future, only that its political behavior will be the outcome of a number of complex interactions and the result of a number of factors, of which strategic power will be only one. It does suggest that one cannot correlate specific attempts to extend Soviet influence or to pursue Soviet objectives with changes in the strategic balance. It also suggests that accretions of strength, even on a comparative basis, do not necessarily induce a more aggressive foreign policy; in fact, one researcher who studied U.S.-Soviet interactions found that the Soviets were more cooperative when their strategic capabilities were improving relative to those of the

United States![30] And it does indicate that the United States should not necessarily regard refusals to acquiesce in American policy, bellicose statements by high-ranking officers, or even displays of power as evidence of Soviet aggressiveness. As John Keep points out: "These [Soviet] exhibitions of nuclear and missile strength serve as a substitute for a more aggressive foreign policy which can no longer be pursued because it entails an unacceptable risk of military conflict and self-annihiliation. They are a means of concealing the painful fact that in the nuclear age the Soviet Union no longer possesses full freedom of action in the international sphere."[31]

Strategic Power and Chinese Behavior

Although the Chinese Communists have tended to be more dogmatic than their Soviet brethren, this dogmatism does not necessarily incline them toward direct military action. Nor have Chinese doubts about the efficacy of "peaceful competition" led them to advocate overt military operations against non-Communist states. Their basic differences with the Soviet Union arise not from a belief that nuclear war (or even local aggression) is the best means of advancing the cause of communism but from the conviction that the final overthrow of "imperialism" cannot be brought about unless the Communists maintain their own revolutionary movements within the underdeveloped countries instead of relying on time and the activities of the "national bourgeoisie" to undermine the positions of the Western powers and their indigenous supporters. Thus the Chinese interpretation of Marxism consists largely of a return to the fundamental concepts of the role of the Communist party in arousing class consciousness among the workers and in preparing the way for the proletarian revolution, as against Soviet reliance on the more traditional instruments of diplomatic and financial support, technical assistance, and the sale of arms to win over the third world countries.

Moreover, the Chinese, despite their alleged dynamism, have been exceedingly cautious in employing military force. For instance, although they shelled the Quemoys in 1958 (and intermittently since then), they did not employ their submarines against

Chinese Nationalist shipping, bomb the airfields from which Nationalist planes were flying, attempt to enforce their claim to jurisdiction over a twelve-mile belt of coastal waters, or otherwise engage in operations which might have intensified the level of warfare or threatened to involve them with the United States. Their clashes with India in 1962 were both limited in extent and brief in duration, despite their military successes along the northeast frontier. And their participation in the Vietnam war has been restricted to the use of engineer troops along the railway from Laokay to Hanoi, despite their obvious interest in a Viet Minh success and all the advantages of proximity. As Alice Hsieh points out, Peking's aim is "to avoid any military initiatives that might lead to a direct confrontation with U.S. forces, conventional or nuclear."[32]

One reason for this caution is fear of a U.S. nuclear strike which, the Chinese purportedly estimate, could "kill from one-half to two-thirds of the Chinese population, destroy most major military facilities and economic and population centers, and eliminate regular communications networks."[33] Although the Chinese seemingly believe that their politico-social structure and their trained militia would enable them to survive such an attack and to "swallow up" U.S. forces, this is in the context of the inevitable American aggression against China.[34] The Chinese concern is not how to maneuver militarily under the shield of *their* nuclear deterrent, but how to avoid a deliberate attack by the United States, to which end they have, among other things, pledged themselves not to be the first to use nuclear weapons, consistently sought to place limitations on the employment of such weapons, and conducted themselves so as not to provoke nuclear war.[35]

Another reason for caution is that any overt Chinese Communist attacks on neighboring states could precipitate an American tactical nuclear strike, against which Chinese forces would be virtually defenseless. All that has been said earlier with respect to the vulnerability of Soviet troop concentrations, supply centers, and supporting weapons would apply in even greater degree to the Chinese, who have nothing like the air defense capabilities possessed by the USSR. More importantly, the Chinese have no way of deterring U.S. tactical nuclear strikes without extending and intensifying the conflict and no way of retaliating save by employing their "strategic" forces, which, as of 1970, consisted of a handful of obsolete light and medium bombers. (In fact, one analyst suggests that the inability of the Chinese Communists to wage limited nuclear war on anything like equal terms may lead them to concentrate on the development of tactical nuclear weapons systems, rather than of strategic ones.)[36]

A third reason for caution is that the Chinese People's Liberation Army is so deficient in transport, in communications, and in logistic services that it cannot bring its full power to bear over any distance, a circumstance which led one commentator to characterize it as "the best Army in Asia—fifty yards outside the Chinese frontier." Moreover, the Chinese Communists are essentially limited to ground operations against neighboring states; the Chinese Nationalists probably have a greater capability to conduct airborne and amphibious operations than do their rivals.[37] Given the comparative weakness of Communist China, the internal upheavals through which it has been going, and the technical and economic costs of modernizing its army, navy, and air force (which will require more time and effort than the building of at least a regional nuclear force), it is questionable whether Chinese "forces of intervention" will increase significantly over the next decade. And even if they should, it is doubtful if the Chinese could overmatch American mobile units, even on the "dark and bloody ground" of Southeast Asia.

At the moment the Chinese tendency toward caution is reinforced by internal weaknesses: divisions among the leaders of the regime, separatism in the provinces, a decline in industrial production, and the virtual loss of a generation of students, to name just a few. Whatever the long-term consequences of the "Cultural Revolution," it is obvious that it failed in smashing the Chinese version of the Establishment and in replacing it with a more utopian, more revolutionary leadership. Whoever succeeds Mao will still have to deal with the problem of reintegrating the political machinery, reinvigorating the party, and renewing the process of industrial growth—in short, with domestic affairs. Although the Chinese will still pay attention to outside threats, both internal and external developments suggest that "there is little room in Chinese thinking for high-level aggression in the [Far Eastern] area."[38]

Strategic Power and Chinese Aggression

All this suggests that relative levels of strategic power are largely inapplicable to the deterrence of overt Chinese aggression, which is not the preferred instrument of the Chinese leaders, which could be both difficult and costly, and which could precipitate a disastrous nuclear war. As a matter of fact, the U.S. advantage in strategic nuclear capabilities is so great, and for the foreseeable future will continue to be so great, that the United States could not only easily destroy the fifty cities which contain 50 million people and over half of China's industrial capacity but could go on to knock out every town with over 5,000 inhabitants and to blanket most of China with lethal radioactive materials. Nor need it draw down its deterrent to Soviet attack in order to do this; given probable Chinese Communist air defense capabilities, the U.S. bomber fleet alone—or even the 250-odd B-52s scheduled to be placed on active reserve—could virtually obliterate China, by making repeated runs over target areas. Furthermore, the United States could, with a relatively small fraction of its programmed forces, launch counterforce strikes against Chinese missile sites, air bases, and nuclear facilities, thereby drastically reducing Communist China's retaliatory capabilities.

As indicated previously, this does not mean that the Chinese Communists could not inflict some damage on the United States, nor that they might not program their ICBMs to fire on warning, in order to be certain of retaliating to an American attack. This is, however, a far cry from suggesting that they would provoke such an attack by nuclear strikes against Japan or other Asian allies of the United States, as envisaged by Mr. Laird.[39] It is even further from suggesting that the Chinese would attempt to face down the United States in a crisis or confrontation by threatening nuclear war. As Alice Hsieh says, the belief that the Chinese, with embryonic strategic forces, would strike at U.S. cities is "like suggesting a willingness on the part of the Chinese leadership to commit national suicide."[40] And whatever else those leaders may be, they are not suicidal.

Under these circumstances it is doubtful that the credibility of the U.S. deterrent depends on reducing losses from a Chinese attack to very low levels. As Secretary of Defense Laird said, "If one believes that a Communist China armed with a force of ICBM's could still be deterred by our overwhelmingly greater strategic offensive forces, then an ABM defense need not be deployed against that threat."[41] While Mr. Laird professes not to believe this and supports the installation of the Safeguard ABM system, others may question the need for ballistic missile defenses —especially since the Nixon administration is apparently prepared to give them up in order to induce the Soviets to limit their strategic strike forces.[42]

Even when the Chinese achieve a significant nuclear capability (as they could by 1980), this may not alter pronouncedly their willingness to engage in any high-risk military policy; they will still have to live with the vast military-technological gap between their capabilities and those of the United States, with the possibility that overt Chinese military operations could precipitate an American nuclear response, and with the knowledge that this response could be made without drawing down the forces earmarked for deterrence of Soviet attack. Furthermore, they must (unless present trends are reversed) consider not just the probability that the USSR will not help them but the sobering possibility that it may join with the United States against them. What, however, if the USSR and Communist China move closer together, thereby requiring the United States to cope simultaneously with two nuclear powers?

Obviously, under such circumstances some strategic postures might look more desirable than they now do; for example, superiority in deliverable warheads and/or launch vehicles would obviously be of great importance if one had simultaneously to wage war with Communist China, to preserve assured destruction forces against a first strike counterforce attack by the USSR, and to prepare to penetrate Soviet ballistic missile defenses. Politically and psychologically a degree of superiority sufficient to cope simultaneously with the two great Communist states would demonstrate U.S. determination and intent to do just that. It would preclude a possible Sino-Soviet coalition (such as might arise after the death of Mao Tse-tung) from appearing so much stronger than the United States as to weaken U.S. prestige and influence. Given the present state of the world, some might consider such superiority a necessary hedge against the re-formation of such a coalition or a cementing together of the fractured Communist bloc.[43]

Against these strong arguments in favor of superiority, it might be pointed out that U.S. forces smaller than those of the USSR and Communist China combined could, in the event of war, inflict unacceptable damage on either or both of those countries, even after undergoing a first strike. Moreover, for the foreseeable future, the United States should be able to deal with Communist China without drawing to any significant degree upon its strategic strike forces. Its nuclear-armed air and naval units along the Asian littoral could in all probability destroy the fifty Chinese cities whose prospective loss Mr. McNamara believed would serve as a deterrent to Chinese aggression.[44] And if the threat of Soviet intervention or of retaliatory attacks from as yet unused Chinese missiles inhibited such a response, these same forces could, in conjunction with relatively small numbers of long-range bombers and ICBMs, launch counterforce strikes against Chinese weapons sites. Thus even for war-fighting purposes strategic superiority may be unnecessary.

As for deterrence of Soviet-supported Chinese aggression, or of joint Sino-Soviet military operations, the existence of superior strategic strike forces—or even of a nuclear deterrent—is only one among many factors which will influence Soviet and Chinese behavior. Perceived opportunities, domestic pressures, estimates of the will and intent of the United States, changes in the method if not the aim of Communist ideology, and so on, are all likely to have a significant impact upon the willingness of the USSR and Communist China to wage—or to risk—war against the United States. At the moment China's policy of fomenting revolutionary violence and of expelling American and Soviet influence from mainland Asia has tended to alienate the Soviet Union and to induce common interests between the U.S. and the USSR.[45] Even were the USSR and Communist China to move closer together politically and ideologically, the divergence in their interests, their attitudes, and their willingness to take risks might well preclude the Soviet Union from giving to Communist China the kind of support for its own efforts that the latter would like to see.[46]

If, however, the USSR did support and encourage Chinese Communist aggression against neighboring states, it by no means follows that U.S. strategic superiority would be either helpful or necessary. In the first place, the threat of escalation would probably inhibit the kinds of military actions which a greatly superior America might take, even as it would inhibit the Chinese (and the Russians) from attempting too much in the face of even inferior U.S. strategic strike forces. In the second place, the Chinese might be unwilling to place too much reliance on the Soviet Union, which could only "protect" China against American nuclear strikes by itself initiating general nuclear war; as Chinese Foreign Minister Chen Yi said in 1963, "Soviet protection is worth nothing to us."[47] In the third place, the United States and its probable allies already have in being local forces which, as Mr. McNamara put it, "provide both a strong deterrent and the ability to defend important areas."[48] And finally, to the extent that deterrence was both stable and mutual, the United States would have a relatively freer hand to employ tactical nuclear weapons against Communist forces operating outside their own territories.

In short, while strategic superiority may have the greatest military utility in deterring or coping with threats from two or more nuclear powers (which in practice means the USSR and Communist China), it is questionable whether its advantages warrant efforts to maintain it. For one thing, it may not be necessary: the mere existence of the deterrent will inhibit Chinese and Soviet actions, and other factors will affect the success or the failure of these actions. For another, only superiority in inflicting and limiting damage would be truly meaningful, and that is virtually impossible to attain vis-à-vis the USSR. For a third, as Chinese nuclear capabilities grow, corresponding increases in U.S. forces may appear to threaten the USSR, which in turn might step up its own procurement of strategic weapons systems, thereby accelerating the arms race. Hence, while some may deem it desirable that the United States maintain a clear strategic advantage over Communist China,[49] this may neither be necessary nor, in the long run, feasible.

Strategic Power and Chinese Risk-taking

As already pointed out, Communist China is economically weak, internally divided, and largely preoccupied with domestic affairs, including the sharing of power both while Mao is alive and following his death. It is quarreling with the Soviet Union, and that quarrel not only deprives it of economic and military assistance which could enable it to pose more credible threats to the United States but also diverts its energies and its resources to other tasks, such as the safeguarding of its borders with the USSR. Furthermore, its leaders have a keen appreciation of the destructive capacity of nuclear weapons and a strong desire not to precipitate a nuclear war.[50] For these and other reasons Communist China has been cautious in deeds, if belligerent in words.

It is conceivable that Chinese behavior could change with increases in strategic power, which will open to the Chinese a number of options ranging from counterdeterrence of U.S. tactical nuclear strikes to the possibility in a crisis of threatening the Japanese with annihilation if they do not force out U.S. troops and aircraft. Although stronger nuclear capabilities may make the Chinese more confident of limiting responses to low-level pressures, they do not necessarily add to their ability to apply such pressures. For one thing, only Hong Kong and Macao are immediately vulnerable to Chinese economic sanctions or political maneuvers, and these cities are more valuable outside Communist China than in it. Although Japan could be hurt by trade restrictions, it would not be crippled, nor even necessarily induced to change its political stance; moreover, the Chinese economy would suffer. China could conceivably pressure Burma into further readjustments of its northern border or encroach on territory claimed by India, but the returns would scarcely seem worth the effort—much less the risk that moves against India might again motivate the United States and the USSR to support that country. Threats of military action against most of China's neighbors are likely to be ineffectual, if only because the Chinese lack the air, naval, and amphibious units needed to make them credible. And actions against Korea, Taiwan, and other countries within reach would again bring the Chinese into a direct confrontation with the United States.

As for attempts at the direct employment of nuclear power for political gains, these might prove both risky and counterproductive. Although none of China's Asian neighbors has nuclear weapons, the United States has pledged itself to shield them if they are pressured.[51] And even if it is unwilling to threaten nuclear retaliation (or the Chinese refuse to believe the threat), the United States can take many measures to heighten the risk of war, and to instill confidence in its allies—to give just one illustration, by deploying on Quemoy nuclear-armed shells for the 155-mm guns which were emplaced there a decade ago. It is, moreover, hard to imagine a Communist China so stimulated by the possession of a modest and not very secure nuclear force that it would attempt to pressure the United States out of major bases or to force its withdrawal from vital positions in the western Pacific under the threat of nuclear war. As the distinguished Sinologist Allen S. Whiting says, "It is difficult to write a credible scenario for Chinese nuclear blackmail or nuclear confrontation at Chinese initiative."[52]

Not the least of the reasons for Chinese restraint is that China has many other interests which would be adversely affected by undue bellicosity, interests ranging from a potential loss of trade to the stimulation of a Pan-Asian anti-Communist alliance. Even an unsuccessful attempt at nuclear blackmail might bring about a reversal of the Nixon Doctrine and insure an American presence in the western Pacific for another decade. And a successful one could inspire the Indians or the Japanese to build nuclear armaments, thereby creating new obstacles to the future extension of Chinese power and influence.

It is possible that the growth of Chinese nuclear power may make them more willing to support "wars of national liberation," which they consider the best way both to weaken the imperialists *and* to avoid nuclear war.[53] In the past, however, their efforts in this direction have not been very fruitful, as evidenced by their ouster from Mozambique and their expulsion from the Democratic Republic of the Congo. Not even in Southeast Asia have the Chinese been able (or willing) to promote new insurrections: their supporters in Burma, the White-Flag Communists, number less than a thousand, and their partisans in northeast Thailand have (according to one eyewitness) caused less trouble than have the local cattle rustlers. While the Chinese have aided and abetted dissident elements in Vietnam, in Laos, and latterly in Cambodia, these are not wholly subject to Chinese control nor are their activities necessarily models for others to copy. Even skeptics of the "domino theory" must acknowledge that the outcomes of these conflicts are likely to have more of an impact on Chinese decisions to foment new ones than will any given levels of nuclear forces.

So far the Chinese have been extremely circumspect in aiding nationalist or pro-Communist elements in other countries. Many of their activities, such as road-building in Yemen, are of such a nature that the United States would find it difficult to justify military countermeasures—much less to threaten nuclear war. While they have sent advisers as well as arms to North Vietnam, these have not, so far as is known, gone into battle, and the only Chinese troops in that country have been occupied in repairing railroads. Nor did the Chinese, despite American bombing raids within a few miles of their southern border, "lend" airplanes to the North Vietnamese air force or themselves engage in combat. That these low-level activities in support of "friendly" governments will continue is almost axiomatic; that they will, with the growth of Chinese nuclear power, be undertaken on such a scale or in such areas as to threaten vital American interests is much less certain. As Arthur Huck says, "Any *régime* calling itself Communist will probably continue to pay lip service to the doctrine of continuous revolution in the Third World but this is very different from advocating or becoming involved in military adventures far afield."[54]

Even should the Chinese come to adopt a more aggressive stance, it is hard to see how they could exert significant pressures upon the United States and its allies. Unless these come to believe that there are *no* circumstances under which the United States would risk war on their behalf, Chinese nuclear blackmail is likely to be ineffective. Direct attack would almost certainly prompt an American response and large-scale military intervention in civil wars might well do so, but lesser actions (such as providing "volunteer" pilots or "transferring" submarines to other countries) are unlikely to affect their outcomes. Although support to dissident groups, such as the Hukbalahap in the Philippines, could be expanded, their success will depend more on the policies and practices of the local government than on the nature and level of Chinese assistance. And while the Chinese can certainly demonstrate weapons capabilities, mass troops, issue threats, and otherwise attempt to overawe their neighbors, this may signify only that more direct methods of achieving Chinese objectives may be too risky and too costly.

All this does not mean that the Chinese Communists are going to give up their efforts to promote more friendly—and perhaps more ideologically compatible—regimes in Southeast Asia, to establish Chinese hegemony over that area, and to achieve Chinese political primacy both in the Far East and among the world Communist parties. It does, however, suggest that both these aspirations and the methods by which the Chinese may pursue them are largely unrelated to the balance of strategic power between the United States and Communist China. And it further suggests that the success of the United States and its allies in precluding too rapid and too effective an extension of Chinese influence will also depend less upon the strategic balance than upon the political, social, and economic alternatives which they can offer to the peoples of the Far East.

The Implications for U.S. Strategic Nuclear Forces

As the previous discussion suggests, estimates of the level and nature of strategic nuclear forces required to "deter" a prospective enemy depend in large measure upon judgments concerning his aims, his intentions, and his probable behavior. If, as much official American opinion holds, that enemy is aggressive, willing to run risks in pursuit of his national or ideological objectives, and inclined to the use of force, then strategic superiority may be a *sine qua non;* on this basis one can understand Mr. Nixon's remark that "what has kept the peace . . . has been the immense

[U.S. strategic] superiority."[55] According to this thesis, the achievement by the USSR of strategic parity, however defined, could "liberate" forms of conflict that had been precluded previously, including "even military action against allies of the United States."[56] As Mr. Laird argued, Communist China's acquisition of a minimum deterrent could encourage that country to practice nuclear blackmail, to attack America's Asian allies, and even to threaten the United States with nuclear war.[57]

If taken literally such phrases would require U.S. programs even larger than those now envisaged, since the latter would maintain the U.S. lead over the USSR only with respect to numbers of warheads, leaving the Soviet Union ahead in numbers of launch vehicles and in deliverable megatonnage.* Or if one interprets them to mean that the United States should retain a relative advantage with respect to the ability to inflict damage (which is probably the only meaningful criterion), they would require not only increases in strategic strike forces but also the extension and/or the thickening of the Sentinel ABM system, which could not cope with large-scale Soviet attacks nor, over the long run, with those which the Chinese Communists could launch. And they certainly would rule out that "equitable limitation on strategic nuclear weapons"[58] proposed by Secretary of State William P. Rogers—at least as long as *equitable* is translated to mean "conferring a significant advantage upon the United States"

In this and the previous chapter it has been suggested that deterrence does not necessarily depend on the ability to inflict high levels of damage on an opponent nor on insuring an advantageous outcome to a nuclear exchange: the mere prospect of such an exchange may well suffice to induce caution. This is particularly true because of the uncertainties associated with nuclear war, the difficulty of achieving meaningful gains through force and the threat of force, and the risks attendant on initiating military operations against vital areas. Furthermore, it has been argued that the potential costs of such actions may in themselves inhibit aggression, regardless of the possibility of nuclear war. And finally, questions have been raised about the view that Com-

---

* See table 5. If one also counts Soviet SLCMs, IRBMs, MRBMs, and medium bombers, the USSR would probably lead in all categories.

munist revolutionary zeal, alleged disregard for human life, and expansionist tendencies preclude the United States from accepting equal or inferior deterrent forces. Obviously, this view of deterrence could lead to different estimates of the requirement for strategic nuclear forces.

For one thing, it suggests that, whatever their utility in fighting a war, increases in strategic defenses and/or improvements in the ability of U.S. strategic strike forces to limit damage may not be essential to deterrence as such. (As General John P. McConnell, former Chief of Staff of the Air Force, phrased it, "Regardless of whether you have a nuclear superiority or not, as long as you have the capability to destroy one another, then I don't see why we [Americans] should be less concerned than they are [about nuclear war], or why they [the Soviets] should be less concerned than we are.")[59] For another, it raises doubts about the necessity for major new programs designed to offset the growth (or the potential growth) of Soviet and/or Chinese Communist strategic nuclear forces; as Mr. Bundy said with respect to the credibility of the American deterrent in Europe, "Relative numbers of [strategic nuclear] weapons have never been decisive."[60] Although such programs may affect the strategic balance, they will do so only marginally; for example, Mr. McNamara testified in 1965 that the entire U.S. bomber fleet could increase by only 1 to 2 percent the damage to Soviet industrial facilities which American missiles could cause in a retaliatory strike during the early seventies.[61] Thus, while shifts in the strategic balance may cause U.S. policymakers to worry about the stability of deterrence, it does not follow that they will have a corresponding impact on prospective adversaries.

Nor will such shifts necessarily increase the propensity of these adversaries to take risks. Even in the unlikely event that the Soviets achieved "superiority" in numbers of launch vehicles or in megatonnage, it does not automatically follow that they would press harder against the United States; Soviet behavior will still be influenced by other factors, such as a loss of revolutionary *élan*, a preoccupation with domestic affairs, the divisions within the Communist world, and, above all, the adoption of political goals whose attainment requires Western cooperation. It is possible that the growth of Soviet strategic power may, as some analysts argue, tempt the USSR "to undertake a more extensive, more acute, and more dangerous range of risks in order to . . . reshape the world according to its own dogma,"[62] but it is equally possible, as others maintain, that this growth may be "a precondition for reaching a stable understanding with the United States."[63] If the USSR does not achieve such an understanding, or if it abandons efforts to reach one, the consequences may be more dire than those attendant on any foreseeable shift in the strategic balance.

As for the Chinese, it is conceivable that their development of a small nuclear deterrent might incline them to run greater risks in the pursuit of their political objectives. However, U.S. strategic superiority will still be so pronounced, and Chinese vulnerability to a disarming strike so high, that Chinese leaders cannot rely on their nuclear force for other than defensive purposes. In any case factors other than the balance of strategic power will also influence the Chinese propensity to risk confrontations with the United States and their behavior during them. One of them is their inability to stand up to the United States without Soviet support, which has not been readily vouchsafed to the present regime, and which presumably would not be available to a future one except at a price. Another is that the Chinese, whatever the bellicosity of their pronouncements, have espoused a cautious and defensive foreign policy, which they show no sign of altering. A third is that the Chinese, for both practical and doctrinal reasons, place reliance on other and less provocative means of advancing their interests, such as support of existing guerrilla organizations and operations, aid to revolutionary movements in other countries, and even the more traditional forms of technical and economic assistance to other governments. Even when the Chinese acquire a meaningful counterdeterrent, as they could by 1980 or 1985, this may not alter pronouncedly their behavior, although it could impose additional restraints upon the United States and hence affect the nature of any response to Chinese pressures against neighboring countries.

Moreover, even if the future leaders of the USSR or Communist China choose to adopt more bellicose, expansionist foreign policies and seek to capitalize upon their growing strategic nuclear capabilities, the prospects for success are not very good. For one thing, it is hard to exploit strategic power for political purposes: the difficulty of making threats credible and the variety of ways in which these threats can be countered militate against compelling another country to grant concessions or to make changes in policy. Furthermore, attempts at "compellence" not only may risk nuclear war but may carry other penalties, among them the possibility of heightening tensions, promoting allied solidarity, stimulating larger defense expenditures, and inducing nonnuclear states to acquire their own deterrents. And finally, success in exerting pressures under the protection of a "nuclear umbrella" may depend more on the importance of the issue at stake, the degree of interest in a given outcome, and the extent of the commitment to such an outcome than on the number of ribs in the umbrella; hence it does not follow that even superior strategic nuclear forces would enable the USSR to win every showdown by default, or that the vulnerability of the United States to Chinese Communist ICBMs would induce crisis outcomes favorable to China.

All this is not to argue for a precipitate cut in U.S. strategic nuclear forces or even for a passive stance in the face of continuing Soviet and Chinese Communist buildups, but only for less concern that these may markedly weaken the American position in the world at large. In retrospect it is clear that the United States overreacted to the earlier shift in the strategic balance occasioned by the Soviet development of a meaningful counterdeterrent,[64] which did not induce the greater Soviet bellicosity and higher propensity to take risks which many had assumed it would; no more may the present shift. As for the Chinese, it is possible that their development of a small strategic nuclear force might incline them to run greater risks in the pursuit of their political objectives; however, it is also possible that Chinese spokesmen are sincere when they characterize their nuclear weapons program as intended primarily to deter the American— and the Soviet—imperialists from attacking Communist China.[65] It may, therefore, be unnecessary for the United States to maintain strategic forces more powerful than those of the USSR, or to insist on extremely advantageous war outcomes vis-à-vis Communist China, on the ground that only thus can these two countries be restrained from pursuing more aggressive policies.

6
Strategy, Strategic Power, and Alliance Relations

Since the end of World War II, it has been the policy of the United States to oppose the forcible extension of Communist control over other countries and other peoples, both because some such extensions could directly threaten the vital interests of the United States and because their continuation could lead ultimately to a world in which the United States could not comfortably live. However, while this policy has been constant, the strategy for its attainment has undergone a number of transformations, from one in which nuclear weapons were deemed auxiliary to conventional forces to one in which they were predominant, from one in which their use was viewed as a last resort to one in which consideration was given to their employment at an early stage, at least for limited tactical purposes or for communicating intent.

These alterations reflect changes in a number of important variables: Communist strength, American and allied perceptions of the threat, characteristics of weapons systems, and so on. They also reflect the fact that the United States must help to defend countries in virtually every part of the globe, countries whose military capabilities, economic potential, level of technology, proximity to Communist neighbors, and accessibility to American forces vary almost infinitely. Accordingly, the United States has developed different strategies for coping with threats in various areas, with particular reference to threats to employ nuclear weapons for either military advantage or political gain. In Europe the United States has conceived and espoused the concept of "flexible response," under which conventional forces are to play a primary role in coping with Soviet aggression, tactical nuclear weapons are to be used only when it is clear that a Soviet advance can be checked in no other way, and strategic nuclear forces are to be employed as a last resort or in response to a Soviet nuclear attack on Western Europe. In Asia the United States has relied more heavily on atomic weapons to deter large-scale Chinese Communist attacks, with American and allied conventional forces relegated to the secondary roles of handling local incursions by China, North Korea, or North Vietnam and (until recently) of coping with Communist-supported insurrectionary movements. In both Asia and other parts of the world, the United States has pledged itself to shield nonnuclear states against nuclear aggression or the threat of such aggression,[1] though without specifying precisely how this is to be done.

Questions can be raised—indeed books can be written—about the validity of these strategic concepts, the adequacy of programs to support them, and the utility of ancillary measures such as providing equipment but little or no manpower for counterinsurgency operations. Not only, however, is the topic too broad to cover here but books *have* been written about it.[2] Instead, this chapter will consider to what extent U.S. programs for the development of strategic nuclear forces and U.S. concepts for their employment are acceptable to the nations for whose protection they are designed and will ask whether stronger U.S. nuclear forces than those now envisaged and/or improved U.S. strategic defenses would enhance the sense of security of these nations and promote solidarity between the United States and its allies.

Before attempting this, however, it might be useful to consider the fundamental shifts in the nature and purpose of alliances which have taken place in recent years and which affect both the questions asked above and the answers to them. Prior to the atomic age alliances could be viewed as augmenting the strength of each member state by pooling the resources of all. In this way small nations increased their bargaining power, enhanced their ability to deter stronger neighbors, and sometimes got a free hand in dealing with weaker ones. However they gave as much as they received, if not more. Not only did they provide bridgeheads across physical barriers, as Burgundy did for England in the fifteenth century, or assure control of strategic passages, as Turkey has for over five hundred years, but they contributed men and material to the common cause. These contributions were meaningful because technology did not confer significant military advantages on a "great power," at least until World War II. Hence, even small states could affect the pace—and perhaps the outcome—of a war between larger ones, as the kingdom of the Netherlands did in 1815 and the kingdom of Serbia a century later.

The advent of atomic weapons altered all of this. In the first place, it made nonnuclear states ultimately, if not absolutely, dependent for their security on nuclear-armed allies. In the second place, it diminished the value of territory, except as this afforded advanced bases for bombers and missiles; by 1950 the *glacis* which the USSR had so painstakingly erected along its western frontier had already lost much of its utility. In the third place, it downgraded the military contributions of smaller countries, which were meaningful only in conventional operations and were, even then, frequently contingent upon the willingness of the senior partner to provide advanced weapons and logistical support. Thus what an ally gave to a nuclear power became devalued in comparison to what it got.

The strain these developments placed on the Western Alliance became intensified when the USSR developed strategic nuclear forces which could devastate the United States. The Soviet counterdeterrent made the United States less willing to retaliate to an attack on one of its allies, even as it made some of those allies more nervous about the possibility of such an attack. The allies reacted by seeking even firmer pledges of American support and almost automatic U.S. involvement in any threat to their security or to their interests. The United States, for its part, responded ambivalently, repeating and enlarging its pledges even as it sought, through controls on the proliferation of nuclear weapons and through the development of new strategic concepts and force postures, to reduce the possibility of being embroiled in quarrels not of its own choosing.

Such a dichotomy between words and deeds is neither stupid nor Machiavellian but represents a logical solution to the problem of deterring aggression without becoming fully committed to initiating nuclear war should deterrence fail. It also reflects the fact that in a showdown between two superpowers, allies can only be liabilities, in that they multiply the risks of nuclear war without adding significantly to the ability to deter it—a judgment which applies even more to allies who possess nuclear weapons than to those who do not. Thus, whatever their cultural affinities, their economic and military contributions, and their political ties, the allies of one superpower are bound to feel somewhat exposed in the face of threats from the other, a point which should be kept in mind during the forthcoming assessments.

Strategy, Strategic Forces, and the European Allies

As noted previously, the United States and its allies have been concerned almost since the end of World War II lest the Soviet Union utilize its powerful ground and tactical air forces to over-run Western Europe, or, at the very least, use them to exert both political and military pressures against the Western Alliance. For a time, this concern was mitigated by a belief that the USSR would not undertake actions which might precipitate an over-whelming retaliatory strike by U.S. strategic forces; however, the steady growth of Soviet nuclear power, and particularly their early lead in the development and deployment of intercontinental ballistic missiles, generated fears that the United States might be either powerless to respond to Soviet aggression or unwilling to do so. By 1959–1960, European and American government officials, military men, and political analysts were arguing that the advent of strategic parity virtually nullified the American deterrent and gave the USSR greater freedom to exploit its presumed advantages in conventional forces.

These views were shared both by President Kennedy and by key policymakers in his administration, who generally assumed that the USSR would continue to exert pressures against vulnerable points, would attempt nuclear blackmail, and would perhaps even engage in "limited brushfire wars."[3] Furthermore, they were fearful lest the Soviets "capitalize on their conventional military power by the threat of bringing it to bear in situations where they have local conventional superiority."[4] In short, they believed that with the decline in the credibility of the American strategic deterrent there would be an increase in Soviet belligerence and risk-taking, including the possible use of force against the Western allies.

The Kennedy administration sought to cope with this problem in four ways. First, it stepped up the Titan, Minuteman, and Polaris missile programs, with the aim of achieving and maintaining a marked superiority over the USSR in relatively invulnerable strategic delivery vehicles. Secondly, it developed a doctrine for the employment of strategic forces which encompassed alternative uses ranging from initiating massive retaliatory attacks to withholding any nuclear strike in order to bargain with the USSR, with emphasis on limiting damage to both the United States and its allies.[5] Thirdly, it sought to raise the level of conflict at which it would be necessary to utilize either tactical or strategic nuclear weapons and thereby to increase the ability and the willingness of the allies to respond in kind to Soviet conventional operations against Western Europe. And fourthly, it sought to convince both the Soviets and the NATO allies that these measures (particularly the buildup of conventional capabilities) signified a continuing American willingness to defend Western Europe by whatever means might be deemed necessary—including the use of nuclear weapons.

Whatever the validity of this approach from the point of view of American officials, it had some drawbacks from that of their European counterparts. To the extent that the United States, in the interest of avoiding a nuclear exchange, sought to decouple Soviet aggression and nuclear retaliation, it may, in the eyes of some Europeans, have diminished the credibility of the deterrent; as the former Supreme Allied Commander, General Lauris Norstad, allegedly informed the White House in 1961, "Every document we [Americans] submitted stressing conventional warfare cast doubt on our nuclear resolve."[6] Since most Europeans wanted, in the words of former British Secretary of State for Defense Dennis Healey, "to prevent war, not to fight one, or even to win one,"[7] they reacted adversely to the American strategy of flexible response. The Germans, for example, insisted that "in NATO's military arrangements the prevention of war by deterrence should be given absolute priority over the conduct of operations in the event deterrence failed."[8] And former Premier (now President) Georges Pompidou charged that the U.S. strategy was not only adopted without French assent and without regard to French objections but that it was designed to enable the United States to avoid the consequences of nuclear war by limiting operations to the battlefields of Europe.[9]

These sentiments reflected in part national interests and national policies, but they also reflected a keen appreciation of the costs of war. Even tactical nuclear operations could have killed or wounded millions of people, and a larger-scale exchange could have devastated Western Europe. Since the Europeans had no means of coping with the Soviet MRBMs and IRBMs targeted against their countries—much less with the longer-range missiles of the Strategic Rocket Force—they had of necessity to rely on the United States to limit damage from a nuclear strike. That country, however, was both unwilling to provide NATO with its own medium-range missiles, lest this make more difficult the control of any conflict, and unable, in the face of growing Soviet power, to guarantee that it could or would initiate counterforce attacks against Soviet weapons sites.*

Although the growth of U.S. armed forces, the adroit American handling of the Cuban missile crisis, the Sino-Soviet split, and a number of other factors resulted in a lessening of European worries about the possibility of Soviet aggression, changed circum-

---

* Success would in any case depend on the Soviets refraining from attacking European targets during the early stages of a war—and some, at least, doubt that they would withhold their nuclear weapons. See "The Atlantic Alliance: Unfinished Business," a study submitted by the Subcommittee on National Security and International Operations to the Committee on Government Operations, U.S. Senate, 1 March 1967, which says, "The Soviet Government cannot suppose that a large-scale attack on Western Europe could be even briefly restricted to conventional forces, and therefore, if a massive attack is to be made it will surely begin with a nuclear strike against Western Europe and North America, not a march of great armies across NATO's eastern boundaries" (p. 6). Reprinted in U.S. Congress, Senate, Report of the Combined Subcommittee of Foreign Relations and Armed Services Committees on the Subject of United States Troops in Europe to the Committee on Foreign Relations and the Committee on Armed Services, *United States Troops in Europe*, 90th Cong., 2d sess., 15 October 1968, p. 57.

stances have again brought to the fore the concerns of the early sixties. One of these circumstances was the erosion of American strategic superiority as a result of major increases in Soviet defense programs. A second was the drop in NATO capabilities for conventional defense, resulting in part from the inability to base units on French territory or to plan on the use of French troops and in part from the failure of the NATO nations to meet their prescribed force goals; even though the member states agreed to concentrate on qualitative improvements rather than to expand beyond the 1968 levels, there may still be significant shortfalls some years hence. And finally, the continuing modernization of land, air, and naval units, the occupation of Czechoslovakia, and the appearance in the Mediterranean of a sizeable fleet strengthened the already formidable Soviet forces poised on or near the borders of NATO Europe.

Taken together these developments seemed to some members of NATO to mean that the United States would be less willing to initiate nuclear war in response to Soviet aggression and less able to limit damage to itself or to its allies in the event of war. They also seemed to mean that the allies would be handicapped in dealing with any Soviet thrusts and in responding to any Soviet pressures, both because of the disparity in conventional capabilities and because of the increasingly disastrous consequences attendant on the use of nuclear weapons. And finally, they seemed to some to presage a greater Soviet willingness to employ force, either directly, against exposed positions, or indirectly, in an outflanking move through the Mediterranean.[10]

The U.S. reaction apparently has been to reiterate the strategy of "flexible response," with minor modifications. First of all, the United States has committed itself to keep large numbers of American combat troops in Europe and to maintain a capability for their rapid reinforcement in the event of a crisis. Secondly, it has worked out procedures for the limited use of tactical nuclear weapons in the early stages of a conflict, in order not only to communicate intent but to increase the threat of escalation and thereby give warning to the USSR.[11] Thirdly, it has continued to rely on the nuclear deterrent to inhibit the USSR from launching a major assault on Western Europe.[12] And fourthly, it has sought to ease the fears of some Europeans that this deterrent might not be employed in support of their interests by offering them a voice in selecting targets for attack and in determining the nature and timing of any nuclear strike.

European participation in planning for nuclear war has been largely assured by the opportunity to name representatives to the Joint Strategic Targeting Group at the Strategic Air Command headquarters in Omaha and to join in the special studies concerning the employment of tactical nuclear weapons in Europe conducted by the Nuclear Planning Group. A role in decision-making has, to a lesser degree, been afforded to the Europeans by their involvement in the work of this group and in the deliberations of the larger Defense Planning Committee. So far, however, the United States has reserved to itself ultimate control over the nature and the timing of any nuclear response to Soviet aggression. Moreover, the United States has kept outside of NATO not only the Strategic Air Command and the bulk of the missile-carrying submarines but even the Sixth Fleet in the Mediterranean, and it has installed on the tactical nuclear warheads furnished to NATO units electronic locks releasable only by the Supreme Allied Commander (who is a U.S. general) and positive arming devices operable only by Americans.[13]

The allies have not been entirely happy with these arrangements which, as Hedley Bull pointed out, leave them with "a feeling that one of the options concerned, the nuclear option, is not unambiguously available to them."[14] So far, however, all save the French have accepted them, partly because of the dearth of feasible alternatives, partly because the Soviet threat has only intermittently been so pronounced as to incite the allies to take stronger measures. It may be that this will continue to be the case, especially if the USSR continues its present moderate policy toward Western Europe and/or negotiations on the reduction of both nuclear and conventional forces succeed. If, however, the Europeans came to feel that their security were endangered by new Soviet armaments or by shifts in Soviet behavior, they might both seek additional reassurances from the United States and take steps of their own to improve their defense posture.

If past preferences are any guide, the United States would like the Europeans to respond by beefing up NATO conventional forces so that these could deal with almost any assault by troops of the Warsaw Pact, thereby reducing dependence on the strategic deterrent and limiting the cases in which atomic weapons would have to be employed. This, however, may not be politically and economically feasible, especially since the United States government is (as President Nixon acknowledged) under pressures to cut back American troop strength in Europe and is asking the allies to contribute more largely to the support of those units that do remain.[15] Even if a buildup of conventional forces were feasible, it might not be successful in achieving the desired objective: the vulnerability of some areas (such as northern Norway), the lack of depth in allied positions, the ability of the Soviets to utilize interior lines of communication, and the advantages of surprise would make it very difficult for NATO troops to defend successfully the territories of all the member nations.[16] Furthermore, conventional forces, however strong, could not preclude the Soviets from initiating tactical nuclear strikes in support of their ground and air operations (as called for by Soviet military doctrine), from waging limited strategic war, or from inflicting massive damage on Western Europe should they choose to do so. Since, moreover, the Europeans are as little interested in refighting World War II as they are in experiencing World War III, it is questionable whether they would exercise this option.

Another possibility would be to make the deterrent more credible in European eyes by restoring the ability of the United States to wreak heavy damage on the Soviet Union without itself suffering severely from a nuclear exchange. However, as already stated, attempts to do this through multiplying the number of American missiles, enhancing their accuracy, and/or improving their information and control systems seem doomed to failure*— and most European officials and analysts recognize this. A more promising approach would be to build strategic defenses capable of blunting a nuclear strike, but this depends largely on Soviet forbearance. And even if this were forthcoming, and prospective U.S. fatalities were reduced from 120 million to 10 to 20 million

* See chapter 3, pp. 29–32.

(which Mr. McNamara estimated could be done), it is questionable whether the Europeans would feel very much safer, in view of statements by American officials that still lower levels of damage might cause them to back down before a Chinese Communist threat![17] Despite the contribution which ballistic missile defenses could make to the security of U.S. retaliatory forces and of the United States itself, and despite the improvement in damage-limiting capabilities resulting from this, from increasing the number of launchers, from installing MIRVs, and so on, there is no assurance that even a vastly more powerful United States would in fact initiate nuclear war. Hence, even though one might agree with President Nixon that "the nuclear capability of our strategic and theater forces serves as a deterrent to a full-scale Soviet attack on NATO Europe,"[18] this does not solve the problem of persuading the Europeans of this.

A third option would be to reduce the levels of damage which the Europeans themselves might suffer from a nuclear attack, thereby making them more willing to resist aggression and more confident, therefore, that it would not take place. This, however, would present some problems.

First of all, damage-limiting strikes against the numerous IRBM and MRBM sites and bomber bases in the western USSR would require hundreds if not thousands of warheads. If NATO tactical nuclear forces were to be used for this purpose, they would have to be strengthened by the addition of more and longer-range missiles, their intelligence and control systems enlarged, and their command structure revamped so as to enable them to direct such strikes and to coordinate their activities with those of the Strategic Air Command and the U.S. missile-submarine fleet—to say nothing of British and French nuclear forces. If U.S. strategic nuclear forces were to initiate these damage-limiting strikes, this would add to the demands already imposed on them by the necessity to inflict assured destruction even on a USSR defended by ABMs, to preclude repetitive strikes by Soviet long-range bombers and intercontinental missiles, and to survive increasingly powerful counterforce attacks by growing Soviet forces. Moreover, if the United States, (which needs 1,200 reentry vehicles to inflict as much damage as the USSR could with 200) argued that it or its

NATO allies should have another 1,000 or 2,000 deliverable warheads to counter Soviet MRBMs and IRBMs, this could arouse Soviet concerns about the security of their own intercontinental ballistic missiles, lead to counterclaims on their part, and complicate markedly the current talks on the limitation of strategic armaments. (In fact, the Soviets have been reluctant to count MRBMs and IRBMs as strategic weapons systems unless all American aircraft capable of delivering tactical nuclear warheads on the USSR are also counted.)

From the European point of view, a more significant problem would be that, under current arrangements, both tactical and strategic nuclear forces would still be controlled by the United States. Since large-scale attacks against military targets in the western USSR would be very likely to provoke a Soviet strike against the United States, that country might be understandably reluctant to authorize such attacks. And since any delay in so doing would enable the Soviet Union to devastate Western Europe, the allies might not have much confidence that an American-run counterforce operation would actually reduce damage to their countries.

Many Europeans feel that defensive systems offer the best—if not the only—chance of markedly reducing damage from a nuclear exchange. Moreover, they appreciate the extent to which even embryonic ballistic missile defenses could complicate Soviet planning for a nuclear strike, cause problems in the tactical use of atomic weapons, and lend credence to the British and French deterrents. So far the members of NATO seem to feel that the technical difficulty of constructing air and missile defenses which could be effective against the numerous and diverse Soviet delivery vehicles, the economic costs of such defenses, and the political problems of installing, coordinating, and controlling them rule out antiballistic missiles as a viable option for Europe.[19] If, however, the United States was largely secured against damage from a nuclear strike but Europe was left vulnerable, their views might change: the more extensive American ballistic missile defenses are, the more likely it is that the Europeans would want defenses of their own. Since a decision to improve the effectiveness of European air and missile defenses could put pressures on the United States to share its technology, to contribute to the costs, and even to provide radar and interceptor missiles (to say nothing of warheads for them), such a development might not be altogether in the American interest, even were it feasible.

Perhaps the least desirable option, from the point of view of the United States, would be for the Europeans to strengthen existing national nuclear forces or to build new ones. Even the former could make more difficult coordinated nuclear planning, create strains within NATO, and raise anew the specter of German atomic armaments, while the latter would in practice mean just that: a West German nuclear capability. Even if this did not split NATO, it would exacerbate East-West relations, jeopardize the talks on the limitation of strategic armaments, endanger the Nuclear Nonproliferation Treaty, and conceivably lead to a dissociation of the United States from plans for the defense of Western Europe.

Somewhat more acceptable would be the creation of an Anglo-French nuclear force under European control or the construction of a more truly multinational force, which would include elements from various countries; indeed the United States is on record as supporting such arrangements. If properly constituted, either of these forces could probably give the Europeans a greater sense of security. As Pierre Hassner points out, even a comparatively small European force could "be 'held in trust' for the coming of a Federal Europe and of a negotiated settlement [of East-West issues], or to limit the damage in the case of a break-down of the alliance. More immediately, it would increase the uncertainty of the aggressor and the probability of escalation, or, more specifically, it might serve to offset the possible Russian calculation of intimidating the United States by holding Western Europe as hostage, or of waging 'limited general war by proxy'. . . . The main protection against most types of attack would still be the American one, and the European deterrent would only be a method of influencing its character and its timing and would supplement it in the case of certain specific contingencies based on possible Soviet calculations."[20] However, entirely aside from the technical problems, the financial costs, and the political difficulties of constructing, operating, and controlling even a limited European deterrent,

it is not at all certain that official American approval would necessarily mean enthusiastic American acceptance, especially if the
European deterrent were, as Mr. Hassner hinted, to be used to
trigger the American one. Hence the development of an acceptable strategy for Europe depends largely on whether Europeans
can gain sufficient control over the American deterrent to feel
secure without gaining so much that the United States (or the
Soviet Union) feels insecure.

Although such a balance might be difficult to achieve, a beginning could be made by revamping U.S. strategy to place greater
emphasis on deterrence than on defense. Such a revamping need
not—and should not—rule out a conventional response to any
Soviet probes or local incursions, but it should favor concepts for
the quick (if limited) employment of nuclear weapons against
large-scale assaults, rather than those calling for protracted conventional operations. It would imply greater emphasis on securing
otherwise vulnerable points through the reenforcement of present
garrisons and hence some alterations in operational plans, military
policies, and troop deployments in Europe, which are still largely
oriented towards the strategy of "flexible response." It may—failing agreement by the Soviet Union to limit its own Strategic
Rocket Forces—require the deployment to NATO Europe of
medium-range missiles and/or the virtually irrevocable allocation
of the U.S. missile-submarines now in the Mediterranean and of
the Sixth Fleet, with its nuclear-armed carrier aircraft. It may
necessitate giving the Supreme Allied Commander in Europe
(who has traditionally been, but need not always be, an American) authority to employ tactical nuclear weapons under prescribed circumstances and against specified targets. And it will
certainly require more meaningful participation by the allies in
planning for and deciding on the use of nuclear weapons and
greater willingness on the part of the United States to outline the
kinds of circumstances under which it would authorize their use.*

* The views expressed above run counter both to current American policy, which
calls for the maintenance within NATO of forces capable of engaging in large-scale
conventional operations for months at a time, and to the thinking of some analysts
about the desirability of employing nuclear weapons, even for purposes of signaling
intent. A good review of prevailing policies and proposed alternatives will be found

Even if adopted, such measures would not solve all the problems of NATO, some of whose members are concerned about the vulnerability of exposed positions, nervous because of the powerful Soviet presence in Central Europe and in the eastern Mediterranean, and sensitive to shifts in Soviet policy. They could, however, better equip those states to adjust to such shifts, to resist any future Soviet pressures, and to preserve their own equanimity in the face of any new Soviet threats. However difficult their implementation may be for the United States, it is less difficult than trying to restore allied confidence by achieving strategic superiority or by building comprehensive ballistic missile defenses. And it would probably be more meaningful than any given level of strategic nuclear forces, offensive or defensive.

Strategy, Strategic Forces, and the Asian Allies

American strategy for the protection of U.S. and allied interests in Asia is less well defined, and the situation confronting it is vastly different from that in Europe. For one thing, Communist China is not nearly so powerful militarily as the Soviet Union, either in conventional forces or in nuclear capabilities. For another, the interests of America's Asian allies and their estimates of the intensity and the nature of the threat from Communist China differ even more widely than do those of the members of NATO. For a third, the United States is bound to these allies by a series of individual pacts, not an overall treaty, so that there is no common willingness to aid one another, no automatic involvement of one Asian nation in the event of an attack upon another. Finally, even if an Asian Treaty Organization existed, the geographic dispersal of the possible participants, their relatively low

---

in Timothy W. Stanley, *NATO in Transition: The Future of the Atlantic Alliance* (New York: Frederick A. Praeger, 1965), esp. pp. 243–305, and a reasoned argument for continuing to rely heavily upon conventional forces in the article by Alain C. Enthoven and K. Wayne Smith, "What Forces For NATO? And From Whom?" in *Foreign Affairs*, 48, no. 1 (October 1969), pp. 80–96. That opinions concerning the contributions to deterrence of such forces are by no means unanimous is evidenced by Bernard Brodie's *Escalation and the Nuclear Option* (Princeton, N.J.: Princeton University Press, 1966).

economic, technical, and military capabilities, and their lack of naval and air forces would probably require the United States to assume a larger share of the defense burden than it does in NATO.

For all of these reasons, the United States has pursued in Asia a strategy very different from that for Europe. Although the United States attempted to bolster the capabilities for local defense of Korea, Japan, and the Nationalist government of the Republic of China on Taiwan, it was reluctant to station many ground forces in these countries; in fact, only political exigencies prevented it from drawing down before now the two divisions left in Korea following the 1953 armistice. Elsewhere, it concentrated primarily on developing forces which could maintain internal security and guard borders against minor incursions. Until the outbreak of the war in Vietnam, American soldiers were conspicuous by their absence from Southeast Asia, primary reliance being placed on naval, air, and amphibious units—reinforced as necessary from the United States—to handle overt threats by China or other Communist states. Even so, the United States seemed determined to "avoid a strategy which relies almost wholly on the use of tactical nuclear weapons to cope with the enemy's 'massive' ground forces,"[21] and by the late sixties U.S. and allied units were credited with the "ability to defend important areas" against Chinese attack without recourse to nuclear weapons.[22]

Within the last few years, however, two factors have induced changes in U.S. military policy. One of these was the traumatic experience of the war in Vietnam, which seemingly convinced American officials of the undesirability of engaging in large-scale and protracted wars in Asia. In consequence, the Nixon administration has set limits to the support it will give governments faced by insurrectionary movements or by attacks from North Korea or North Vietnam and has begun to cut back on American forces in the Pacific. Although the United States will, as President Nixon said, remain an Asian power, it will have fewer troops in countries like Korea and Thailand and fewer bases in places such as Okinawa.

Implicit in this policy, and in the promise to provide a shield against any nuclear power which threatens America's allies, is greater reliance on atomic weapons to deter Chinese pressures of all kinds and to cope with any large-scale Chinese military operations. Here, however, the United States must consider another new factor: Communist China's acquisition of nuclear weapons. Whereas in the past the United States was immune from attack, and its bases and its allies in the western Pacific virtually so, it must in the future consider the possibility that the Chinese may launch nuclear strikes against the Japanese islands, Taiwan, the Philippines, or the United States itself.

The American reaction to this emerging threat has been to plan, through a combination of counterforce strikes and strategic defenses, to reduce Chinese Communist intercontinental delivery capabilities to virtually zero. As indicated earlier this does not really require any buildup of U.S. strategic strike forces; even if the Chinese do build the ten to twenty-five ICBMs which Secretary of Defense Laird estimates they could deploy by 1975,[23] these will amount to fewer than 1 percent of American launch vehicles, not counting regional capabilities in the form of aircraft carriers in Asian waters, fighter-bombers on Asian bases, and so on. And American strategic defenses are necessary only if the United States considers it essential to reduce Chinese Communist first strike capabilities from low levels to very low levels—that is, if it wants to raise its advantage in a nuclear exchange from six to one to fifty to one. Only if the United States both abandoned its program for the construction of ballistic missile defenses and drastically reduced its strategic strike forces could the Chinese hope to improve these exchange ratios and even then probably not before the 1980s.

Politically the question is whether the maintenance of American strategic superiority—and particularly of the capability to reduce damage from a Chinese attack to very low levels—is essential to maintain the credibility of the deterrent in the eyes of the Asian allies. Successive administrations have argued that it is, on the ground that the Chinese are so willing to risk and to lose lives in pursuit of their objectives that deterrence is difficult and chancy.[24] Moreover, U.S. officials have noted that population dispersal in Communist China was such that the United States could not, by destroying fifty Chinese cities, kill a percentage of the people equal to that which it could kill in the Soviet Union by striking at the same number of cities. (They have generally sloughed over the fact that, because of China's larger population, such an attack would nonetheless kill almost as many people as it would in the USSR.) Without defenses the United States could suffer 7 to 23 million casualties from a Chinese Communist nuclear strike, which could come in the form of a preemptive attack, originating out of a fear on the part of China that the United States would destroy its forces unless it launched them immediately, or in retaliation to U.S. tactical nuclear strikes at targets such as Chinese air bases and other military installations used in support of local operations against Asian nations. This American vulnerability might, it is said, make the Chinese Communists more confident that they could deter both U.S. conventional counteractions and the U.S. use of tactical nuclear weapons and hence more prone to exert pressures against their Asian neighbors or even to employ force against them. And the elimination or erosion of the Chinese capability to damage the United States could, it is claimed, serve not only to restrain the Chinese but also to reassure its allies about American willingness to support them in a showdown.[25]

It cannot be said how persuasive this argument is to the Asian allies, since these have vastly different perspectives and interests and varying degrees of confidence in the United States. Certainly all of them are vulnerable to Chinese Communist nuclear strikes, since each has at least one or two large cities (Bangkok, Melbourne, Manila, Taipei), and central Japan is virtually one continuous metropolitan area. Furthermore, with the exceptions of Japan and, to a limited degree, Nationalist China and Australia, they have virtually no defense against Chinese Communist air strikes, much less against the IRBMs and/or submarine-launched missiles which China could build over the next decade. Finally, while they have some potential delivery systems, they have no nuclear warheads—and hence no indigenous counter-deterrent—nor is there any indication that United States proposes to provide them with one.

Despite this there seems to be relatively little concern with the possibility of a Chinese Communist nuclear attack. To some countries, such as Japan, this threat seems remote, since there are no outstanding issues between the two countries and since Chinese utilization of Japan's industrial capacity could probably be more effectively assured by political and psychological means than by military force.[26] While Nationalist China, Thailand, and the Philippines may be more worried, nuclear aggression is not of as much immediate concern to them as are other forms which do not involve the use of atomic weapons. And even if they should come to feel threatened, the Asian allies must recognize that a Chinese nuclear strike is virtually certain to trigger a U.S. response, since it would directly challenge the credibility of alliance arrangements, constitute a *casus belli* not only under these but also under the Nixon Doctrine, and have a shock effect on American decision makers which would be almost independent of levels of strategic power.

To most allies, Chinese nuclear blackmail must seem almost as remote a possibility. First, it is hard to envisage a cause—except possibly the recovery of Taiwan—to warrant Communist China's threatening nuclear war against any of its neighbors, and there may be better and less provocative means of achieving even that objective. Secondly, there is the real difficulty of practicing nuclear blackmail, whose success must depend on a belief that the Chinese actually would employ nuclear weapons despite the virtual certainty that this would provoke American retaliation. Thirdly, there are a number of ways in which the United States could raise the risk of a nuclear war and enhance the confidence of its Asian allies, as by dispatching fighter-interceptor squadrons and surface-to-air missile battalions to threatened countries, redeploying nuclear-armed fighter-bombers and carrier aircraft to adjacent areas, and temporarily disseminating tactical nuclear weapons to allied units, should this seem warranted. And finally, there is the prospect that the USSR might, according to its pledge in conjunction with the Nuclear Nonproliferation Treaty, join in countermeasures again Communist China, thereby more or less permanently cementing an anti-Chinese alliance between the two superpowers.

Many types of overt Chinese aggression, such as an assault on the offshore islands or a large-scale invasion of Southeast Asia, should also be deterred, since the Chinese Communists cannot be sure that the United States would be inhibited from employing nuclear weapons by the fear of Chinese counterreprisals. The allies, however, may be less certain of this, not because of any relative increase in Chinese Communist nuclear capabilities but because of doubts about American willingness to fight on their behalf. Already there are questions in Asian minds about the degree of American interest in them, questions arising not only out of differences in culture, in race, and in equality of treatment, but out of the lack of a political and military commitment parallel to that which the United States has made in Europe. Furthermore, although the President has assured the Asian allies that the Nixon Doctrine does not mean an end to American support of their governments but only a shift in the means of support, they may not see things the same way. Indeed, the measures taken to implement the Nixon Doctrine, such as the retrocession to Japan of Okinawa, the planned cutback in U.S. forces in Korea, and the efforts to put an end to the war in Vietnam (and to the American presence there) may all tend to persuade the allies that U.S. support is less likely in circumstances meaningful to them: internal threats, low-level operations, proxy wars, or simply Chinese Communist politico-military pressures.[27] In the long run some may begin to come to terms with Communist China, whether or not the United States builds ballistic missile defenses or adopts other measures to insure its strategic predominance. And while political accommodation in the Pacific may be essential to peace, too rapid or too far-flung a movement in this direction could unduly encourage the Chinese Communists and inspire them to greater belligerency rather than to compromise and conciliation.

All this suggests that U.S. willingness to support its Asian allies may have as much or more influence on their sense of security as levels of strategic strike forces or the deployment of ballistic missile defenses.* It further suggests that the United States may

---

* For contrary views about the importance to the Asian allies of an American capability to limit damage from Chinese Communist ICBMs, see Harry G. Gelber, "The Impact of Chinese ICBM's on Strategic Deterrence," Orbis, XIII, no. 2 (Summer 1969), pp. 407–34, and D. Carlton, "Anti-Ballistic Missile Deployment

have to continue to give evidence of that willingness, through more meaningful joint planning for contingencies, through the maintenance of a visible (if less obtrusive) American presence, and through arrangements for the dispatch of air and naval units if and as needed. It also suggests that the United States stop emphasizing its unwillingness to stand up to the Chinese except under ideal (and virtually unattainable) circumstances. Whatever may be its utility in "selling" weapons programs to a reluctant Congress, this approach is both illogical (in view of parallel statements about the ineffectiveness of French and British nuclear forces in deterring Soviet actions) and counterproductive (in that it makes the allies more nervous). In the long run the United States *will* have to face a Communist China which possesses powerful strategic nuclear forces; if it now exaggerates their meaning for Asian security it may make more difficult both the maintenance of American interests in that area and the reconciliation of those interests with the aims and aspirations of Communist China which is the sole basis for lasting peace in Asia.

Strategic Power and the Nuclear Guarantee

A similar problem arises with the maintenance of a credible "shield" over nations "vital to our security and the security of the [Asian] region as a whole"[28] and to other guarantees against nuclear aggression and nuclear blackmail. Although sophisticated analysts and officials in foreign countries may recognize the advantages conferred by powerful strategic offensive and defensive forces, they are unlikely to equate continued American nuclear superiority with security against threats to their national interests. For one thing, they must recognize that interests vital to them, such as the maintenance under Indian control of the Aksai-Chin area, or the safeguarding of Israeli positions along the Suez Canal,

---

and the Doctrine of Limited Strategic Nuclear War," in *Implications of Anti-Ballistic Missile Systems,* eds. C. F. Barnaby and A. Boserup, Pugwash Monograph II (New York: Humanities Press, 1969), esp. pp. 134–37. Other views covering the potential utility and desirability of ABMs in strengthening the U.S. (or Soviet) deterrent against third world countries will be found on pp. 27–34, 111–14, 146–54, 162–69, and 217–19.

may be of lesser concern to the United States. For another, they may doubt the willingness of the United States to commit its nuclear power in their defense, not so much in the unlikely case of overt nuclear attack as in the case of threats or pressures or, more significantly, small-scale military operations carried out under the cover of the nuclear deterrent.[29] For a third, they must know that concerns other than those arising out of the strategic balance will influence American decisions; even if it were unquestionably superior to the USSR, the United States might be unwilling to back Israel openly and openhandedly, lest it further antagonize the Arab states and promote that extension of Soviet influence in the Middle East which it is trying to curb. Thus the question to be asked about American "nuclear guarantees" is not so much, "What are the relative levels of strategic power between the United States and the USSR, or between the United States and Communist China?" but, "What is the United States willing to do to safeguard the security of countries which feel threatened by either present or potential Nth powers?"

From the point of view of a nonnuclear state, the ideal "security guarantee" would probably be a promise by one or more nuclear powers to come to its assistance should it be attacked by, or threatened by, still another nuclear power. To the extent that such a guarantee extended a "nuclear umbrella" over the nonnuclear state, it could both deter a nuclear strike and provide reassurance against nuclear blackmail. To the extent that the promised assistance included support against conventional attacks, it could ease fears of local incursions. And to the extent that the promises were buttressed by staff talks, military aid, and troop deployments to adjacent areas, they could, even in the absence of formal commitments, be made more meaningful to all concerned.

The present American nuclear guarantee falls considerably short of this mark. The declaration of October 1964 by President Johnson said only that, if nonnuclear states "need our strong support against some threat of nuclear blackmail, then they will have it"—a statement which former Secretary of State Dean Rusk interpreted to mean that a country "specifically threatened with the use of nuclear weapons, would have the entire international community, including the United States, register its support in whatever appropriate way would be necessary in the circumstances."[30] And the guarantee by President Nixon, quoted previously, leaves unanswered the question of which states may be deemed "vital," as well as that of how the U.S. "shield" is to be interposed. At the moment it does not seem likely that the United States would offer still stronger guarantees against a Soviet or Chinese nuclear strike, would agree to disseminate nuclear weapons to a nonaligned nation, or would commit itself to furnish troops to repel a conventional attack, in part because of reluctance to treat neutrals better than it treats its own allies, in part because of concern lest these measures automatically involve it in any conflict which the USSR or Communist China might precipitate.

Instead, it has sought to reduce the risks and potential costs of unilateral commitments through joint guarantees by other nuclear powers, such as that given by the United States, the USSR, and the United Kingdom in conjunction with the Nuclear Nonproliferation Treaty.* This, however, may leave something to be desired. For one thing, it covers only parties to the treaty, leaving exposed countries which have not signed it, such as India and Israel, or have signed it but not yet ratified it, such as Egypt and Japan. For another, it implies that assistance will be given only if all three nuclear-weapons states which have adhered to the treaty join in so doing,[31] and it specifically provides that such assistance will be given through the Security Council, where each of the

---

* United Nations Security Council Resolution 255, 17 June 1968, for which these three countries voted:

(1) *Recognizes* that aggression with nuclear weapons or the threat of such aggression against a non-nuclear-weapons State would create a situation in which the Security Council, and above all its nuclear-weapons State Permanent Members, would have to act immediately in accordance with their obligations under the United Nations Charter; [and]

(2) *Welcomes* the intention expressed by certain States that they will provide or support immediate assistance, in accordance with the Charter, to any non-nuclear-weapons State party to the treaty on the Non-proliferation of Nuclear Weapons that is a victim of an act or an object of a threat of aggression in which nuclear weapons are used.

For the complete text of the resolution, see the *New York Times*, 18 June 1968, p. 2.

guarantors (as well as France and Nationalist China) has a veto.*
Moreover, while both the resolution and various declaratory
statements make reference to the "inherent right of individual or
collective self-defense . . ." under Article 51 of the UN Charter,
this is apparently intended as an assurance to present allies
rather than as an extension of American commitments; Secretary
of State Rusk testified that the new arrangements would not obli-
gate the United States to take any actions outside of those already
required by the UN Charter and by existing treaties of alliance.[32]
  Even so, the various assurances given by and in connection
with Security Council Resolution 255 might be more meaningful
to nonnuclear states if it were not for three other problems. The
first is that the guarantor powers may not always see eye to eye
on actions to be taken, especially if the alleged threat to use
nuclear weapons is made by, or directed against, one of their
allies. The second is that the already difficult task of acting
through the Security Council will become virtually impossible if

---

  * The operative paragraphs of the U.S. declaration preceding the Security Council vote were:
  Aggression with nuclear weapons, or the threat of such aggression, against a
  non-nuclear weapons State would create a qualitatively new situation in
  which the states which are permanent members of the Security Council would
  have to act immediately through the Security Council to take the measures
  necessary to counter such aggression or to remove the threat of such aggression in accordance with the United Nations Charter, which calls for taking
  'effective collective measures for the prevention and removal of threats to the
  peace and for the suppression of acts of aggression or other breaches of the
  peace'. . . .
  The United States affirms its intention, as a permanent member of the
  United Nations Security Council, to seek immediate Security Council action
  to provide assistance, in accordance with the Charter, to any non-nuclear
  weapons State party to the Treaty on the Non-proliferation of Nuclear Weapons that is a victim of an act of aggression or an object of a threat of aggression in which nuclear weapons are used. . . .
  The United States vote for the resolution before us, and this statement of
  the way in which the United States intends to act in accordance with the
  Charter of the United Nations, are based upon the fact that the resolution is
  supported by other permanent members of the Security Council which are
  nuclear-weapons States and are also proposing to sign the Treaty on the Nonproliferation of Nuclear Weapons, and that these states have made similar
  statements as to the way in which they intend to act in accordance with the
  Charter. (*New York Times*, 19 June 1968, p. 2)

and when Communist China (against whom Resolution 255 was obviously aimed) secures its "rightful" seat as a permanent member of the Security Council—and with it the prerogative to veto any proposed operations. And the third is that the guarantee covers only nuclear aggression or the threat of aggression, thereby leaving open the possibility of conventional operations, such as a Soviet thrust into Yugoslavia or an Israeli advance into Egypt.

This last possibility—that a country may insist on security against nonnuclear aggression—is not only the most difficult to handle but perhaps the most likely to induce further proliferation. Thus Israel, fearful lest it be overwhelmed by a resurgent Arab League, may build a nuclear deterrent rather than rely on outside help. The United Arab Republic, worried about the Israeli development of a token nuclear force, may itself seek to acquire atomic bombs. India may decide that tactical nuclear weapons offer the best possibility of checking new Chinese advances. Or Pakistan, alarmed over the possibility that India might "go nuclear," may look to Communist China for weapons of its own. And while the acquisition of atomic weapons by Israel or Egypt is not likely to start a stampede for nuclear rearmament, it may strengthen the hands of those in other countries who argue for such a step.

Moreover, to persuade India, Pakistan, Israel, Egypt, and other nonallied countries that under such circumstances their security can be assured by means other than national nuclear forces will be difficult indeed. As indicated above the present nuclear guarantees contain so many ambiguities and gaps that no country whose interests are threatened can fully rely upon them. And while unilateral American measures, such as the deployment of troops and the dissemination of nuclear weapons, might deter potential aggressors, it is questionable whether Egypt, India, or Yugoslavia would accept them—and even more questionable whether the United States would further extend its commitments, to these or to other states outside its network of alliances.

If, therefore, the United States is seriously interested in precluding nuclear proliferation, it may have to adopt new and different ways of reassuring potential Nth powers against threats to their security. At the very least these would have to incorporate more precise statements concerning the circumstances which would trigger the guarantee and the ways in which the United States would implement it, including ways in which nuclear weapons would be employed. They would have to include some assurances against nonnuclear aggression from whatever source. They presumably would have to be worked out with the USSR, both to remove the onus attaching to unilateral U.S. actions, to achieve political acceptance of these actions, and, above all, to avoid precipitating a confrontation with the Soviet Union. And while no one can say that even the last of these would be easy, it might be easier than persuading potential Nth powers that vague American promises, coupled with the construction of ballistic missile defenses, will insure their security over the next decade.

Strategic Power and Reassurance

Whatever measures are taken to reassure countries which feel threatened must be credible in the eyes of three different groups of leaders: those of the United States, those of the USSR and Communist China, and those of the nations whom the measures are supposed to protect. The burden of chapters 4 and 5 was that the deterrent was highly credible to Soviet and Communist Chinese decision makers, and probably credible to American officials, despite the doubts of some about the effect of shifts in the strategic balance.* The sense of this chapter is that the deterrent may be less credible to allied leaders—and still less so to the leaders of potential Nth ·powers—but for reasons having little to do with perturbations in the strategic balance.

This does not mean that these men are unconcerned about levels of strategic power: they certainly would react adversely to

---

* It is difficult to determine with any accuracy whether American leaders *are* worried about the effectiveness of the deterrent, since efforts to muster support for, or obtain congressional approval of, particular programs sometimes lead military officers and civilian officials to engage in exaggerated statements of the threat and to put forward somewhat rhetorical descriptions of future situations in which the desired weapons system may be "essential." The fact that the amounts budgeted for strategic nuclear forces dropped by $2 billion during the first year of the Nixon administration would suggest less concern than might be inferred from statements by high officials of that administration.

deep unilateral cuts in U.S. strategic strike forces, which, under present circumstances, could only be interpreted as an abdication of responsibilities and as evidence of a drop in interest. Furthermore, most allied officials would agree that the ability to inflict heavy damage on a potential aggressor is important and that the ability to do so without suffering comparable damage is highly desirable. While this view may to some extent be motivated by a belief that strategic superiority will enable the United States to cope with threats which are beyond their own ability to handle— such as Soviet MRBMs or Chinese medium bombers—it may more largely reflect a belief that the maintenance of this capability is essential in U.S. eyes. This is probably still more true with respect to strategic defenses, which may seem irrelevant to the deterrence of Chinese aggression, or even counterproductive, in that they may enable the United States to decouple itself from events in Europe or Asia. (As Professor A. Doak Barnett indicated, "if the United States focuses on such a defense strategy rather than relying on the continued applicability of mutual deterrence, the Japanese may conclude that America in a crisis situation might concern itself only with its own defense and abandon interest in allies not protected by such [ballistic missile] defenses.")[33]

If this assessment is accurate, it means that conveying a sense of security to allies and to states falling under the aegis of the nuclear guarantee may depend more on tangible assurances of U.S. interest than on statements about American strategic nuclear capabilities, and more on irrevocable guarantees of U.S. support than on references to low levels of damage from a Chinese strike. Such assurances have been forthcoming, in the form of declarations, treaties, arms aid, the dissemination of nuclear weapons, the deployment of U.S. forces, and even assistance in combat, as to South Korea and South Vietnam. However, guarantees that the United States will furnish meaningful support to a nation under all circumstances are somewhat harder to come by. For one thing, U.S. interests in all countries are not equal; while it can be said with some validity that a free, non-Communist Western Europe is vital to American security, the same is not necessarily true of South Vietnam, South Korea, or even Iran. Secondly, the ability of the United States to provide meaningful support is very uneven, and it can do more to block the Fulda Gap in West Germany than it can to close the passes between Communist China and India. Thirdly, the threats to various allies will differ, and so will the consequences of counteractions; at the present time the use of tactical nuclear weapons against Chinese Communist air bases is both more feasible and less risky than their employment against Soviet or even East European airfields. Finally, the United States—quite understandably—wishes to reserve to itself decisions on the use of nuclear weapons and the conduct of nuclear war, which many regard as the *sine qua non* of American guarantees.

One cannot say that this is wrong from the American point of view, just as one cannot say that it is wrong for the Indians to seek more precise assurances before they pledge themselves never to "go nuclear," or for the Israelis to ask for more extensive military aid before they agree to a truce in the Middle East. One can only point out that in a period when the United States is not only not extending its commitments but is reinterpreting and limiting them, the states which are more or less dependent on its military power may become nervous, even to the extent of considering building national nuclear forces. (In fact, the respected newspaper *Asahi Shimbun,* in commenting on an American reinterpretation of the U.S.-Japanese security treaty which places on the Japanese almost complete responsibility for their own defense, indicated that "the lure of nuclear arms [for Japan] will increase!"[34])

Under present circumstances there would seem to be four major ways of precluding greater nervousness on the part of these countries. One would be to give the allies a larger voice in decisions to employ nuclear weapons, in the targets against which these are to be directed, and in the timing and magnitude of any nuclear strikes. To some extent this process is already underway in Europe, even though the United States formally retains control over decisions to employ weapons and, for all practical purposes, over the weapons themselves.* In Asia the process will be incom-

---

* This control does not, of course, extend to British and French strategic nuclear forces; however, it does include British tactical delivery systems in Germany and did include those tactical weapons provided to the French prior to 1967.

parably more difficult, since there is no cohesive alliance, and since the interests of the allies vary from security and noninvolvement on the part of Japan to a desire on the part of the Chinese Nationalists to engage the arms and the power of the United States in support of a "return to the mainland." However, these difficulties should not be permitted to stand in the way of political consultations about the circumstances under which atomic weapons might be employed and the procedures for so deciding, which could be meaningful to virtually every one of the allies —and, in time of crisis, to those states covered by the "nuclear guarantee."

A second way of alleviating nervousness would be to attempt to ameliorate actual or perceived threats; it may well be that American perceptions of future threats and of programs required to deal with them have fed the fears of allies and neutrals alike. (After all, if Communist China's development of a few ICBMs requires the United States, despite its overwhelming strategic nuclear power, to install ballistic missile defenses, why should not Australia worry?) Until the United States comes to assess more accurately the threats to its own security, and to cope with these threats by means other than arms buildups, it is unlikely to persuade its allies that these are unnecessary or that the American failure to maintain a strategic advantage, for whatever reason, does not weaken their security.

A third way would be to try to work out with the United Kingdom and the USSR procedures for multilateral support to countries threatened by a nuclear power (as agreed under UN Security Council Resolution 255), and to provide that support under UN auspices, rather than unilaterally. At the very least, such an effort would help to educate the Soviet Union to the long-term consequences of pressuring potential Nth powers, such as Israel. It could create mechanisms for considering and endorsing American (or Soviet) measures to uphold the "guarantee," even if it did not achieve agreement in advance on their implementation. And despite the divisions between the United States and the USSR on other issues, it might produce a unified response to possible Chinese Communist moves which could both deter the Chinese from ever making them in the first place, reassure those who might otherwise feel "let down" by the United States, and remove from the latter both the onus and the risks of unilateral action to "contain" Communist China.

Fourthly, it would seem that allied concerns about the credibility of the deterrent could be lessened by altering the nature of the threat, at least in Europe. To the extent that talks on strategic arms limitations result in some measures to control or to reduce the Soviet missiles and bombers targetable against NATO, the allies might be less worried about nuclear war or nuclear blackmail. To the extent that reductions in strategic armaments are accompanied by "mutual and balanced force reductions" on the part of NATO and the Warsaw Pact, concerns about Soviet local operations in a period of strategic parity can be eased, if not completely eliminated. Such arrangements—and even more the political atmosphere which would both precede and accompany them —could go a long way to alleviate allied nervousness; as Robert E. Osgood stated, "The [NATO] allies felt secure because even a low degree of credibility was regarded as sufficient for deterrence under the new political conditions of *détente*."[35] And while in the short run agreements on arms control with Communist China do not seem possible, this does not mean that efforts to achieve them should be ruled out; in fact, it is conceivable that China might accept some tacit restraints on both the deployment and the use of nuclear weapons—a subject which will be explored further in the next chapter.

7
Arms Control and Strategic Power

In the past the United States government has, to say the least, displayed marked ambivalence toward measures for the control of armaments.* Sometimes these were judged largely in terms of their impact on world opinion and were designed to maximize that impact rather than to be negotiable or even feasible. Some people viewed arms control as a means of reducing international tensions, others as an objective which could not be reached unless and until modifications in political behavior had taken place. Some arms control measures won approval because (like the freeze on U.S. and Soviet strategic strike forces suggested by President Johnson in 1964)[1] they would perpetuate an advantage, others (like the proposal for burning obsolescent American and Russian bombers) because they would not really affect the strategic balance. Only as it became apparent that minimum U.S. objectives with respect to strategic nuclear forces could be achieved through agreed limitations on armaments, and that maximum objectives could not be achieved at all, did the United States begin to take seriously the possibility of arms control.

---

* The phrase *arms control* is intended to encompass all bilateral or multilateral understandings, arrangements, or agreements, whether formal or informal, explicit or implicit, which set limits to the size, capabilities, or deployment of the armed forces of a country. It does not include unilateral measures to reduce the vulnerability of those forces, to improve command and control systems, or otherwise to enhance their security against an enemy and their responsiveness to their own duly constituted authorities—largely for the reason that what one country might deem a step toward the control of armaments, another might consider threatening, if not provocative.

134

As outlined by officials in the Johnson and Nixon administrations, these minimal objectives included the maintenance of strategic strike forces which could, under the worst of circumstances, inflict on the USSR and/or Communist China unacceptable damage and, in the case of the Soviet Union, damage comparable to that it could inflict on the United States. These forces were to be so secure against a first strike as to give the USSR no incentive to preempt in a crisis, and thereby precipitate nuclear war. Moreover, the strategic nuclear forces, and particularly strategic defensive systems, were to protect the United States against small-scale missile strikes, such as Communist China might be able to deliver in the mid-70s, as well as against accidental or unauthorized launches from any source.[2] Both administrations rejected as infeasible the aim of attempting to preclude significant damage from a Soviet nuclear attack, but Mr. Nixon went one step further by ostensibly abandoning the goal of maintaining superiority over the USSR which had been set by his predecessors and which he had endorsed during his Presidential campaign.

More importantly, Mr. Nixon voiced the view that "sharp increases [in U.S. strategic nuclear forces] might not have any significant political or military benefit. Many believe that the Soviets would seek to offset our actions, at least in part, and that Soviet political positions would harden, tensions would increase and the prospect for reaching agreements to limit strategic arms might be irreparably damaged."[3] And he suggested, as had other senior officials before him, that this prospect be pursued.

There are good reasons for the American interest in limiting strategic armaments. First of all, particular arms control measures might be helpful in warding off specific threats to the security of the United States. For example, a mutual halt to the further construction of ICBMs would leave the U.S. Minuteman force relatively safe (at least in the short run) and would obviate the need to deploy ballistic missile defenses around weapons sites. Alternatively, an agreement to limit the installation of antiballistic missiles could minimize fears that the Soviet Union would deploy extensive defenses and thus remove much of the incentive to install MIRVs on U.S. missiles. And provisions for cutbacks in the Soviet MRBMs and IRBMs targeted against Western Europe could not only diminish European concerns about Soviet aggression and partially reduce the damage from a nuclear exchange but also lessen some of the worries about the erosion of the U.S. damage-limiting capability. Hence it is not surprising that the Nixon administration announced its readiness to seek to maintain U.S. security "through cooperative efforts with other nations to provide greater security for everyone through arms control."[4]

However, the reasons for American willingness to set limits to strategic nuclear forces go beyond the narrow one of heading off particular threats. For one thing, arms control measures might preclude technological developments which could cast doubt on the maintenance of the deterrent, induce new and continuing efforts to keep up with an opponent, and create greater uncertainties about that opponent's capabilities and intentions—such as the Soviet motives for building so many SS-9 ICBMs or the American ones for developing MIRVs.* For another, the resultant competition in armaments tends to absorb resources, talents, and energies which could be better employed in supplying rising domestic demands. And for a third, this competition could well increase both the damage from a nuclear exchange and the tensions and

---

* This process has been illustrated as follows:

1) The Soviet deployment of antiballistic missiles triggered a U.S. decision to install MIRVs on its missiles in order to penetrate Soviet ballistic missile defenses.

2) Since MIRVs could enable U.S. counterforce strikes against undefended Soviet ICBMs, the USSR then had to multiply its own kill capabilities by installing MIRVs.

3) Since Soviet MIRVs could threaten American ICBMs, the United States had to build ABMs, in order to safeguard its strategic deterrent.

4) Since the United States will have ABMs, the Soviets must devise some means of insuring that the United States does not "give them a double whammy," and so on (From the remarks of Sen. Jacob Javits during his interrogation of Deputy Secretary of Defense David Packard in U.S. Congress, Senate, Committee on Foreign Relations, Subcommittee on International Organization and Disarmament Affairs, *Hearings, Strategic and Foreign Policy Implications of ABM Systems*, 91st Cong., 1st sess., 1969, pt. I, pp. 317–20).

In all probability U.S.-Soviet interactions are much less closely linked than this; however, there is apparently a general tendency by both sides to consider each other's postures and programs in deciding on their own (Testimony of Professor Alex Inkeles in U.S. Congress, Joint Economic Committee, Subcommittee on Economy in Government, *Hearings, the Military Budget and National Economic Priorities*, 91st Cong., 1st sess., 1969, pt. 3, p. 868).

hostilities between the United States and the USSR, which in turn might enhance the likelihood of such an exchange. As President Nixon has said, echoing others before him, "the traditional course of seeking security primarily through military strength raises several problems in a world of multiplying strategic weapons."[5]

Obviously, the imposition of limits on strategic armaments will not satisfy those Americans who are desirous of achieving meaningful strategic superiority, since it is highly unlikely that this would be acceptable to the other side. Nor will they please those who have argued for comprehensive ballistic missile defenses—unless, that is, both sides agree that these are desirable and are prepared to limit their reactions to the introduction of such defenses. And they may arouse concerns about everything from the effect of particular constraints on weapons systems development to the overall implications of any agreement for future Communist behavior. While it is impossible in this chapter to deal adequately with all the relevant factors, an attempt will be made to discuss briefly some of the major questions, such as:

1) How could agreements to limit strategic armaments enhance U.S. security?

2) What would be the impact on the strategic balance of various types of arms control measures?

3) To what extent are particular measures likely to affect the credibility of the U.S. strategic deterrent?

4) What might be the effect of arms control agreements on the attitudes toward the United States of the European allies, of the Asian allies, and of the states covered by the nuclear guarantee?

Arms Control and National Security

Although no arms control agreement can cope with all the problems of insuring security in the nuclear age, and those measures likely of acceptance will probably be even less inclusive, arms control can do some things. For one, it can reduce the risk of war by accident, by establishing tight controls over missile launches and bomber flights and by creating a climate in which these controls are deemed acceptable, despite the fact that they may make retaliation less certain or less rapid. It can help avoid war by miscalculation, by providing means for rapid and secure communication between two parties and by enabling them to verify through reliable sources what is actually taking place; thus had the Soviets—or the Egyptians—checked on the rumors of Israeli deployments against Syria, the six-day war might never have occurred. It can preclude deployments which may seem threatening or be provocative, such as the introduction of missiles into countries near an adversary's homeland. It can assure that adversary that one is not contemplating a first strike, by revealing that essential elements such as missile-submarines are not in position to participate in such a strike. And it can, most importantly, reduce the advantage accruing from striking first, by stabilizing the forces on either side.

This stability can be achieved in three ways: by setting limits on numbers of weapons, by imposing restrictions on new types of weapons, and by discouraging measures to make existing weapons systems markedly more effective than they now are. The first approach would attempt to insure, by limiting, freezing, or reducing the number of authorized launch vehicles on each side that neither one had (or could quickly acquire) a degree of superiority in numbers of launch vehicles or deliverable warheads which would enable it to knock out an opponent's strategic retaliatory forces. As far as the two superpowers are concerned, this would be relatively easy, since their forces are already so large and so diverse that neither qualitative improvements in existing weapons nor sizable increases in current forces would be likely to give either one a meaningful damage-limiting capability;* moreover, any such developments could be quickly detected, as they are today. And while the establishment of a crude parity in numbers might cause problems with respect to "equality" in the ability to inflict damage, or in connection with the capability to attack or defend other nuclear powers, it would certainly help maintain stability of the strategic balance.

Constraints on numbers of launch vehicles would, however, not

* See chapter 3, pp. 38–40.

help as much as would limitations on the introduction of new weapons, which by their very nature may threaten strategic stability and which will, whatever their military-technical impact, probably induce countervailing actions. True, improvements in the accuracy of unpowered reentry vehicles might make them about as useful a counterforce weapon as maneuverable warheads, but the latter will undoubtedly be more disturbing. True, one could offset either development by shifting from ICBMs to bottom-based or sea-borne missiles, within agreed limits on total numbers, but this may not be wholly satisfying. And true, such innovations may be less meaningful when the limits on total numbers are low rather than high (because expenditures for counterforce strikes may reduce the damage which could be inflicted by the remaining weapons below that level regarded as unacceptable), but this argument may not be wholly persuasive to an alarmed Congressman. Thus both the maintenance of a sense of security under any arms control agreement and the continuance of the agreement itself could depend in part on controlling new weapons.

This is particularly true where innovations threaten to offset the benefits obtained through dispersing, protecting, or defending strategic retaliatory forces. For example, even though the Soviet FOBS (fractional orbital bombardment system) may be comparatively inaccurate, its large warhead, low trajectory, and potential ability to circumnavigate the globe would enable it to knock out U.S. airfields before all the bombers based thereon could take off. Similarly, accurate MIRVs would enable the United States to destroy Soviet ICBMs, even if the latter were covered by ballistic missile defenses. Hence both the desire to insure the security of retaliatory forces and the need to make meaningful any limitations on the size of such forces and any agreements for their protection argue for curbing the introduction of new weapons. Furthermore, such curbs could avoid the necessity for taking costly countermeasures, which might in turn simply stimulate additional weapons deployments by the other side.

There are, however, other incentives to the arms race than the introduction of new and exotic weapons and other means of blunting them. One incentive is provided by the upgrading of existing offensive weapons systems, which may induce counter-vailing measures—such as the expansion of antisubmarine warfare forces to deal with more silent submarines carrying longer-range missiles. Another is the augmentation or improvement of strategic defenses, which may inspire qualitative changes in the weapons system attempting to penetrate them: the reverse of the previous illustration. Unfortunately, one cannot expect existing weapons to last indefinitely; even ICBMs deteriorate over time. Nor can one expect replacement weapons not to be better; even if the United States wanted to, it could not today produce B-52 bombers, which were built in an era of less advanced technology. For this reason it may be necessary to curb qualitative improvements by imposing gross restrictions on weapons system characteristics (such as the weight of bombers or the thrust of missiles) or by introducing selective constraints on equipment, such as the number of launch control radars for ABM systems. It may also be necessary to curtail the expansion of weapons systems which either could themselves threaten to degrade strategic retaliatory forces or which could be adapted to that purpose—on both of which counts Mr. Laird has expressed concern about the Tallinn surface-to-air missile system built by the USSR.[6]

Unfortunately, only drastic (and very unlikely) reductions in strategic strike forces would markedly reduce damage from a nuclear exchange, and some measures (such as curbing defensive systems) which might make such an exchange less likely would also make its potential consequences more disastrous. Since one objective of arms control is to reduce damage from a nuclear war, other means to this end must be sought.

One possibility would be to seek agreement both on the nature and scope of strategic defensive systems and on the kinds of reactions to these which would be permitted—that is, to try to achieve "Arms Control Through Defense" as suggested by Herman Kahn and Donald Brennan.[7] Under such an arrangement, the United States and the Soviet Union could install ballistic missile defenses, but each would agree also to freeze or to reduce its strategic strike forces, thereby heading off a new arms race. As these defenses were progressively improved, the ability of each party to limit damage would also rise, thus making them comparatively secure against attacks by one another and almost invulnerable to those by lesser powers. Alternatively, the two superpowers could, by mutual agreement, employ defenses only to protect communications facilities, command centers, and loci of political authority, thus enhancing their ability to wage a controlled war and bring about a quick peace, at lesser costs to both.

They could also do this by restricting nuclear weapons to targets such as air bases, missile silos, and other strategic installations, thereby limiting civilian fatalities to those arising from fallout or occurring because key military facilities were located in cities, as is the Polaris storage and repair site in Charleston, South Carolina. Agreement to detonate nuclear weapons only at sea or in the upper atmosphere, not to employ them outside one's own territory, or even not to use them at all, except under extreme and rigidly specified circumstances, could also reduce levels of damage—admittedly at the risk, in some eyes, of weakening the credibility of the deterrent. As a corollary, restraint in the use of nuclear weapons, or agreement on measures to safeguard critical facilities, could make war termination easier, partly by insuring that there would be political leaders left to make decisions about peace or war, partly by enabling them to talk quickly and directly to one another rather than having to improvise systems of communication. Furthermore, the preservation of political and communication centers would enable national leaders to control the dissemination of nuclear weapons to operating units, to maintain their authority over the use of such weapons, and to restrict the targets against which such weapons might be directed. Failing this, decisions concerning weapons employment might be left to junior military commanders, whose concepts of local needs might override their perceptions of the importance of restraint; as one worried Italian pointed out, in case of tactical nuclear war captains and lieutenants could well be deciding against which targets in Milan atomic warheads should be directed!

This brief rundown does not list—much less describe—the full range of measures which could be employed to limit strategic armaments.[8] Nor does it argue that all the measures outlined should be adopted forthwith; for instance, the proposal for "Arms Control Through Defense" may enhance strategic stability at the expense of stability in other areas and at different levels of conflict.[9] What it attempts to do is to indicate that there are arms control measures which could help insure stable strategic deterrence, head off threatening technological developments, reduce the costs of maintaining strategic nuclear forces, and, conceivably, reduce damage should these forces ever be utilized.

Arms Control and Strategic Power

Which arms control measures (if any) are actually put into effect depends on the strategic objectives and the national interests of the powers concerned. At the moment, the United States seems to feel that its interests would be served by the four types of measures outlined below, which it has proposed in the so-called Strategic Arms Limitations Talks with the USSR;[10] accordingly, more detailed analyses will be made of measures which could:*

1) Limit the numbers of U.S. and Soviet strategic nuclear delivery vehicles
2) Freeze qualitative improvements as well as quantitative increases in offensive forces
3) Constrain or bar antiballistic missile systems
4) Restrict the deployment of new weapons such as MIRVs

Limiting Numbers of Strategic Delivery Vehicles

The first measure outlined—that of setting limits to U.S. and Soviet strategic delivery vehicles—is probably the most impor-

---

* While there are certainly other measures, including agreements on rules of engagement, understandings about the "no first use" of nuclear weapons, restrictions on defense budgets, etc., which could also promote national security, they pose so many and such difficult problems that they are not under consideration at the moment. For instance, U.S. estimates of Soviet defense expenditures vary from 5.9 percent to about 15 percent of gross national product, so that the first step in imposing budgetary restrictions would have to be a complete exchange of information on military and associated budgets—a step which neither side is likely to find palatable. Similarly, although there may be considerable merit to restricting the use of nuclear weapons, this seems more likely to apply in tactical nuclear war than in the case of a strategic exchange, and its implications for both deterrence and alliance relationships are so great as seemingly to rule out its immediate consideration by the United States and the Soviet Union.

tant, because of the political and psychological connotations of advantages in numbers of launchers, in deliverable warheads, and/or in deliverable megatonnage. Although both concerns about such connotations and military-technical considerations (such as the asymmetries in population distribution previously mentioned) might suggest that the United States attempt to perpetuate its current lead, this is probably impractical. In the first place, while there are formulae for equalizing the capabilities of strategic strike forces, these are so dependent on variables such as the reliability of missiles and the effectiveness of early warning radar as to be largely inapplicable—and certainly nonnegotiable. (If the French and the Germans spent four years arguing over the relative value of conscripts and long-term professional soldiers, as they did from 1928 to 1932, how long would it take the United States and the USSR to reach agreement on equalization factors?) In the second place, the Soviets have consistently maintained that they will settle for nothing less than "equality" with the United States, and while there are many ways of defining equality, the simplest is in terms of numbers. In the third place, the United States seems prepared to accept this as the basis for agreement, if the Soviet Union will grant concessions on other measures.[11] And in the fourth place, U.S. and Soviet forces are so large and so varied that "equality" in intercontinental delivery vehicles, at whatever level one may reasonably expect to be set, would not in and of itself meaningfully alter the damage each side could inflict on the other.*

---

* It could, however, affect the ability of the United States to launch counterforce strikes against the 1400 to 1500 Soviet missiles and bombers targeted against its allies, and hence their confidence that the United States is looking after their interests as well as its own. It would seem desirable, therefore, to reduce the numbers of these weapons in consonance with increases in Soviet intercontinental delivery forces or at least to freeze the Soviet MRBMs, IRBMs, and medium bombers at their current levels. Unfortunately, the introduction of this question into negotiations could (and did) immediately raise questions about the inclusion in any agreement of U.S. carrier-based aircraft in the Mediterranean, American nuclear-armed fighter-bombers, and tactical nuclear missiles in Western Europe. Hence, while the issue of limiting Soviet medium-range rockets and bombers cannot be left unresolved forever, it may be better dealt with separately, perhaps in a forthcoming European security conference. At any rate, it is assumed in this analysis that controls will be imposed only over intercontinental delivery vehicles.

If the outcome of any arms control negotiations is to be
"equality" between the United States and the USSR, the United
States may wish to keep the number of launchers at or near the
present level, which would leave the Soviet Union ahead in
deliverable megatonnage and the United States in deliverable
warheads—thereby enabling the leaders of each country to tell
their domestic audiences that they had "superiority." Whether the
numbers are kept high or reduced by 20 to 25 percent is, however,
less important than whether controls are imposed over each type
of weapons system (bomber, SLBM, and ICBM) or over strategic
strike forces as a whole. If the limits were by type of weapons
system, the USSR would either have to cut back on its current
ICBM force or allow the United States to build another 400 missiles, in either case reducing its own ability to eliminate through
counterforce strikes the land-based component of U.S. strategic
power. While the Soviets could in time build more—and more
modern—submarine-launched missiles to match the 656 now possessed by the United States, these missiles, because of their lesser
warhead yield and longer reaction time, would not give them a
counterforce capability equivalent to that obtainable from an
equal number of ICBMs. In either case, the short-run ability of
the Soviet Union to degrade American strategic retaliatory forces
would be reduced, and its long-run ability made even more
dependent on the development of MIRVs than is now the case.

An overall limit on strategic delivery vehicles would permit the
USSR (which has fewer than 150 bombers compared to over
500 for the U.S.) to build up both its SLBM and its ICBM components, thereby increasing its ability to launch counterforce
strikes. However, the effectiveness of such strikes depends not
only on Soviet progress in developing MIRVs, in improving the
accuracy of its missiles, and in devising a shoot-look-shoot missile
control system, but also on the United States doing nothing. As
previously noted, the United States could harden its ICBM sites,
defend them, or move the weapons themselves out to sea—and
a "flexible freeze" would both permit and encourage this.[12] Thus
it is difficult to see how the Soviet Union would be any better off
(or the United States any worse off) if both countries were free

to adjust the composition of their strategic strike force: each could still destroy the other, as it can now (see table 7).

TABLE 7: Hypothetical U.S. and Soviet Force Postures Under Arms Control, Circa 1975

	A Freeze by Classes of Weapons		An Overall Freeze on Weapons	
	U.S.[a]	Soviet[b]	U.S.[c]	Soviet[d]
ICBMs				
Large (SS-9)	—	280	—	280
Medium (Titan II, SS-8, etc.)	54	200	54	—
Small (Minuteman II & III, SS-11, etc.)	1,000	960	500	971
SLBMs				
Polaris A-3 or SSN-6	160	448	160	640
Poseidon	496	—	496	—
Bottom-based or ship-borne missiles	—	—	500	—
Bombers	326	145	326	145
Total launchers	2,036	2,033	2,036	2,036
Total warheads (approximate)	12,000	2,900	12,000	2,900
Deliverable megatonnage (approximate)	3,900	7,000	3,900	6,200
Ballistic missile interceptors	0–100	0–100	0–100	0–100

a. Assumes that United States continues with forces now programmed for 1975 (see table 4), save for keeping all Titan IIs.

b. Assumes that number of SS-8s, SS-9s, and similar missiles is frozen at 1970 levels, that MIRVs are installed only on SS-9s, and that USSR will not scrap excess missiles until bomber force is built up, which cannot be done by 1975.

c. Assumes United States puts all Minuteman IIIs on or under the water.

d. Assumes USSR destroys all medium missiles, installs MIRVs only on SS-9s, and builds as many missile-submarines as possible without scrapping its more modern ICBMs or reducing its bomber forces.

There are, however, three caveats to this estimate. One is that unless qualitative controls were also imposed, the Soviets could in time improve the accuracy of their ICBMs and/or trade off smaller missiles for larger ones, thereby increasing significantly their ability to launch both counterforce and countervalue strikes against the United States. A second is that ballistic missile defenses might degrade attacks by smaller or less powerful ICBM forces; in fact, if MIRVs were precluded and ABMs permitted, U.S. officials might feel surer of their ability to launch retaliatory strikes but less certain about the effectiveness of those strikes! And the third, of course, is that some combination of increases in long-range delivery vehicles, higher-thrust rockets, and MIRVs might enable the Soviets to knock out most of the American land-based missiles and bombers, thereby reducing the ability of the United States to limit damage from Soviet strikes against NATO, if not its competence to retaliate against the USSR. Obviously, no agreement to limit strategic armaments is likely to survive this kind of development.

Freezing Qualitative Improvements

For this reason it is probably desirable to preclude at least some qualitative improvements in weaponry, most notably increases in the size and throw-weight of ICBMs. Large missiles, with or without multiple warheads, could be more devastating against civilian targets, for which fewer would be needed, could free additional weapons for counterforce attacks, could (by virtue of their large-yield warheads and, in the long run, their greater accuracy) make such attacks more effective, could enable the installation of MIRVs on vehicles which might not now be able to carry them (presumably thereby benefiting the Soviet Union), and could enable both sides to install more and better penetration aids—only the last of which would necessarily be beneficial to the United States. Thus it would seem in the American interest to restrict the numbers of large missiles which each side might have.

If the USSR agreed to this—perhaps in return for American acceptance of the principle of "equality"—its near-term ability to destroy U.S. missile silos would be reduced, since it is the combination of an increase in the number of SS-9s and of MIRVs for these high-thrust rockets which makes them a potential threat. And while the Soviet Union could in time lighten its reentry vehicles, improve the accuracy of its missiles, and thus acquire in another way more meaningful counterforce capabilities, these might be viewed as less threatening than has the recent growth of the SS-9 force and provoke different American reactions. (For one thing, under an arms control agreement no one will have to think up reasons why the United States should build ABMs.)

At first sight it might also seem desirable to constrain other improvements in weaponry, lest Soviet-American competition shift to the qualitative area, and the upgrading of missiles or bombers upset both the strategic balance and any arms control agreement designed to preserve it. Admittedly, neither the United States nor the USSR would be entirely happy to see the other side building quieter submarines or faster airplanes; however, such developments are no more likely to alter the basic situation under arms control than without it. Moreover, freedom to make qualitative improvements may assuage the concerns of those who would otherwise fear "cheating" by the adversary, as was the case with the Nuclear Test Ban Treaty. And it may, in conjunction with continued research and development, seem a prudent hedge even to those who may not be so concerned.

More importantly, many of the qualitative changes could not be precluded except by intensive and intrusive inspection. It might, for example, be desirable to constrain improvements which could add to the accuracy or increase the thrust of smaller missiles; however, this would be difficult to do without either detailed inspection of the missile sites or extensive monitoring of test firings, either of which might be hard to arrange. Furthermore, weapons are continuously upgraded during the life cycle of the system and are replaced (at least in theory) only by better ones. Precluding the kinds of improvements that take place during overhaul (such as the installation of new guidance packages in missiles or the placement of better radar sets in bombers) would be virtually impossible. Preventing a country from introducing a new launch vehicle in place of an old one would probably be unacceptable; neither the United States nor the USSR would agree to replicate the missile submarines built ten years ago, even if this were technically feasible. Thus, with rare exceptions, qualitative controls will probably have to be forsworn.

Constraining Strategic Defenses

One of these "rare exceptions" may be in the case of ballistic missile defenses, which could either be banned *in toto*, limited to the protection of certain areas, or restricted so far as the installation of radars or the deployment of antimissile missiles is concerned. The total abolition of ballistic missile defenses would resolve the need for MIRVs on U.S. ICBMs and SLBMs; however, it would also preclude the United States from defending its land-based missiles against Soviet MIRVs and would require it to rely on hardening missile sites, shifting to mobile missiles, or changing to a more powerful sea-based deterrent. Moreover, the absence of ballistic missile defenses could leave U.S. bombers vulnerable to attack by missile-submarines, which can approach closely enough to reduce the warning time available; hence, unless there were constraints on either Soviet SLBMs or Soviet MIRVs or both, the United States might continue to face some hazards from a total ban on antiballistic missiles. More importantly, such a ban would leave it defenseless against one of the threats to which the administration attaches great importance: that of Chinese Communist ICBMs. Mr. Nixon has argued that a defense against Chinese ICBMs ten years from now is "absolutely essential," that it "gives the United States a credible foreign policy in the Pacific which it otherwise would not have," and that "some kind of defenses" are necessary to prevent Peking from indulging in nuclear blackmail against the United States or its Asian allies.[13] If the United States accepts severe restrictions on the deployment of ballistic missile defenses, it may find it hard to "swallow its rhetoric" and to maintain among those allies that confidence in the deterrent which it has insisted depended on ballistic missile defenses.

However, partial ABM deployments would also present grave problems. For one thing, it is by no means certain that the Soviets would be interested in defending missile sites and air bases, except as a by-product of coverage for the major cities of the western USSR. For another thing, Soviet strategic rockets—especially their MRBMs and IRBMs—are generally closer to concentrations of population than are those in the United States, so that defenses designed to protect missile sites could reduce Soviet fatalities relative to those of the United States. Hence any Soviet ABM deployment would, *de facto* or *de jure,* afford protection to large numbers of people and should be judged in that light.

This in itself would not affect the strategic balance, as even a system comparable to Safeguard could not markedly degrade U.S. retaliatory strikes. However, once the radars for such a system were built, the USSR could quickly enhance its effectiveness by deploying additional interceptors, thereby gaining a psychological advantage, if not a military one. Furthermore, there is always the possibility that the Soviets might upgrade their extensive air defense system, which relies heavily on surface-to-air missiles, so that it could cope with incoming warheads.[14] Hence, entirely aside from "antigravity and antimatter, plasma (ball lightning) . . . lasers (death rays) . . ." and other exotic devices mentioned by Marshal Vassili D. Sokolovskii, former Chief of the Soviet General Staff,[15] the United States may be so concerned about current Soviet ABM technology that it would be unwilling to accept sizable cuts in missiles or restrictions on penetration aids and multiple warheads unless there were fairly rigid constraints on Soviet ballistic missile defenses, especially on the number and location of Soviet missile-tracking radars.

It is, however, unlikely that the Soviet Union would accept restrictions on the construction of radars or the installation of interceptors unless these applied equally to the United States— and as already indicated, equal restrictions can have very unequal impacts on damage-limiting capabilities. The United States would either have to accept these constraints and redesign its ABM system (with perhaps a reduction in its ability to cope with more sophisticated, second-generation Chinese ICBMs) or give up ballistic missile defenses completely, or almost so.* As of early 1971 it seemed to be opting for the latter choice—although this would be contingent on Soviet agreement to other arms control measures.[16]

---

* The focus on ballistic missile defenses reflects the key role these can play both in limiting damage and in preventing the degradation of air defenses and antisubmarine warfare systems. It also reflects the fact that air defenses are too complex, the number of elements involved too large, and some of these (such as fighter-interceptors) too capable of multipurpose uses for restrictions to be readily enforceable or easily verifiable. This is even more true in the case of antisubmarine warfare forces, which encompass everything from passive sonars to aircraft carriers, and include elements such as destroyers which are capable of everything from shadowing enemy submarines to bombarding coastal defenses. Although it is possible, by imposing restrictions on radar and other detection devices, to limit the effectiveness of air defense and antisubmarine warfare forces, such restrictions are not only difficult to enforce but asymmetrical in their impact on Soviet and U.S. capabilities—and hence unlikely.

Restricting the Deployment of New Weapons

The imposition of controls over missiles is more a matter of choice (or of bargaining outcomes) than of necessity, since none of the options described is likely to affect markedly the strategic balance between the United States and the USSR; as indicated in chapter 3, there are dozens of ways of killing people and relatively few ways of protecting them.* The choice made will be more significant in terms of its impact on the allies than on levels of strategic power, and in terms of its effect on arms control agreements and defense expenditures than on numbers of people killed or saved. This is particularly true since one of the counters to antiballistic missiles is MIRV, and multiple independently-targetable warheads have characteristics which make them potentially destabilizing. One is that they can multiply the ability to destroy most soft targets and some hard ones, as shown in table 8. Another is that the missiles carrying them present more lucrative targets, thereby making counterforce attacks more tempting. And a third is that once MIRVs are installed on a missile they can be detected only by instrusive inspection, thereby forcing each side to assume the worst about enemy capabilities and to plan accordingly. Unless, therefore, MIRVs are banned, the United States must assume that in the long run the USSR will have both improved counterforce capabilities and a greater incentive to employ counterforce strikes, since presumably it could then knock

TABLE 8: Comparative Effectiveness of Two Hypothetical Missile Payloads

	Number of Targets Destroyed by:	
Type of Target Destroyed	Ten 50 KT Warheads	One 10 MT Warhead
Airfields	10.0	1.0
Hard missile silos	1.2–1.7	1.0
Cities of 100,000 population	3.5	1.0
Cities of 500,000 population	0.7	1.0
Cities of 2,000,000 population	0.5	0.6
Total megatonnage	0.5	10.0

SOURCE: U.S. Congress, House, Subcommittee on Military Applications of the Joint Committee on Atomic Energy, *Hearings, Scope, Magnitude and Implications of the United States Antiballistic Missile Program*, 90th Cong., 2d sess., 1969, p. 48.

* See chapter 3, pp. 32–38.

out three or more U.S. reentry vehicles on every Minuteman III or other ICBM; similarly, the USSR will have to reckon with more extensive American capabilities.

The concerns which MIRVs could cause, and the strains on any arms control agreement which measures designed to offset the effects of MIRVs could generate, argue for banning them entirely, especially if ABMs are also banned or severely constrained. In fact, the U.S. has indicated that, if ABMs were constrained, it would be willing to scrap its program and to dismantle the MIRVs already installed.[17] This would, however, leave it with the potential of installing proven—if low accuracy—MIRVs clandestinely, and the Soviets with a similar potential for installing multiple reentry vehicles (MRVs), which do not yet have an independent targeting capabilitiy but could readily be given one. To some extent, increases in the accuracy of American MIRVs, and independent targeting capabilities for Soviet MRVs, could be slowed down by limiting the testing of such weapons. Although there are technical problems in so doing, most tests by both countries—particularly those which take place over the oceans—can be verified by national intelligence systems; furthermore, even greater assurance could be obtained if both sides would agree to test all missiles only over certain specified ranges which could be readily monitored by each other's national intelligence system. Even so, assurance will not be absolute and, barring on-site inspection (which the Americans have insisted be authorized under any agreement precluding MIRVs and the Soviets have rejected as too intrusive), each side will have to proceed on the basis that the other has workable MIRVs and program its forces accordingly. The horse has already left the stable, and locking the door will do little good now.*

This does not mean that failure to control MIRVs will automatically result in the United States or the USSR gaining an advantage: as indicated in chapter 3, the forces on both sides are

---

* This is probably true also of powered reentry vehicles (RVs), that is, maneuverable warheads which (like space rockets) can be reaimed and refired during flight, thus bringing their accuracy below the two-tenths of a nautical mile which is currently considered the limit for unpowered vehicles. If powered reentry vehicles were also equipped with homing sensors and/or television cameras, there is no reason why they could not be directed right onto the target.

too powerful, too diverse, and too widely deployed for this to happen. It does, however, suggest that the United States may either have to accept the resultant degradation in its land-based forces (relying on MIRVs to maintain its capability for assured destruction), build a "hard-point" missile defense system, perhaps utilizing smaller radars and short-range interceptors such as Sprint,[18] or make its ICBMs mobile, thereby handicapping targeting for a first strike.

Although neither of these latter steps would necessarily be incompatible with arrangements to limit strategic armaments, they would make agreement more difficult and implementation more complex. Even an ABM system designed specifically to protect hardened silos, submarine pens, and so on, could be upgraded into more extensive defenses—or so the Soviets might believe; moreover, their own system does not include short-range interceptors, so that they would either have to redesign it or have to accept asymmetries in American and Soviet defensive capabilities. More importantly, since land-mobile ICBMs would still be comparatively vulnerable and the people living near them even more so, a sea-borne or bottom-based system might be preferable. These, unfortunately, may be hard to keep track of, especially if one turns to underwater barges, bottom-mounted missiles, and other devices whose construction would take less time and be easier to conceal than that of a missile-submarine. At the very least, therefore, this kind of offset requires some exchange of information between the two sides, some method of verifying transfers from one type of weapons system to another. (For example, one cannot just assume that a missile taken out of its silo is gone and that therefore it is all right to deploy a sea-based missile as a replacement; the old ICBM could be stored, for launching by crane or gantry in a city-busting operation, thereby saving other missiles for counterforce strikes and building up strategic capabilities in excess of those allowed.)

Combinations of Arms Control Measures

This brief analysis of the arms control measures now under consideration by the United States suggests that each offers advantages and suffers from disadvantages. Which combination of measures is chosen depends on one's priorities. If the primary purpose of arms control is to save money, then the immediate imposition of all four measures (limitations on numbers of weapons, by types; a freeze on obvious and significant qualitative improvements; constraints on strategic defenses; and restrictions on the deployment of new weapons) would seem warranted, since it would both preclude costly new programs and maintain the strategic balance more or less at present levels. The great disadvantage to this approach is that it is almost impossible: both the United States and the USSR have developed multiple warheads whose installation could, in the absence of very intrusive inspection, take place clandestinely. Even though this installation probably would not significantly affect strategic stability, it could increase the ability of both sides to inflict damage and, as missile accuracy increased or maneuverable reentry vehicles were introduced, their ability to launch counterforce strikes. Such developments could, over the long run, arouse concern about the vulnerability of land-based weapons systems and generate pressures for a shift to sea-borne missiles, for the construction of ballistic missile defenses, or for both. Thus it is unlikely that this particular combination of measures could be either agreed upon or long maintained if it were indeed adopted.

If one's primary purpose is to reduce damage from a nuclear war, then restrictions should be placed on numbers of weapons, by type, on qualitative improvements, and on innovations such as MIRV, but not on ballistic missile defenses. Selective controls of this nature would enable the United States and the USSR to insure themselves against damage from small-scale attacks by other countries or from accidental launches—both of which are American objectives. The expansion and improvement of ABM systems could (assuming they were effective) also enable these two countries to knock down increasingly higher percentages of each other's incoming missiles, thereby appreciably reducing losses from a nuclear exchange, without necessarily lessening the deterrent effect of such an exchange. And it is conceivable that the resultant sense of security would encourage the United States and the Soviet Union to agree on cutbacks in their strategic strike forces. Whether, in the absence of effective controls on MIRVs, this approach would be feasible, or whether, in view of the apparent desire of the Soviets to ban or to curb ballistic missile defenses, it would be acceptable, are perhaps other questions.

If, however, one's primary aim is to come as close as possible to achieving the overall American objectives of maintaining an adequate capability to deter an all-out surprise attack, providing no incentive for the Soviet Union to strike first in a crisis, preventing the USSR from inflicting considerably greater damage than the United States could inflict in a nuclear war, *and* precluding major damage from small attacks or major launches,[19] other combinations of measures might seem more rewarding. For example, overall limitations on strategic strike forces, rather than limitations on each type of launch vehicle, would enable the United States to shift from fixed weapons systems to mobile ones, or from land-based systems to sea-borne ones, thereby both maintaining relatively secure retaliatory forces and minimizing the possibility that the USSR could gain any advantage from striking first. If this measure were combined with one controlling the numbers of high-thrust missiles which each side could have, this would inhibit improvements in first strike capabilities resulting from the installation of multimegaton maneuverable warheads, or from very large-yield single ones, as well as reducing the damage which a force of any given size could inflict. Furthermore, authorization for the limited deployment of antiballistic missiles would enable the United States to guard against improvements in the accuracy of Soviet reentry vehicles which might threaten its land-based weapons systems or against the introduction of MIRVs, if these were not also precluded by agreement or if one were worried that the agreement might not be foolproof.

Unfortunately, this combination of measures (which is basically the one initially advanced by the U.S. during the talks on the limitation of strategic armaments) runs afoul of two difficulties. One is that the likelihood of precluding MIRVs is very low and the possibility of constraining maneuverable warheads even lower, so that the Safeguard system of ballistic missile defenses now programmed may not be able to protect U.S. weapons sites throughout the 70s. The other is that the process of upgrading that system to cope with advances in either Soviet or Chinese missile technology might enhance the ability of the United States to blunt a large-scale retaliatory strike, thereby arousing Soviet concerns about the effectiveness of their deterrent and inducing the USSR to take countermeasures. Thus even if the American "package" put forward in the summer of 1970 had become the basis for agreement, it might not have long survived the pressures placed upon it.

In point of fact, it seems unlikely (as of early 1971) that any agreement which might be reached would authorize nationwide ballistic missile defenses or would incorporate those procedures for the inspection of missile sites which the United States deems a prerequisite to the banning of MIRVs. (According to Chalmers Roberts, who has reported extensively on the negotiations, the Americans have dropped from the "package" the proposal for a ban on MIRVs.)[20] The United States is apparently willing to accept the Soviet proposal that ABMs be deployed only around Moscow and Washington, even though this may mean giving up its objective of preventing damage from small (Chinese Communist) missile strikes or from accidental launches. If, in return, the United States achieves its goal of imposing overall limitations on strategic delivery vehicles and some restriction on the number of large ICBMs each side could have, strategic stability would be enhanced, at least in the short run.

However, this package would not preclude other weapons programs which could threaten, or seem to threaten, the American strategic deterrent and which could spark a technological arms race. If, therefore, the United States wants to achieve the broader objectives of reducing costs and alleviating tensions set forth by President Nixon, it may have to seek agreement on other measures for the control of armaments.

One such measure could be a ban on the introduction of new weapons systems, even where this ban is not fully enforceable; for instance, it might be possible to inhibit the further development of MIRVs by prohibiting flight testing, as reportedly recommended by the President's Advisory Committee for the Arms Control and Disarmament Agency.[21] Since space-borne launch vehicles potentially capable of carrying nuclear warheads are likely to be even more provocative and tension-inducing than

MIRVs, missile-intercept systems such as Bambi and its variants should also be barred. Furthermore, if and as the United States and the USSR begin to construct space platforms and to operate space shuttles, concerns about the potential use of space vehicles for military operations may grow. And while only the orbiting in outer space of nuclear weapons is prohibited by UN agreement, it may be desirable to give proof to the other side that not even conventionally armed interceptor missiles are carried, and that only "normal" activities such as monitoring communications, photographing installations, and so on, are being carried out aboard space platforms.

It may also be necessary to preclude or to restrict some adaptations of existing weapons, such as the sea-based antiballistic missile system (SABMIS) which some in the United States have been advocating. Although this could provide protection and assurance to some allies (such as the Japanese or the Indians), it cannot cover many of them, notably the Europeans. Moreover, to the extent that it is designed to intercept an ICBM during the early or middle parts of its flight, it would have to move close to the USSR or Communist China, in which case those countries might begin to worry not only about its effect on their launch capabilities but about its potential for initiating nuclear strikes, a potential which it would indeed possess. Finally, geography makes such a system more useful to the United States than to the USSR and hence less likely to be acceptable to the latter.

Particularly useful in achieving the broader objectives of arms control would be the imposition of more stringent limitations on the size and/or the weight of bombers and missiles. Although such restrictions might not be wholly effective (as shown by the German construction of "pocket battleships" during the interwar period), they could preclude gross improvements, such as the upgrading to intercontinental range of the 700 Soviet MRBMs and IRBMs. They could also inhibit modifications in launch vehicles—such as the change from Polaris to Poseidon submarine-launched missiles—which would facilitate the installation of MIRVs. Thus qualitative controls might take on increased importance in the aftermath of any agreement to freeze the size of strategic strike forces.

This would be even more true if the United States and the USSR ever agreed on sizable reductions in these forces. However unlikely this may seem at the moment, it is a possible (and a desirable) follow on to any more limited arrangements. Even if strategic offensive forces were cut by half—to, say, 1,000 launch vehicles apiece—this would not alter notably the damage each party could inflict on the other, because these cutbacks would also affect its ability to launch counterforce strikes; yet such a measure could significantly reduce costs, favorably influence perceptions of intent, and perceptibly improve the prospects for international stability and peace.

The preceding analysis does not mean that all arms control agreements must be comprehensive; indeed, the insistence of one side or the other on "general and complete disarmament," or upon drastic reductions in all or most classes of weapons systems, has in the past been a major obstacle to agreement. It does, however, indicate the difficulty of devising measures for the limitation of strategic nuclear forces which will not give (or seem to give) an advantage to one side or the other, or which will not simply shift research efforts to other types of weapons or expenditures to other categories of forces. It does suggest that arms control is a dynamic rather than a static process, one which will inevitably have an impact on almost all defense programs. And it does say something about the likelihood of obtaining approval for such measures as may be devised—a subject which will next be discussed.

The Prospects for Agreement

Although arms control measures such as those outlined above could stabilize the strategic balance between the United States and the USSR, this does not necessarily ensure their adoption. Both sides face certain problems which will make it difficult for them to come to terms. One is the sheer complexity of the subject, in which limitations on one weapons system, or on one component of strategic nuclear forces, can have far-ranging implications for the strategic balance, for the political and psychological impact of strategic nuclear power, and for the future of research, development, and procurement. Another is that both sides must cope with the technical momentum of weapons system development, which (as in the case of MIRVs) may carry them past crucial decision points before they can really decide to impose or accept limitations. A third is the time lag in conceptualization of ideas within the bureaucracy and their acceptance among both elites and the public at large; although the United States and the USSR have been negotiating more or less continuously on measures to limit armaments since 1946, and have concluded several treaties covering marginal areas, this is the first time that a real chance of agreement on meaningful issues has seemed near. And finally, there is the fact that both sides are concerned about the attitudes of nonparticipating powers, whether these be the Chinese, the Indians, or the European allies.

Furthermore, the attempt to limit strategic armaments comes at a time when both the United States and the USSR are making significant alterations in their force postures. As suggested earlier, increases in an adversary's strategic strike forces, or his introduction of new weapons systems, have two effects: one on the strategic balance and one on the perceptions of that adversary. In some cases the latter may be more pronounced than the former; thus Secretary of Defense Laird interpreted the continuing construction of SS-9s by the USSR as evidence that the Soviets were attempting to achieve a first strike counterforce capability—and reacted accordingly.[22] Similarly, MIRVs, powered reentry vehicles, space-borne missile interceptors, and other new weapons may have less impact on the strategic balance than on the more fragile psychological balance, on the tenuous bonds of trust which are being woven in the negotiations on strategic arms limitation. Under these circumstances the deployment of new weapons systems or the expansion of old ones could drastically reduce the prospects for adoption of any agreement, yet neither side seems willing to halt its programs pending the outcome of those negotiations.

Although this may in part reflect bargaining tactics, it also reflects deep-seated distrust and the interplay of domestic politics. In the United States, powerful and influential forces are against limiting strategic armaments, partly because this would mean giving up all hope of achieving strategic superiority, partly because it might rule out effective defenses against a nuclear strike. Even some of those favoring arms control might object to arrangements which obliged the United States to accept the uncertainties of nationally monitored arms control agreements or to trust the Soviets to keep those agreements. And some might fear the effect on Soviet behavior or on allied solidarity of any agreement which seemed to reflect "equality" between the United States and the USSR.[23] Even though the political climate has changed since then, the long and sometimes acrimonious debates preceding ratification of the Nuclear Test Ban Treaty indicate something about the difficulty of obtaining approval of any arrangements for limiting U.S. and Soviet strategic forces, even if there is no further change in force postures.

A number of factors will also affect the willingness of the USSR to come to terms. On the positive side, these are the same ones that have motivated the United States: minimization of uncertainties about the strategic balance, avoidance of destabilizing technological developments, and reductions in the cost of present or future strategic nuclear forces. The USSR may also have a number of other (and not so acceptable) reasons: the desire to secure formal confirmation of nuclear equality, a belief that it may thereby gain greater freedom of action, a desire to shift the arms race to areas where the Soviets would have an advantage, and finally, a belief that strategic arms limitations would undermine alliance confidence within NATO.[24] This does not, however, mean that the Soviet Union will necessarily jump at the opportunity to impose mutual limitations on strategic armaments. First of all, the USSR (like the United States) includes people with varying views on the proper size of deterrent forces, the level of damage these should be able to inflict, and whether or not they should be stronger than those of the adversary. Secondly, some elements among the Soviet military are so opposed to arms control that they have taken the almost unprecedented step of deleting from the speeches of political leaders favorable references to that topic.[25] And while the military may ultimately be controllable by the Communist party, the current leadership may be either unable or unwilling to exercise that control, especially since other elements in party and bureaucratic elites may likewise have little enthusiasm for strategic arms limitations.

Furthermore, the Soviet leaders have two sets of concerns about Communist China, both of which may induce them to move cautiously. One is that they may not wish to lend too much credence to Chinese Communist charges of "collusion with the imperialists," which could further damage Soviet prestige and influence among the various Communist parties in different nations. Secondly, and perhaps more importantly, they may not wish to weaken their deterrent to Communist China, either by accepting substantial reductions in numbers of medium bombers, MRBMs, and IRBMs or by wholly abandoning ballistic missile defenses.[26] And finally, there are groups in the Soviet Union which do not trust the Americans, just as there are groups in the United States which do not trust the Soviets.

All this suggests that U.S.-Soviet agreements on strategic arms limitation are likely to be difficult rather than easy. In consequence they are also likely to be simple rather than complex, partial rather than comprehensive, and aimed more at limiting further increases in strategic nuclear forces than at reducing those now on hand. And they are unlikely to affect the strategic balance, partly because neither side will agree to accept constraints that would do so. What, however, about their political and psychological effects, to which reference was made previously? And what about their potential impact on Soviet and Chinese Communist behavior? It would not be wise to enter into agreements intended to stabilize the strategic arms race, only to find that, as a result of political and military pressures at lower levels, greater expenditures for conventional forces were required. Thus, before deciding whether or not limitations on armaments are in the U.S. interest, these other questions should be answered—at least to the extent that it is possible to do so.

The Implications of Strategic Arms Limitations

Arms Control and Communist Behavior

As far as arms control agreements with the USSR are concerned, it is necessary to start by repeating that these simply represent a mutual recognition of reality, which is that meaningful strategic superiority is not possible. As a corollary, it follows that the present levels of forces are not necessary, since even lower ones could inflict heavy damage and since quantitative and qualitative controls over weaponry can prevent any attempt to take advantage of the situation by again seeking "strategic superiority." As President Nixon pointed out, since neither of the superpowers can win a nuclear war, whatever their force postures, it makes sense to collaborate in reducing those forces.[27]

At the very least, agreements along the lines described previously will leave the United States no worse off than if there were no limitations on armaments: the USSR will in any event have an effective deterrent. What arms control may do is give the Soviets a vested interest in maintaining strategic stability, which means avoiding not only strategic postures and programs which might induce the United States to resume its own force buildup but also local pressures which would cause the United States to abrogate any agreement. Thus, rather than encouraging or facilitating threats to the security of the United States and its allies, arms control agreements should inhibit them.

This does not mean that the Soviets will never challenge the United States, never act against allied interests, never press for concessions; in fact, as it emerges from its geographic and ideological shell, the USSR may be more inclined to behave like a great power, with all that this implies. It could, however, add one more to the numerous restrictions on Soviet behavior of this nature: too strong an action and you may find yourself again engaged in a strategic arms race. And although some would regard this as an unimportant consideration, or even one which the Soviets would dismiss as unlikely to eventuate, there are indications that the USSR realizes that threats and pressures may be counterproductive—not least among them its eight-month suspension of the deployment of SS-9 missiles during the 1969–1970 negotiations on the limitation of strategic armaments.*[28]

* Following the installation, in June 1970, of MIRVs on the first flight of Minuteman III ICBMs, the Soviets again started building silos for SS-9s. Early in 1971, they shifted to what Mr. Laird characterized as "a new—and apparently extensive—ICBM construction program" (*Washington Post*, 23 April 1971, p. 15).

As for the Chinese, they are likely to remain a source of political embarrassment to the USSR and a military threat to both sides—a factor which may restrict the scope of any U.S.-Soviet agreement or lead to its modification or abrogation at some future time. It is entirely possible that such an agreement may make the Chinese even more suspicious of U.S.-Soviet intentions and confirm their belief that the two superpowers are collaborating against China. But this is a far cry from saying that they will react by becoming more belligerent.

In the first place, even the most far-reaching limitations discussed would still leave the United States (and the USSR) with strategic strike forces ten to twenty times as large as those which China will have a decade hence. In the second place, even the most severe restrictions on qualitative improvements are not likely to affect the kinds of strategic weapons systems (such as bombers) which would be most useful against China, and even a ban on new weapons would not preclude the United States from maintaining strategic nuclear capabilities far superior to any that China could hope to develop. Thirdly, no foreseeable U.S.-Soviet agreement is likely to affect long-range fighter-bombers, carrier aircraft, and other elements of the tactical nuclear forces, which could alone inflict heavy damage on Communist China. Hence the only way in which limitations on armaments could significantly affect Chinese capabilities vis-à-vis the United States (and, in the eyes of some, Chinese behavior) would be by abrogating or curtailing American ballistic missile defenses.

As has been argued *ad nauseam*, the view that the Chinese will, in the absence of American ABMs, become more belligerent, more prone to take risks, more inclined to engage in military operations against their neighbors, and more willing to launch a preemptive nuclear attack on the United States, lacks validity; to quote Alice Hsieh, if there is any uncertainty about Communist China's behavior in a confrontation with the United States, "it is an uncertainty which we will have created for ourselves by attributing to the Chinese a degree of recklessness and adventurism which does not in fact exist."[29] Indeed, to the extent the Chinese fear that the United States and the USSR are building ballistic missile defenses in order to wage preventive war, constraints on those defenses may make them less nervous, and perhaps less belligerent. And to the extent that these constraints, together with those imposed on strategic offensive forces, help Communist China, through its own nuclear arms buildup, to achieve a credible deterrent, they may make the Chinese less inclined to take moves which could provoke a reversal of this process.

This does not mean that Communist China itself is likely to agree to restrict nuclear armaments. First of all, the Chinese have tended to view with great suspicion previous U.S.-Soviet discussions and agreements, regarding the Nuclear Nonproliferation Treaty as directed against them. Secondly, the Chinese have said repeatedly that they will not agree to any arms control measure in whose negotiation they did not take part. Thirdly, their past proposals have been of a type unlikely to generate much interest on the part of the United States or the Soviet Union, as in their calls for a mutual pledge on the "no first use" of nuclear weapons, their suggestions that a nuclear-free zone be established in the western Pacific, and so on.

If the Chinese do come to accept any arms control arrangements, this may only be after they have acquired a minimal deterrent and the United States and the USSR have acknowledged both its existence and the claim to respect which this gives China.[30] The Chinese may then be willing to consider agreements on or understandings concerning the nondissemination to others of information about nuclear weapons, measures to inhibit the proliferation of nuclear weapons (in contrast to their present position that this is good), and other actions to minimize the likelihood of dangerous and unpredictable instabilities in the international environment. It is also conceivable that they may then become interested in measures to avoid accidental or inadvertent war, such as the exchange of information on control systems, a better forum than the Warsaw Ambassadorial Talks for the quick exchange of reassuring information, perhaps even a Peking-Washington hot line. In the longer run they may unilaterally restrict the deployment of their weapons systems in return for similar U.S. and Soviet restrictions on deployments in the western Pacific or in central and eastern Siberia, in effect establishing a tacit nuclear-free zone. And it is possible that they may agree to set upper limits to the number of IRBMs and ICBMs which they construct, in return not for similar limitations on U.S. forces but for U.S. behavior in the Pacific, concessions with respect to Taiwan, entrance into the United Nations, and other political aspirations. The reluctance of the Chinese Communists to accept —or even to approve—measures for the limitation of strategic armaments does not mean that they are reckless and bellicose, only that they pursue their objectives in a different fashion, that they see other ways of avoiding the risks of war and the damage from war, and that they are not inclined to join the United States and the USSR in arms control agreements—at least, not at this time.

Arms Control and the Allies

One should not expect from the allies either wholehearted approval or unqualified disapproval of any American agreement to limit strategic armaments: their views will vary not only with the nature of the agreement but with their own interests and positions. Some will see any accommodation with the USSR as evidence of a weakening in the U.S. resolve to oppose communism and to support them against threats and pressures; others will look on it as a positive move toward a more peaceful and more stable world. Some will consider the agreement as simply fulfilling the obligations assumed under the Nuclear Nonproliferation Treaty to "pursue negotiations in good faith on effective measures relating to cessation of the nuclear arms race at an early date and to nuclear disarmament,"[31] while others will criticize it because it does not go far enough in that direction. Some will welcome it on the ground that it will free additional American resources, part of which should come to them, while others will regret it because it may necessitate higher defense expenditures for conventional forces.

The views of the European allies are not likely to run this gamut, since most of them have a clearer understanding of the military situation and a somewhat sharper perception of their own interests. In general, as the former British Secretary of State for Foreign Affairs said, "All members of the [NATO] Alliance must recognize the advantages of setting any agreed level of strategic armaments as low as possible."[32] They would, however, probably balk at levels so low that these adversely affected the American ability to launch counterforce strikes against Soviet MRBMs and IRBMs or required the withdrawal of the U.S. missile submarines now under the operational control of the Supreme Allied Commander, Europe. Most, like German Defense Minister Helmut Schmidt, would like to see Soviet MRBMs and IRBMs also reduced in number and would oppose limitations on allied tactical nuclear weapons and delivery vehicles in Europe, as the Soviets have suggested, except in trade for such reductions.[33] And none, so far, have indicated any desire to have French and British strategic strike forces counted in the totals or brought under the aegis of any agreement.

Meaningful restrictions on upgrading existing weapons or introducing new ones might be looked at favorably as giving the Europeans a chance to catch up technologically. Constraints on ballistic missile defenses would probably be received even more warmly, partly because such defenses could degrade Anglo-French strategic forces and NATO tactical nuclear capabilities, but more largely because they would leave an unprotected Europe as the potential site of a third world war. Conversely, the Europeans would probably oppose any agreement (such as one authorizing both parties to build "light" antiballistic missile systems) which reduced the Soviet fear of escalation and thereby weakened, or seemed to weaken, the credibility of the U.S. deterrent. As a corollary, the Europeans would reject any arrangement which seemingly required greater emphasis on conventional forces, in part because they have resisted this trend all along and in part because they view these as likely to be cut in the near future.

In short, the Europeans are ambivalent, recognizing that limitations on strategic armaments can contribute to the stability of the strategic balance—and hence of the deterrent—but fearful lest this stability be achieved at their expense. They see arms control as reducing the risk of war but also, just possibly, as leading the Soviets to believe that the United States may be less willing than previously to launch a nuclear strike, should this prove necessary. They are generally nervous about U.S.-Soviet bilateral negotiations, which could conceivably lead to the delineation of "spheres of influence," might simply ratify the *status quo,* and could leave unchanged the differences between the two powers which contribute in large measure to European tensions and uncertainties.[34] And even though the United States has been scrupulously careful to brief its allies on the nature of U.S. proposals and the status of the negotiations, some elements of distrust and concern may linger.

In general, the Asian allies are only mildly interested in arms control agreements which would limit Soviet strategic nuclear forces; as previously indicated, none of them seems particularly worried about Soviet attack. Most of them probably recognize that U.S. capabilities would be more than sufficient to deal with Communist China, that the agreement would enhance the possibility of U.S.-Soviet cooperation against China (or at least would further reduce the likelihood that the USSR would back up Communist China in a crisis), and that it might free more American resources for employment in Asia. To the extent, however, that any agreement seemed to reduce the credibility of the deterrent vis-à-vis China, either because it restricted ballistic missile defenses or because it signified an American willingness to come to terms with the Communists, it could be interpreted unfavorably. Thus the Asian allies, like the European ones, will tend to view arms control measures in terms of what these mean for their security, which depends very heavily on the readiness of the United States to come to their support.

In the case of nonaligned nations, this will be even more true. The Indians might welcome an agreement not only as furthering Article VI of the Nuclear Nonproliferation Treaty, for whose adoption they fought, but even more as presaging U.S.-Soviet collaboration against any future Chinese Communist threats; the actual effect of the agreement on U.S. strategic power might never be considered. As for other countries covered by the nuclear guarantee, the degree of American strategic superiority is largely irrelevant; the question the Israelis may ask each other is not, "Is the United States stronger than the USSR?" but, "Will the United States support us in any showdown with the USSR and its adherents in the Arab League?" And the answer to that cannot be found by counting missiles.

Arms Control and American Interests

Earlier in this chapter, it was asked whether limitations on strategic armaments were in the U.S. interest. The answer given was that this depended first on the nature of the agreement, second on its effect on U.S. (and Soviet) strategic power, and third on its implications for Communist behavior and for U.S.-allied relations.

Although no one can forecast precisely the nature of any U.S.-Soviet agreements, it would seem that these could include limiting the size of strategic strike forces, restricting qualitative improvements in important weapons systems, banning or constraining ballistic missile defenses, and possibly precluding the introduction of new weapons. In general, it can be stated that a prudent combination of these measures would, in the short run, tend to maintain the security and the retaliatory capabilities of the U.S. strategic deterrent, although perhaps in a shape somewhat different from that now programmed. In the longer run, a number of developments could again threaten parts or all of the U.S. deterrent; for instance, MIRVs, if not banned; new Soviet submarine-launched missiles, if not precluded or limited by agreement; improvements in the accuracy and thrust of missiles, if these are not somehow proscribed; lasers and other exotic defensive weapons, if these are not ruled out, could all have an effect. The virtual certainty that these and similar developments can take place suggests that the United States, in order to maintain the desired level and balance of strategic power, may have to seek agreement on the imposition of constraints on new types of weapons, may have to maintain an ability to shift from one type of weapons system to another, and may have to continue research and development which is aimed at offsetting any destabilizing innovations. In short, arms control is a dynamic, not a static, process.

If the United States should work out arrangements for the types of constraints outlined above, it would gain broadly, in terms of greater stability of the strategic balance, in terms of lower costs, and, even more, in terms of ameliorating tensions between itself and the USSR. It would, however, have to pay a price for these gains, by giving up its previous aim of maintaining a meaningful strategic advantage over the Soviet Union and possibly by abandoning or modifying some of its other strategic objectives, such as that of precluding damage from small-scale attacks. It does not follow that either or both of the latter will necessarily incline the Soviets (or the Chinese Communists) to become more bellicose or more aggressive; on the contrary, it could be that the USSR, which would not come to terms unless it were in its interest to do so, would subsequently avoid actions which could result in the abrogation of any arms control agreement. And while some arrangements for the limitation of armaments might adversely affect relations with some allies, they could strengthen them with others—especially if the United States takes care, as it apparently has, to consider their wishes in formulating its proposals.

The answer, then, is that it *is* in the U.S. interest to attempt to reach agreement with the USSR on the limitation of strategic armaments. Prudence requires that the United States follow the advice of former President Johnson and "assure that no nation can ever find it credible to launch a nuclear attack or to use its nuclear power as a credible threat against us or our allies." However, it also requires that the country heed his further counsel to do this by slowing down the arms race,[35] as a prelude to that larger-scale understanding toward which both the United States and the USSR have been groping during the past decade.

8
Power and Security in the Nuclear Age

The question raised at the beginning of this book was whether and to what extent the security of the United States depends on the maintenance of particular levels or types of strategic nuclear forces, or of a favorable ratio between its strategic power and that of its potential adversaries. It specifically asked whether the continuation of strategic superiority over the USSR and Communist China and the construction of comprehensive and effective strategic defenses are, as some have argued, essential to dissuade these countries from attacking the United States, from exerting pressures against its allies, or from encroaching on its interests. As those who have read this far undoubtedly realize, the answer is a cautious "no." Although the United States may, in the present state of the world, have no choice save to maintain strong and effective strategic nuclear forces, these do not necessarily have to be larger and more powerful than those of an opponent in order to deter him from starting a war or risking a confrontation.

There are a number of reasons for this, chief among them the fact that only a few nuclear weapons are required to kill millions of people; if, for instance, a single 20 MT warhead were delivered on the city of Pittsburgh, it would kill over a million Americans—more than have been killed in all the wars the United States has fought since its inception. Once a nation has sufficient weapons to inflict unacceptable damage—whatever that may be—the means of delivering these, and the further means of safeguarding its delivery vehicles until they must be used, then additional forces become of declining importance. In contrast to what Napoleon once said, God is no longer on the side of the heaviest battalions.

Within this context increases or decreases in comparative levels of damage may be of interest only to defense analysts; a national leader may view 50 million casualties with as much horror as 80 million or deem 10 million fatalities as unacceptable as an incomprehensible 100 million dead. Moreover, attempts to shift the balance of deaths from 80–80 to 80–50 or 80–10 have major and sometimes undesirable consequences. For one thing they require a sizable investment in offensive and defensive weapons. At the moment, for example, the United States has approximately 2,300 strategic delivery vehicles (bombers, submarine-launched missiles, and ICBMs) to the Soviet Union's 1,900; if the ratio were 230 to 190, the United States could still inflict unacceptable damage, as defined by Mr. McNamara. And although the force levels on both sides reflect factors other than a conscious decision to seek strategic superiority, the desire to maintain a significant advantage was a major motivation, at least on the part of the United States.

Another adverse effect of attempts to achieve a favorable strategic balance is that these may induce the other side to take countervailing measures. While these may not be aimed specifically at offsetting a particular technical development or weapons system deployment (i.e., at installing MIRVs to penetrate ballistic missile defenses or building ABMs because the other side has them), they nevertheless represent a general reaction to increases in strategic nuclear forces. As two prominent Soviet social scientists said, "It is clear that the USSR and the entire socialist camp will have to respond with an appropriate reaction in response to the US imperialism's attempt to insure for itself nuclear-missile superiority."[1]

Furthermore, attempts to achieve strategic superiority or to construct strategic defenses can generate fears and create tensions, largely because the Soviets and the Chinese Communists tend to believe that the United States has aggressive intentions. These are not simply "mirror images" of American beliefs but a result of historical experiences and ideological preconceptions. Thus Ralph K. White, after analyzing Soviet elite opinions, concluded that "either active or passive [U.S.] defenses would probably be interpreted not as a sign of genuine fear on our part but as a sign that our 'ruling circles' intended to attack them and were trying to mitigate the effects of the inevitable Soviet counterattack."[2] And Allen S. Whiting testified that the Chinese Communists interpreted the announcement that the United States would deploy antiballistic missiles "as a step taken by U.S. imperialism to continue their nuclear blackmail and nuclear threats against Communist China. . . . If we continue with the ABM and its present justification, we will perpetuate the suspicion, if not the conviction, in Peking that we are determined to maintain maximum military superiority over China so as to act at will in pursuit of our interests."[3]

In consequence of these incitements to arms buildups, and the fears and tensions which both precede and accompany them, efforts to achieve or to maintain a superior military posture may increase the likelihood of war and diminish security rather than enhance it: the great danger is not that one side or the other will deliberately launch a nuclear strike but that it may become so obsessed with threats and so influenced by perceptions of hostility as to miscalculate an adversary's intentions and mistakenly initiate nuclear war. The danger of a "preemptive strike" in time of crisis looms larger because both sides are apparently attempting to structure forces which could launch damage-limiting attacks, even as they are attempting to reduce their vulnerability to such attacks. And although the United States has insisted that the Soviet Union "cannot reasonably interpret [American forces] as being intended to threaten a disarming attack,"[4] it so interprets the Soviet buildup of ICBMs—which suggests at least the possibility that the USSR may similarly interpret (or misinterpret) measures taken by the United States.

All these costs and risks might be acceptable if advantages in strategic power were necessary to deter a potential aggressor or to influence his political behavior; however, one cannot say that this is so. For one thing, the levels of damage which he might suffer may not be as important as his evaluation of the risks and uncertainties of conflict, his calculation of the potential costs and benefits of exerting pressures, or his estimates of the long-term consequences of either succeeding or failing in efforts to extend his influence. For another, strategic power is only one among many factors which will influence decisions: his political philosophy, his perceptions of threat, his confidence in being able to achieve his objectives by other means, even his domestic political position, may all affect the choices made by a national leader. Thirdly, there are trends within the Communist countries which suggest that less weight be given to revolutionary militancy as a factor making for aggressive behavior. As Professor Marshall Shulman, Director of the Russian Center at Columbia University, says, peaceful coexistence "has now been extended [by the Soviet Union] into a long-term strategy, implying a continuing acceptance of the necessity for an indirect and more political way of advancing Soviet interests than the militant advocacy of revolution and the use of force."[5] And although the Chinese may not be as willing as the Soviets to coexist with the outside world, they are equally as aware of the need to be peaceful.

This does not mean that the Communists will never employ force, that all dangers of a clash are gone, and that the United States can therefore look forward to a largely peaceful world. It does, however, suggest a different view of the factors influencing Communist behavior and the forms which that behavior might take from some which are advanced as a rationale for military programs. (For example, a close reading of Lin Piao's celebrated article calling for the "global encirclement" of capitalism by revolutionary movements in the underdeveloped areas indicates that these movements must succeed largely on their own; a Communist state cannot actually win a revolution for a foreign people.)[6] And it suggests that strategic superiority may not be *the* determinant of such behavior, as some have implied.

Nor can one say that strategic superiority, strategic defenses, or particular levels of relative strategic power are essential to allied solidarity. This depends more on demonstrations of U.S. intent, on tangible evidences of U.S. support, and above all on U.S. willingness to consult with and cooperate with its allies than it does upon the strategic balance. This is particularly true of consultations on the possible uses of nuclear weapons and the circumstances under which the United States may employ them.[7] And it is even more true with respect to those states over which the U.S. has informally extended a "shield" against nuclear aggression than it is with respect to those with which it has treaties of alliance.

If this subjective analysis is correct, it has significant implications for the relations between strategic power and national security and for the efforts by the United States to develop or maintain that power and to insure its security. One is that it may be in the U.S. interest to consider measures to limit and even reduce American strategic nuclear forces, in consonance with similar reductions by the USSR. As President Nixon said in a recent telecast, no one can win a war between the two superpowers.[8] If this is the case, it may be desirable to stop trying to do so and to adopt instead measures which could guard against instabilities in the strategic balance, minimize uncertainties about the other side's intentions, inhibit an arms race, and reduce the devastation, should war come. And although this may be difficult and time-consuming, it would seem worth trying.

In the process it is not essential that the United States seek to perpetuate its present strategic advantages over the USSR and Communist China. Neither larger numbers of American strategic delivery vehicles, nor higher levels of defenses, nor greater weights of thermonuclear weapons are very meaningful, except insofar as the United States government attempts to make them so psychologically, to its own people and to those of its allies. Furthermore, it is not possible to regain strategic superiority over the USSR and may not be feasible, in the long run, to keep it with respect to Communist China. In addition, efforts to do so may be very costly. For instance, to keep up the strategic nuclear forces programmed by Secretary of Defense Clifford during his term in office would require about $9.6 billion a year in 1970 dollars for direct support alone, and as much as $18 billion if one considers the costs of other relevant programs. To increase further the damage-limiting capability of these forces, through the development of more and larger missiles, improved air defenses, and a "heavy" ABM system would cost $15 to $28 billion, while less powerful forces, such as might be authorized by an arms control agreement, would run only $7 to $13 billion annually.[9] Although the difference between the highest and the lowest figures is only about 1½ percent of the U.S. gross national product, it is also three times the estimated annual cost of Mr. Nixon's new welfare program. Thus, while no one would wish to be less than prudent in maintaining an adequate defense posture, "adequacy" may vary with circumstances, as will costs.

Moreover, particular attempts to maintain strategic superiority or to insure strategic advantages may be counterproductive as well as costly, as in the case of antiballistic missiles. As already indicated, U.S. construction of ballistic missile defenses might prompt the USSR to increase the number or the capabilities of its own strategic strike forces or might induce it (in or out of any arms control negotiations) to insist on antimissile missiles of its own. If so, the United States would simply have triggered an increase in armaments by both sides which would leave them roughly in the same position afterward. Furthermore, under such circumstances some among the allies may themselves want ABMs; in fact, West German Defense Minister Helmut Schmidt has already said, "The question of the protection of Europe against missile attacks or threats of such attacks should be discussed [in the Strategic Arms Limitation Talks between the United States and the USSR] in case SALT results in an agreement to establish ABM defences in the USA and the Soviet Union or in case the establishment of such defensive systems becomes the *de facto* basis for the bilateral security policy of both the super powers."[10] And while American ABMs may influence Chinese Communist behavior, they may do so in ways that are not wholly desirable; for instance, Dr. Davis B. Bobrow has argued that "the more we [Americans] in word and deed oppose and criticize Chinese policy and declare that the purpose of our weapons system is to deal with China, the more we confirm to them the correctness of the policies that have triggered our opposition."[11]

A further implication of this analysis is that the United States need not—and should not—place increased emphasis upon tactical nuclear or conventional forces, in order to insure its security and to protect its interests. For one thing, the mere existence of powerful strategic forces imposes constraints on the behavior of any country in today's world and tends to limit the size, the nature, and the objectives of any military operations by one nuclear power against another—or against its allies. For a second, there is no indication that the Soviets or the Chinese Communists are prepared to undertake the kinds of actions that could require increases in American or allied troop strength; as President Nixon pointed out, "The nuclear capability of our strategic and theater nuclear forces serves as a deterrent to full-scale Soviet attack on NATO Europe or Chinese attack on our Asian allies."[12] For a third, measures to expand tactical nuclear forces might impair the solidity of any agreement to control strategic strike forces, which could be "trumps" in a limited nuclear war. For a fourth, little would be gained by substituting a conventional arms race for a nuclear one; given the necessity to "whip up" allied enthusiasm for rearmament by stressing the Communist threat, such a development could be more tension-inducing than a U.S.-Soviet strategic buildup. Finally, one must recognize that the Soviet Union, equally with the United States, has much to gain from a slowing of the arms race and from a continuing East-West *détente* and much to lose should it, by renewed pressures, arouse Western fears and incite Western hostility.

This in turn suggests another implication: that the United States make a new effort to reach understandings with the Soviet Union and Communist China, insofar as this may be possible without sacrificing basic American interests or those of its allies. Such an effort will require negotiations not only on the limitation of strategic armaments but on broader political issues, such as the creation of common institutions for a still-divided Germany and the long-term status of Taiwan.

It will require looking to the future rather than to the past; there are many problems, ranging from combating the pollution of the Baltic Sea to administering the exploitation of the ocean bottoms, which are of concern to East and West, North and South, and which will require their cooperative endeavors. It may also require new ideas and new approaches. For example, in all the discussions about the future policies and programs of the Common Market no one has, so far as is known, brought up the subject of Soviet and East European interests in the Market; yet it is obvious that the burgeoning trade of these countries with Western Europe, and their more limited political associations with that area, will both be affected by a larger, stronger, and more independent European economic entity. Why should the Soviets not be informed officially of the course of negotiations, invited to negotiate in parallel on topics of interest to them, or even granted observer status at meetings of the organization? What about asking Communist China to become a guarantor against nuclear aggression and the threats of such aggression, along the lines spelled out in UN Resolution 255? After all, France, though not a signatory to the Nuclear Nonproliferation Treaty, has pledged itself to this course of action; why should not Communist China be afforded a similar opportunity? Admittedly, neither of these approaches may work and both carry with them some danger of Communist exploitation of allied differences, but both also suggest ways in which the United States might shift from its "era of confrontation" into its "era of negotiation."

In the final analysis, as Wendell Wilkie perceptively observed more than a generation ago, this is "One World." Americans, Soviets, Chinese (whether Communists or Nationalists), and all other human beings must live on it. We are progressively rendering this world unfit for human habitation both by wasteful and thoughtless exploitation of its resources and by equally wasteful diversion of those resources to internecine quarrels. We also have developed an ability to make it—or large parts of it—into a desert by engaging in nuclear war. Whatever the difficulties, the dangers, and the uncertainties of trying to ameliorate the present conflicts among nations, this process is more rewarding than that of continuing them. It is also more likely to promote the national security, in the only meaningful sense of that phrase.

Appendix Tables

Notes

Glossary

Index

Appendix Tables

APPENDIX TABLE 1: United States Intercontinental Strategic Strike Forces, End of 1970

Type	Number of Launch Vehicles	Size of Warhead	Number of Warheads	Launched from	Maximum Range Statute Miles	Notes
ICBMs						
Titan II	54	5+ MT	1	Hardened silo	9,000	To be reduced slowly by test firings
Minuteman I	450	1 MT	1	Hardened silo	6,500	Will be phased down as Minuteman IIIs are deployed
Minuteman II	500	2 MT	1	Hardened silo	7,900	Equipped with Mark 12 warhead carrying MIRVs. First flight operational in 1970; deployment of 500–550 missiles to be completed by 1975. All silos being super-hardened to resist pressures of up to 1,000 psi
Minuteman III	50	200 KT	3	Hardened silo	7,900	
SLBMs						
Polaris A-2	208	700 KT	1	Submarine; underwater	1,700	To be replaced gradually by Poseidon C-3 SLBMs
Polaris A-3	288	700 KT	1	Submarine; underwater	2,880	To be replaced gradually by Poseidon C-3 SLBMs
Polaris A-3	160	200 KT	3	Submarine; underwater	2,880	Multiple warheads are not independently targetable
Poseidon C-3	(496)	50 KT	10	Submarine; underwater	2,880	Equipped with Mark 3 warhead carrying MIRVs. First 8 submarines being re-equipped in 1970; program to be completed by 1975
Bombers						
B-52 (C-F)	262	1–5 MT	4	Air	12,500	Excludes bombers engaged in tactical operations in SE Asia. Can carry 1 Hound Dog ASM with a 1 MT warhead. Will be placed in active reserve by 1975
B-52 (G-H)	255	1–5 MT	4	Air	12,500	Can carry 2 Hound Dog ASMs. Will be modified to carry 12 to 20 SRAMs with 200 KT warheads, beginning in 1971

Type	Number of Launch Vehicles	Size of Warhead	Number of Warheads	Launched from	Maximum Range Statute Miles	Notes
ICBMs						
SS-7 (Saddler) ⎫ SS-8 (Sasin) ⎬	200	5 MT 5 MT	1 1	Hardened silo or soft site	6,000 6,000	About 140 of these missiles not in silos; apparently being phased down slowly
SS-9 (Scarp)	280(?)	25 MT	1	Hardened silo	10,000	Could carry three 5 MT warheads or larger number of smaller ones
SS-11	900	1 MT	1	Hardened silo	5,000	Includes VRBMs deployed in the Soviet MRBM/IRBM complexes. Tests of MRVs (and possibly of MIRVs) have been conducted
SS-13 (Savage)	60(?)	1 MT	1	Hardened silo	5,000	Solid-fuelled
SLBMs						
Sark	33(?)	1 MT	1	Submarine; on surface	300	3 missiles on each diesel-electric submarine. Apparently being phased down as Y-class submarines enter service
Serb	45	1 MT	1	Submarine; underwater	650	3 missiles on each nuclear-powered submarine
SSN-6	272	1 MT	1	Submarine; underwater	1300	16 of these missiles, comparable to the obsolete Polaris A-1, are carried on each new Y-class, nuclear-powered submarine
Bombers						
Tu-20 (Bear)	110	1–5 MT	2–4	Air	7,800	About 50 Bear Bs can carry 1 Kangaroo ASM with a megaton warhead
Mya-4 (Bison)	90	1–5 MT	2	Air	6,050	About 50 Bisons used as tankers

APPENDIX TABLE 3: Other Soviet Strategic Strike Forces, End of 1970

Type	Number of Launch Vehicles	Size of Warhead	Number of Warheads	Launched from	Maximum Range Statute Miles	Notes
MRBMs/IRBMs						
SS-4 (Sandal) ⎱ SS-5 (Skean) ⎰	700–750	1 MT 1 MT	1 1	Soft site Soft site	1,100 2,100	The SS-4 is semimobile; a mobile MRBM (Scamp) is under development. The SS-5 is semimobile; a mobile IRBM (Scrooge) is under development
SLCMs						
Shaddock	350(?)	200 KT(?)	1	Submarine; surface launch	300	Mounted on 25 nuclear-powered and 22 diesel-electric submarines capable of carrying up to 8 missiles each. Designed for use against surface ships; however could be employed against targets in the United States
Medium bombers (exclusive of naval aviation)						
Tu-16C (Badger)	550	1–5 MT	4	Air	3,000	About 250 Tu-16Cs have been modified to carry 2 ASMs. Could attack parts of the United States on one-way missions
Tu-22 (Blinder)	175	1–5 MT	4	Air	2,000+	Can carry 1 ASM

APPENDIX TABLE 4: Selected U.S. Strategic Defensive Forces, End of 1970

Type	Number	Range in Statute Miles	Ceiling in Feet	Notes
Fighter-interceptors (F-106A, F-101B, F-102, F-104A)	599	—	—	Excludes Canadian units attached to NORAD and 19 National Guard squadrons operating some 600 F-102s
Surface-to-air missiles				
Hawk	100	5–10	30,000	Conventional warheads
Nike-Hercules	1,050	125+	60,000	To be reduced to 900 missiles by mid-1971; carries nuclear warheads
Bomarc-B	186	440	100,000	Nuclear warheads
Antiballistic missiles				
Spartan	—	400	150,000+	Multimegaton nuclear warhead. Ultimate deployment may reach 800–1,000 interceptors
Sprint	—	25+	100,000	Kiloton-yield nuclear warhead. Ultimate deployment may reach 800–1,000 interceptors

APPENDIX TABLE 5: Selected Soviet Strategic Defensive Forces, End of 1970

Type	Number	Range in Statute Miles	Ceiling in Feet	Notes
Fighter-interceptors (MIG-19, MIG-21, SU-9, etc.)	3,200+	–	–	
Surface-to-air missiles				
SA-2 (Guideline)	8,000	25	60,000	
SA-3 (Goa)	800(?)	25	60,000	More versatile and flexible than SA-2
SA-5 (Griffon)	900	100(?)	100,000(?)	Characteristics largely unknown
Antiballistic missiles				
Galosh	64	100–200	150,000+	1 to 2 MT nuclear warhead

Notes

Chapter 1: Introduction

1. *Statement of Secretary of Defense Melvin R. Laird Before a Joint Session of the Senate Armed Services Committee and the Senate Subcommittee on Department of Defense Appropriations on the Fiscal Year 1971 Defense Program and Budget,* 20 February 1970, mimeographed, p. 102.

2. U.S. Congress, House, Subcommittee on Military Applications of the Joint Committee on Atomic Energy, *Hearings, Scope, Magnitude, and Implications of the United States Antiballistic Missile Program,* 90th Cong., 2d sess., 1969, p. 55.

3. "Vertical Versus Horizontal Proliferation: An Indian View," in *Arms Control for the Late Sixties,* eds. James E. Dougherty and J. F. Lehman, Jr. (New York: D. Van Nostrand, 1967), p. 197.

4. U.S. Congress, House, Subcommittees of the Committee on Appropriations, *Hearings, SAFEGUARD Antiballistic Missile System,* 91st Cong., 1st sess., 1969, pp. 15–16.

Chapter 2: The Backdrop

1. U.S. Congress, House, Subcommittees of the Committee on Appropriations, *Hearings, SAFEGUARD Antiballistic Missile System,* 91st Cong., 1st sess., 1969, p. 11 (hereafter cited as *Hearings on SAFEGUARD ABM System*).

2. "Foreign Policy for the 1970's: A New Strategy for Peace," *New York Times,* 19 February 1970, p. 17M.

3. *Hearings on SAFEGUARD ABM System,* pp. 8–10; see also *Statement of Secretary of Defense Melvin R. Laird Before a Joint Session of the Senate Armed Services Committee and the Senate Subcommittee on Department of Defense Appropriations on the Fiscal Year 1971 Defense Program and Budget,* 20 February 1970, mimeographed, p. 39 (hereafter cited as *Laird Statement, 1970*).

4. *Laird Statement, 1970,* p. 105.

5. This and the preceding information on Chinese Communist delivery systems are from *Hearings on SAFEGUARD ABM System,* pp. 12–14, 17. See also *Laird Statement, 1970,* pp. 108–09.

6. *Statement of the President [on Ballistic Missile Defenses]*, 14 March 1969, mimeographed, p. 2, and testimony of Deputy Secretary of Defense David Packard in U.S. Congress, Senate, Committee on Foreign Relations, Subcommittee on International Organization and Disarmament Affairs, *Hearings, the Strategic and Foreign Policy Implications of ABM Systems*, 1969, pt. I, pp. 290, 293–94 (hereafter cited as *Hearings on Strategic and Foreign Policy Implications of ABM Systems*).

7. "Foreign Policy for the 1970's: A New Strategy for Peace," p. 24M.

8. U.S. Congress, Senate, Committee on Foreign Relations, *Hearings, Intelligence and the ABM*, 91st Cong., 1st sess., 1969, pp. 53 and x–xi.

9. *Hearings on Strategic and Foreign Policy Implications of ABM Systems*, pt. I, p. 258.

10. Quoted in a letter from Secretary of Defense Melvin R. Laird to Sen. J. William Fulbright, reprinted in *Hearings, Intelligence and the ABM*, p. ix.

11. *Hearings on SAFEGUARD ABM System*, p. 29.

12. Statement of Secretary of Defense Melvin R. Laird in ibid., p. 16.

13. U.S. Congress, Senate, Committee on Armed Services, Preparedness Investigating Subcommittee, *Hearings, Status of U.S. Strategic Power*, 90th Cong., 2d sess., 1968, pt. I, p. 5.

14. U.S. Congress, Senate, Committee on Foreign Relations, Subcommittee on Arms Control, International Law and Organization, *Hearings, ABM, MIRV, SALT, and the Nuclear Arms Race*, 91st Cong., 2d sess., 1970, p. 308.

15. *New York Times*, 19 October 1969, p. 1.

16. *Hearings on SAFEGUARD ABM System*, pp. 2, 3.

17. *Statement of Secretary of Defense Robert S. McNamara Before the Senate Armed Services Committee on the Fiscal Year 1969–73 Defense Program and 1969 Defense Budget*, 22 January 1968, mimeographed, pp. 55–56.

18. *Hearings on SAFEGUARD ABM System*, p. 31.

19. "Interview with Secretary of Defense McNamara," *Life*, 29 September 1967, reprinted in *Hearings on Strategic and Foreign Policy Implications of ABM Systems*, p. 420.

20. Excerpts of President Nixon's press conference, 18 April 1969, mimeographed, p. 3.

21. *Hearings on SAFEGUARD ABM System*, p. 16.

22. Henry M. Jackson, "National Security: Basic Tasks" (Address to the Hoover Institute on War, Revolution and Peace, Conference on 50 Years of Communism in Russia, 11 October 1967), reprinted in U.S. Congress, House, Subcommittee on Military Applications of the Joint Committee on Atomic Energy, *Hearings, Scope, Magnitude, and Implications of the United States Antiballistic Missile Program*, 90th Cong., 2d sess., 1969, p. 49.

23. *New York Times*, 22 November 1968, p. 9.

24. Letter to the Honorable Melvin R. Laird, 8 July 1969, reprinted in *Hearings, Intelligence and the ABM*, p. viii.

25. *Washington Post*, 17 June 1969, p. 12. Mr. Anderson's remarks were made in connection with a proposed moratorium on MIRV testing.

Chapter 3: Strategic Power and Nuclear War

1. *Statement of Secretary of Defense Melvin R. Laird Before the Subcommittee on International Organization and Disarmament Affairs of the Senate Foreign*

Relations Committee on the Ballistic Missile Defense System, 21 March 1969, mimeographed, p. 10.

2. Remarks of Secretary of Defense Robert S. McNamara before United Press International Editors and Publishers, San Francisco, 18 September 1967, reprinted in U.S. Congress, House, Subcommittee on Military Applications of the Joint Committee on Atomic Energy, *Hearings, Scope, Magnitude, and Implications of the United States Antiballistic Missile Program,* 90th Cong., 2d sess., 1969, p. 107 (hereafter cited as *Hearings on Scope, Magnitude, and Implications of the U.S. ABM Program).* The emphasis is Mr. McNamara's.

3. Ibid., p. 18. See also the testimony of former Assistant Secretary of Defense Alain C. Enthoven, in U.S. Congress, Senate, Committee on Armed Services, Preparedness Investigating Subcommittee, *Hearings, Status of U.S. Strategic Power,* 90th Cong., 2d sess., 1968, pt. I, pp. 120–22 (hereafter cited as *Hearings on Status of U.S. Strategic Power).*

4. U.S. Congress, Senate, Committee on Foreign Relations, Subcommittee on Arms Control, International Law and Organization, *Hearings, ABM, MIRV, SALT and the Nuclear Arms Race,* 91st Cong., 2d sess., 1970, p. 308 (hereafter cited as *Hearings on ABM, MIRV, SALT and the Nuclear Arms Race).*

5. For a discussion of the options open to the Soviets and the factors likely to affect their choice, see J. I. Coffey, "Soviet ABM Policy: The Implications for the West," *International Affairs* (London), 45, no. 2 (April 1969), esp. pp. 207–11.

6. The phrase is that of Mr. McNamara, who estimated that prospective damage of this magnitude would effectively deter the USSR from initiating nuclear war. *Statement of Secretary of Defense Robert S. McNamara Before the Senate Armed Services Committee on the Fiscal Year 1969–73 Defense Program and 1969 Defense Budget,* 22 January 1968, mimeographed, p. 50 (hereafter cited as *McNamara Statement, 1968).*

7. Secretary of Defense Laird estimated that the activation of four ABM sites under Phase 1 and Option 2A of the Safeguard system would increase the number of Minuteman ICBMs surviving a postulated Soviet strike from 50 to between 250 to 300. U.S. Congress, House, Subcommittees of the Committee on Appropriations, *Hearings, SAFEGUARD Antiballistic Missile System,* 91st Cong., 1st sess., 1969, pp. 27–28 (hereafter cited as *Hearings on SAFEGUARD ABM System).*

8. Ibid., pp. 15–16.

9. Ibid.

10. *Statement of Secretary of Defense Robert S. McNamara Before a Joint Session of the Senate Armed Services Committee and the Senate Subcommittee on Department of Defense Appropriations on the Fiscal Year 1968–72 Defense Program and 1968 Defense Budget,* 23 January 1967, mimeographed, p. 39 (hereafter cited as *McNamara Statement, 1967).*

11. "Foreign Policy for the 1970's: A New Strategy for Peace," *New York Times,* 19 February 1970, p. 24M.

12. *Hearings on Scope, Magnitude, and Implications of the U.S. ABM Program,* p. 49.

13. *New York Times,* 13 May 1969, p. 1. See also the statement of the Secretary of Defense in *Hearings on SAFEGUARD ABM System,* p. 9.

14. Testimony of the former Assistant Secretary of Defense for Systems Analysis, Dr. Alain C. Enthoven, in *Hearings on Status of U.S. Strategic Power,* pt. I, p. 158.

15. Ibid., p. 6

16. Ibid., p. 42.

17. Ibid., p. 145.

18. Sidney S. Winter, Jr., *Economic Viability After Thermonuclear War: The Limits of Feasible Production,* Memorandum RM-3426-PR (Santa Monica, Calif.: RAND Corporation, 1963), p. 160.

19. *Hearings on Status of U.S. Strategic Power,* pt. II, pp. 211–13, 247.

20. Neville Brown, "An Unstable Balance of Terror," *The World Today,* 26, no. 1 (January 1970), pp. 43–44.

21. *Hearings on Status of U.S. Strategic Power,* pt. II, p. 334.

22. Ibid., pp. 327, 334; *Washington Post,* 12 May 1969, p. 1.

23. *McNamara Statement, 1968,* pp. 64–65.

24. Ibid.

25. *Statement of the President [on Ballistic Missile Defenses],* 14 March 1969, mimeographed, p. 1. See also *McNamara Statement, 1967,* p. 53; the *Statement by Secretary of Defense Clark M. Clifford [on] the Fiscal Year 1970–74 Defense Program and 1970 Defense Budget,* 15 January 1969, mimeographed, p. 55; and the statement of Secretary of Defense Laird to the Senate Armed Services Committee, 20 March 1969, excerpted in *New York Times,* 21 March 1969, p. 20.

26. For a further discussion see J. I. Coffey, "The Chinese and Ballistic Missile Defense," *Bulletin of the Atomic Scientists,* 10, no. 2 (December 1965), esp. p. 18.

27. *Hearings on SAFEGUARD ABM System,* pp. 9–10.

28. Ibid., p. 10.

29. In this connection see the statement by Professor George B. Kistiakowsky in U.S. Congress, House, Committee on Foreign Affairs, Subcommittee on National Security Policy and Scientific Developments, *Hearings, Diplomatic and Strategic Impact of Multiple Warhead Missiles,* 91st Cong., 1st sess., 1969, p. 86.

30. *Hearings on Status of U.S. Strategic Power,* pt. II, p. 243. See also the testimony of Dr. John S. Foster, Jr., Director of Defense Research and Engineering, in ibid., pt. I, pp. 105–07.

31. For a more detailed discussion see Hans A. Bethe, "Countermeasures to ABM Systems," in *ABM,* eds. Abram Chayes and Jerome B. Wiesner (New York: Signet Books, 1969), pp. 130–43. A somewhat different view of the effectiveness of chaff, nuclear blackout, and other penetration aids was given by Dr. John S. Foster, Jr., Director of Defense Research and Engineering, in *Hearings on SAFE-GUARD ABM System,* pp. 57, 62–63.

32. "Interview with Secretary of Defense McNamara," *Life,* 29 September 1967, reprinted in *Hearings on Scope, Magnitude, and Implications of the U.S. ABM Program,* p. 116; also the testimony of Dr. Foster in ibid., p. 41.

33. *Hearings on ABM, MIRV, SALT and the Nuclear Arms Race,* p. 308.

34. "Foreign Policy for the 1970's: A New Strategy for Peace," p. 24M.

Chapter 4: Strategic Power and Deterrence

1. This is at least a reasonable inference from Secretary of Defense Laird's testimony that if the Soviets could kill 100 million people and the Americans only 50 million he would not want "that great a disparity," even though the 50 million figure falls within the range prescribed by Mr. McNamara. See the exchange between Mr. Laird and Senator Clifford P. Case in U.S. Congress, Senate, Committee on Foreign Relations, Subcommittee on Arms Control, International Law

and Organization, *Hearings, ABM, MIRV, SALT and the Nuclear Arms Race*, 91st Cong., 2d sess., 1970, p. 311.

2. For a good discussion of both the theory and the practice of deterrence, see Glenn H. Synder, *Deterrence and Defense* (Princeton, N.J.: Princeton University Press, 1961), esp. pp. 9–30. Other works which also treat this subject extensively (and from varying points of view) include: Général d'Armée André Beaufre, *Deterrence and Strategy*, trans. by Major-General R. H. Barry (New York: Frederick A. Praeger, 1966); Phillip Green, *Deadly Logic: The Theory of Nuclear Deterrence* (Columbus: Ohio State University Press, 1966); Henry A. Kissinger, *The Necessity for Choice* (New York: Harper and Brothers, 1961), esp. pp. 10–128; J. David Singer, *Deterrence, Arms Control and Disarmament* (Columbus: Ohio State University Press, 1962), esp. pp. 21–127.

3. *Statement of Secretary of Defense Robert S. McNamara Before a Joint Session of the Senate Armed Services Committee and the Senate Subcommittee on Department of Defense Appropriations on the Fiscal Year 1968–72 Defense Program and 1968 Defense Budget.* 23 January 1967, mimeographed, p. 43. Further details on the capabilities of the U.S. forces programmed for the early seventies will be found on pp. 44–45, 52.

4. Herman Kahn, "Issues of Thermonuclear War Termination" in *How Wars End*, vol. 392, The Annals of The American Academy of Political and Social Science (November 1970), p. 146.

5. McGeorge Bundy, "To Cap the Volcano," *Foreign Affairs*, 48, no. 1 (October 1969), p. 10.

6. U.S. Congress, Senate, Committee on Foreign Relations, *Hearings, Psychological Aspects of Foreign Policy*, 91st Cong., 1st sess., 1969, p. 131. For Mr. Nixon's discussion of "strategic sufficiency," see *United States Foreign Policy for the 1970's: Building for Peace*, 25 February 1971, mimeographed, p. 131.

7. "Foreign Policy for the 1970's: A New Strategy for Peace," *New York Times*, 19 February 1970, p. 20M.

8. Snyder, *Deterrence and Defense*, p. 30. The italics are his.

9. Thomas C. Schelling, *Arms and Influence* (New Haven, Conn.: Yale University Press, 1966), pp. 97–98. The italics are his.

10. Beaufre, *Deterrence and Strategy*, p. 70.

11. Michael Howard, "The Classical Strategists," in *Problems of Modern Strategy, Part One*, Adelphi Paper no. 54 (London: Institute for Strategic Studies, February 1969), p. 22.

12. See, in this connection, the testimony of Secretary of Defense Laird in U.S. Congress, House, Subcommittees of the Committee on Appropriations, *Hearings, SAFEGUARD Antiballistic Missile System*, 91st Cong., 1st sess., 1969, p. 31.

13. U.S. Congress, House, Subcommittee on Appropriations, *Hearings, Department of Defense Appropriations for 1964*, 88th Cong., 1st sess., 1963, pt. I, pp. 30–31, quoted in Bernard Brodie, *Escalation and the Nuclear Option* (Princeton, N.J.: Princeton University Press, 1966), p. 52. See also the remarks by General Earle G. Wheeler, Jr., then Chairman of the Joint Chiefs of Staff, in U.S. Congress, Senate, Committee on Armed Services, Preparedness Investigating Subcommittee, *Hearings, Status of U.S. Strategic Power*, 90th Cong., 2d sess., 1968, pt. I, p. 21 (hereafter cited as *Hearings on Status of U.S. Strategic Power*).

14. Schelling, *Arms and Influence*, p. 70. The italics are his.

15. See N. H Mazer and Jacques Katel, eds., *Conquest Without War* (New York: Simon and Schuster, 1969), esp. pp. 269–71.

16. See the testimony to this effect of Dr. Thomas W. Wolfe, in U.S. Congress, House Subcommittee on Military Applications of the Joint Committee on Atomic Energy, *Hearings, Scope, Magnitude, and Implications of the United States Antiballistic Missile Program*, 90th Cong., 2d sess., 1969, p. 87.

17. Ibid., p. 2.

18. See, for example, the study of decision-making following the invasion of South Korea in Joseph deRivera, *The Psychological Dimension of Foreign Policy* (Columbus, Ohio: Charles E. Merrill Publishing Co., 1968), pp. 132 ff, and that of Elie Abel, *The Missile Crisis* (Philadelphia, Pa.: J. B. Lippincott Co., 1966), pp. 33–37.

19. Abel, *Missile Crisis*, pp. 158–63.

20. See, in this connection, Dean S. Pruitt, "Definition of the Situation as a Determinant of International Action," in *International Behavior*, ed. Herbert C. Kelman (New York: Holt, Rinehart and Winston, 1965), pp. 395–96.

21. Statement by the Soviet government of 11 September 1967, reprinted in David L. Larson, ed., *The "Cuban Crisis" of 1962: Selected Documents and Chronology* (Boston: Houghton Mifflin, 1963), pp. 11–12; address by President Kennedy, 22 October 1962, ibid., pp. 43–44.

22. Beaufre, *Deterrence and Strategy*, pp. 25–26.

23. *Hearings on Status of U.S. Strategic Power*, pt. II, p. 221.

24. Jan F. Triska and David D. Finley, *Soviet Foreign Policy* (New York: Macmillan Company, 1968), p. 346.

25. Michael P. Gehlen, *The Politics of Coexistence* (Bloomington: Indiana University Press, 1967), pp. 126–27.

26. A. Doak Barnett, "A Nuclear China and U.S. Arms Policy," *Foreign Affairs*, 48, no. 3 (April 1970), p. 437.

27. Arthur Lee Burns, *Ethics and Deterrence: A Nuclear Balance Without Hostage Cities?*, Adelphi Paper no. 69 (London: Institute for Strategic Studies, July 1970), p. 3.

28. Oran R. Young, *The Politics of Force: Bargaining During International Crisis* (Princeton, N.J.: Princeton University Press, 1968), p. 310.

Chapter 5: Strategic Power and Communist Behavior

1. See, for example, Robert Strausz-Hupé, William R. Kintner, and Stefan T. Possony, *A Forward Strategy for America* (New York: Harper and Brothers, 1961), pp. 10–11. A more extended discussion of this view may be found in Robert A. Levine, *The Arms Debate* (Cambridge, Mass.: Harvard University Press, 1963), esp. pp. 77–82, 128–41, 212–15.

2. U.S. Congress, House, Subcommittees of the Committee on Appropriations, *Hearings, SAFEGUARD Antiballistic Missile System*, 91st Cong., 1st sess., 1969, p. 15 (hereafter cited as *Hearings on SAFEGUARD ABM System*).

3. Ibid., p. 3.

4. Arnold L. Horelick and Myron Rush, *Strategic Power and Soviet Foreign Policy* (Chicago: University of Chicago Press, 1966), p. 187.

5. See, for example, the testimony of Dr. Philip E. Mosely on the USSR and

of Dr. Alice L. Hsieh on Communist China in U.S. Congress, House, Subcommittee on Military Applications of the Joint Committee on Atomic Energy, *Hearings, Scope, Magnitude, and Implications of the United States Antiballistic Missile Program,* 90th Cong., 2d sess., 1969, pp. 55, 82 (hereafter cited as *Hearings on Scope, Magnitude, and Implications of the U.S. ABM Program).*

6. Ibid., pp. 55, 72–73.

7. See, for example, the column by Joseph Alsop in the *Baltimore Sun,* 13 July 1970, p. A-11, and the statements imputed to Vice Admiral Hyman Rickover, General Thomas Power, USAF-Retired, and Admiral U. S. Grant Sharp, USN-Retired, in the questioning of Mr. Nixon during his telecast of 30 July 1970 *(New York Times,* 31 July 1970, p. 10).

8. Raymond L. Garthoff, *Soviet Strategy in the Nuclear Age* (New York: Frederick A. Praeger, 1958), p. 5. The italics are his.

9. Report to the Plenum of the Central Committee of the Communist Party of the Soviet Union, "On the Struggle for the Cohesion of the International Communist Movement," broadcast over Radio Moscow, 3 April 1964, translated and reprinted in *The Current Digest of the Soviet Press,* XVI, no. 13 (22 April 1964), p. 11 (hereafter cited as *CDSP*). According to Garthoff, this report continued to be circulated in the post–Khrushchev period as a fundamental statement of the Soviet position.

10. *Pravda,* 17 January 1963, translated and reprinted in *CDSP,* XV, no. 28 (7 August 1963), p. 19.

11. *Kommunist,* no. 1, 1961, translated and reprinted in *CDSP,* XIII, no. 4 (22 February 1961), p. 9.

12. Cyril E. Black, "Political Modernization in Russia and China," in *Unity and Contradiction: Major Aspects of Sino-Soviet Relations,* ed. Kurt London (New York: Frederick A. Praeger, 1961), p. 17.

13. Fan Hsiu-Chu, "Struggle Between the Two Lines Over the Question of Dealing with U.S. Imperialism," *Ta Kung Pao,* 26 July 1965, quoted in Raymond L. Garthoff, *Soviet Military Policy* (New York: Frederick A. Praeger, 1966), p. 205.

14. *Statement of Secretary of Defense Robert S. McNamara Before a Joint Session of the Senate Armed Services Committee and the Senate Subcommittee on Department of Defense Appropriations on the Fiscal Year 1968–72 Defense Program and 1968 Defense Budget,* 23 January 1967, mimeographed, p. 39 (hereafter cited as *McNamara Statement, 1967).*

15. *Pravda,* 7 March 1970, translated and reprinted in *CDSP,* XXII, no. 10 (7 April 1970), p. 8. The article by McGeorge Bundy, "To Cap the Volcano," appeared in *Foreign Affairs,* 48, no. 1 (October 1969). The sentence quoted will be found, phrased slightly differently, on p. 11.

16. Marshall V. D. Sokolovskii, ed., *Soviet Military Strategy,* translated and with an analytical introduction by Herbert S. Dinerstein, Leon Gouré, and Thomas W. Wolfe (Englewood Cliffs, N.J.: Prentice-Hall, 1963), pp. 289–93. See also Thomas W. Wolfe, "Trends in Soviet Thinking on Theater Warfare and Limited War," in *The Military-Technical Revolution,* ed. John Erickson (New York: Frederick A. Praeger, 1966), pp. 65–68.

17. Wolfe, "Trends in Soviet Thinking," in Erickson, *Military-Technical Revolution,* p. 69.

18. Donald Brennan, "The Case for Missile Defense," *Foreign Affairs,* 47, no. 3 (April 1969), pp. 433–48.

19. U.S. Congress, Senate, Committee on Foreign Relations, *Hearings, Psychological Aspects of Foreign Policy,* 91st Cong., 1st sess., 1969, p. 37.

20. *McNamara Statement, 1967,* p. 72.

21. For a more extended discussion of this point, see my paper, "Stability and the Strategic Balance," *United States Naval Institute Proceedings,* 93, no. 6 (June 1967), esp. pp. 43–44.

22. Robert R. Bowie, "Strategy and the Atlantic Alliance," *International Organization,* XVII, no. 3 (1963), p. 715.

23. Raymond Aron, "The Evolution of Modern Strategic Thought," *Problems of Modern Strategy, Part One,* Adelphi Paper no. 54 (London: Institute for Strategic Studies, February 1969), p. 9.

24. *New York Times,* 24 November 1968, p. 16.

25. U.S. Congress, Senate, Committee on Armed Services, Subcommittee on Strategic Arms Limitation Talks, *Hearings, the Limitation of Strategic Arms,* 91st Cong., 1st sess., 1970, pt. 2, p. 67.

26. Horelick and Rush, *Strategic Power and Soviet Foreign Policy,* pp. 166–67.

27. This assurance, which carries with it a connotation that these interests are of overriding importance to the United States, was reportedly given by Soviet Foreign Minister Gromyko to former Secretary of State Dean Rusk. *New York Times,* 16 October 1968, p. 1.

28. John H. Kautsky, "Soviet Policy in the Underdeveloped Countries: Changing Behavior and Persistent Symbols," in *The Communist States and the West,* eds. Adam Bromke and Philip E. Uren (New York: Frederick A. Praeger, 1967), p. 204.

29. Michael P. Gehlen, *The Politics of Coexistence* (Bloomington: Indiana University Press, 1967), pp. 211 ff.

30. Walter H. Corson, "United States-Soviet Interaction, 1945–1965: A Quantitative Analysis," Ph.D. diss., Harvard University, 1968, Summary, pp. 2–3.

31. John Keep, "Soviet Foreign Policy: Doctrine and Reality," *Survey,* no. 42 (June 1962), p. 22.

32. Alice L. Hsieh, *Communist China's Military Policies, Doctrine, and Strategy: A Lecture Presented at the [Japanese] National Defense College, Tokyo, September 17, 1968,* Publication P-3960 (Santa Monica, Calif.: RAND Corporation, 1968), p. 21.

33. Davis B. Bobrow, "Chinese Communist Response to Alternative U.S. Continental Defense Postures," in *Weapons System Decisions,* ed. Davis B. Bobrow (New York: Frederick A. Praeger, 1969), p. 198.

34. Alice L. Hsieh, in *Hearings on Scope, Magnitude, and Implications of the U.S. ABM Program,* pp. 78–79.

35. Morton H. Halperin, "China's Nuclear Strategy," *Diplomat,* XVIII, no. 196 (September 1966), p. 112.

36. Alice L. Hsieh, *China's Nuclear Strategy and a U.S. Anti-China ABM,* statement before the Subcommittee on Arms Control, International Law and Organization of the Senate Foreign Relations Committee, mimeographed 9 April 1970, pp. 13, 14.

37. For a comparison of forces see *The Military Balance, 1970–1971* (London: Institute for Strategic Studies, 1970), pp. 58, 62.

38. Hsieh, *Communist China's Military Policies,* p. 22. See also Allen S. Whiting, "Time for a Change in Our China Policy," *New York Times Magazine,* 15 December 1968, p. 28.

39. *Hearings on the SAFEGUARD ABM System*, p. 60.

40. Alice L. Hsieh, *China's Nuclear Strategy*, p. 18.

41. *Hearings on SAFEGUARD ABM System*, p. 60.

42. *New York Times*, 25 July 1970, p. 1.

43. See the questions of Senator Henry M. Jackson and Congressman Chet Holifield concerning this possibility and its implications in *Hearings on Scope, Magnitude, and Implications of the U.S. ABM Program*, pp. 58–61.

44. *Statement of Secretary of Defense Robert S. McNamara Before the Senate Armed Services Committee on the Fiscal Year 1969–73 Defense Program and 1969 Defense Budget*, mimeographed, 22 January 1968, p. 50 (hereafter cited as *McNamara Statement, 1968*).

45. Donald Zagoria, "Russia's New Asian Offensive," *The New Leader*, XLIX, no. 2 (17 January 1966), p. 7.

46. See the testimony to this effect of Dr. Alice L. Hsieh, *Hearings on Scope, Magnitude, and Implications of the U.S. ABM Program*, p. 84

47. Interview with Australian journalist John Dixon, quoted in Arthur Huck, *The Security of China* (New York: Columbia University Press, 1970), p. 65. For subsequent—and more vitriolic—Chinese statements about the undependability of the USSR, see pp. 68–71.

48. *McNamara Statement, 1968*, p. 83.

49. In this connection see Robert Blum, *The United States and China in World Affairs*, ed. A. Doak Barnett (New York: McGraw-Hill, 1966), p. 169 and Jeremy J. Stone, "Arms Control: Can China Be Ignored?" in *Sino-Soviet Relations and Arms Control*, ed. Morton H. Halperin (Cambridge, Mass.: MIT Press, 1967), p. 77.

50. In this connection see Ralph L. Powell, *Communist China's Military Doctrines*, Technical Paper RAC-TP-269 (McLean, Va.: Research Analysis Corporation, November 1967), pp. 23–24.

51. "Foreign Policy for the 1970's: A New Strategy for Peace," *New York Times*, 19 February 1970, p. 20M.

52. "Time for a Change in Our China Policy," p. 112.

53. Yuan-li Wu, *Communist China and Arms Control* (Menlo Park, Calif.: Stanford University, Hoover Institution on War, Revolution, and Peace, 1968), pp. 21–22.

54. Huck, *Security of China*, p. 91.

55. *New York Times*, 30 October 1968, p. 29.

56. Horelick and Rush, *Strategic Power and Soviet Foreign Policy*, p. 180.

57. *Hearings on SAFEGUARD ABM System*, p. 60.

58. *New York Times*, 14 November 1969, p. 8.

59. U.S. Congress, Senate, Committee on Armed Services, Preparedness Investigating Subcommittee, *Hearings, Status of U.S. Strategic Power*, 90th Cong., 2d sess., 1968, pt. II, p. 218.

60. Bundy, "To Cap the Volcano," p. 18.

61. *Statement of Secretary of Defense Robert S. McNamara on an Approach to the FY 1966–70 Program and the FY 1966 Budget*, mimeographed, January 1965, p. 43.

62. Dr. Philip E. Mosely in *Hearings on Scope, Magnitude, and Implications of the U.S. ABM Program*, p. 55.

63. Horelick and Rush, *Strategic Power and Soviet Foreign Policy*, p. 179.

64. Robert S. McNamara, *The Essence of Security* (New York: Harper and Row, 1968), pp. 57–61.

65. *New York Times*, 1 October 1969, p. 12.

Chapter 6: Strategy, Strategic Power, and Alliance Relations

1. "Foreign Policy for the 1970's: A New Strategy for Peace," *New York Times*, 19 February 1970, p. 20M; United Nations Security Council Resolution 255, reported in *New York Times*, 18 June 1968, p. 2.

2. To name just a few, Alastair Buchan, *NATO in the 1960's*, rev. ed. (New York: Frederick A. Praeger, 1963); Henry A. Kissinger, *The Troubled Partnership* (New York: Mc-Graw-Hill, 1965); Robert E. Osgood, *NATO: The Entangling Alliance* (Chicago: University of Chicago Press, 1962); and Morton H. Halperin, *China and the Bomb* (New York: Frederick A. Praeger, 1965).

3. John F. Kennedy, *The Strategy of Peace*, ed. Allan Nevins (New York: Harper and Brothers, 1960), pp. 37–38. See also the address of then Assistant Secretary of Defense Paul H. Nitze before the Cleveland Council on World Affairs, Cleveland, Ohio, 2 March 1963, quoted in William W. Kaufmann, *The McNamara Strategy* (New York: Harper & Row, 1964), 130–31, and the excerpts from speeches and testimony by former Secretary of Defense Robert S. McNamara, pp. 59, 66, 75, 76, 96, 115, 128.

4. *Statement of Secretary of Defense Robert S. McNamara Before the House Armed Services Committee on the Fiscal Year 1964–1968 Defense Program and 1964 Defense Budget*, 30 January 1963, mimeographed, p. 24.

5. Secretary of Defense Robert S. McNamara, address before the Fellows of the American Bar Association, Chicago, Illinois, 17 February, 1962, Department of Defense News Release no. 239–62, 17 February 1962, pp. 6–7.

6. Arthur M. Schlesinger, Jr., *A Thousand Days* (Boston: Houghton Mifflin, 1965), p. 853.

7. Debate in the House of Commons, 4–5 March 1969, reprinted in British Information Services Policy Statement 12/69, *Defence Debate: British Role in NATO*, 7 March 1969, p. 5. For a summation of European views on the importance of deterrence, see Morton Gorden and Daniel Lerner, "The Setting for European Arms Control: Political and Strategic Choices of European Elites," *The Journal of Conflict Resolution*, IX, no. 4 (December 1965), p. 432.

8. Dr. Georg R. Bluhm, *Détente and Military Relaxation in Europe: A German View*, Adelphi Paper no. 40 (London: Institute for Strategic Studies, September 1967), p. 12.

9. Statement by Premier Georges Pompidou before the French National Assembly, 13 April 1966, Speech and Press Conference no. 243A, April 1966, p. 4.

10. For a summary of actions—and reactions—see *Strategic Survey, 1968* (London: Institute for Strategic Studies, 1969) pp. 12–16, 19–22, 27–28.

11. *New York Times*, 11 October 1968, p. 10, and "Foreign Policy for the 1970's: A New Strategy for Peace," p. 18M.

12. "Foreign Policy for the 1970's: A New Strategy for Peace," p. 26M.

13. *New York Times*, 21 November 1965, p. 1.

14. Hedley Bull, *Strategy and the Atlantic Alliance*, Policy Memorandum no.

29 (Princeton, N.J.: Center for International Studies, Princeton University, September 1964), p. 33.

15. "Foreign Policy for the 1970's: A New Strategy for Peace," pp. 18M, 19M.

16. For a further discussion of this point, see J. I. Coffey, "The United States and the Defense of Western Europe," *Revue Militaire Générale*, no. 10 (December 1969) and no. 1 (January 1970), esp. pp. 47–52.

17. Mr. McNamara's estimate of the potential effectiveness of U.S. ballistic missile defenses will be found in the *Statement of Secretary of Defense Robert S. McNamara Before the Senate Armed Services Committee on the Fiscal Year 1969–73 Defense Program and 1969 Defense Budget*, 22 January 1968, p. 64 (hereafter cited as *McNamara Statement, 1968*). The statement that the United States would face this choice was repeated several times by Mr. Laird in U.S. Congress, House, Subcommittees of the Committee on Appropriations, *Hearings, SAFEGUARD Antiballistic Missile System*, 91st Cong., 1st sess., 1969, pp. 16, 31, 60 (hereafter cited as *Hearings on SAFEGUARD ABM System*).

18. "Foreign Policy for the 1970's: A New Strategy for Peace," p. 24M.

19. The NATO Nuclear Planning Group came to this conclusion at its meeting of 18–19 April 1968, and the Defense Planning Committee ratified it at its meeting of 10 May. See *Strategic Survey, 1968*, p. 12.

20. Pierre Hassner, *Change and Security in Europe, Part II: In Search of a System*, Adelphi Paper no. 49 (London: Institute for Strategic Studies, July 1968), p. 33.

21. *Statement of Secretary of Defense Robert S. McNamara Before the House Armed Services Committee on the Fiscal Year 1967–71 Defense Program and 1967 Defense Budget*, 8 March 1966, mimeographed, p. 80.

22. *McNamara Statement, 1968*, p. 83.

23. *Statement of Secretary of Defense Melvin R. Laird Before a Joint Session of the Senate Armed Services Committee and the Senate Subcommittee on Department of Defense Appropriations on the Fiscal Year 1971 Defense Program and Budget*, 20 February 1970, mimeographed, p. 43 (hereafter cited as *Laird Statement, 1970*).

24. Ibid.; "Interview with Secretary of Defense McNamara," *Life*, 29 September 1967, reprinted in U.S. Congress, House, Subcommittee on Military Applications of the Joint Committee on Atomic Energy, *Hearings, Scope, Magnitude, and Implications of the United States Antiballistic Missile Program*, 90th Cong., 2d sess., 1969, p. 116.

25. The preceding analysis is drawn from the testimony by Secretary of Defense Melvin R. Laird in *Hearings on SAFEGUARD ABM System*, pp. 15–20. See also the *Laird Statement, 1970*, pp. 42–45.

26. Michio Royama, *The Asian Balance of Power: A Japanese View*, Adelphi Paper no. 42 (London: Institute for Strategic Studies, November 1967), p. 11. Moreover, the Japanese seem confident that the American deterrent will preclude "nuclear wars or large-scale wars" and propose to tailor their forces to cope with limited wars and indirect aggression. "Basic Defence Policies," Japanese White Paper on Defense, 20 October 1970, pt. II, reprinted in *Survival*, XIII, no. 1 (January 1971), p. 3. See also the Notes on the White Paper, pp. 4, 5.

27. See, for example, the alleged opposition of the Asian allies to American efforts to reduce the U.S. presence in, and its commitments to, the Pacific region, in the *New York Times*, 9 July 1970, p. 1.

28. "Foreign Policy for the 1970's: A New Strategy for Peace," p. 20M.

29. See, for example, Bishwanath Singh, "National Defense in the Nuclear Age: Dilemma of India," *Political Scientist*, 2, no. 1 (January–June 1966), pp. 1–17, and "India: What's a Nuclear 'Guarantee' Worth?" *The Economist*, 16 March 1968, pp. 31–33.

30. U.S. Congress, Joint Committee on Atomic Energy, *Non-Proliferation of Nuclear Weapons*, p. 12, quoted in William Bader, *The United States and the Spread of Nuclear Weapons* (New York: Pegasus Books, 1968), p. 110.

31. France, although separately indicating its willingness "to go to the assistance of any non-nuclear nation that was threatened with nuclear aggression," abstained from voting on Resolution 255 and has indicated that it will not sign the Nuclear Nonproliferation Treaty. *New York Times*, 18 June 1968, p. 2.

32. *New York Times*, 11 July 1968, p. 16.

33. A. Doak Barnett, "A Nuclear China and U.S. Arms Policy," *Foreign Affairs*, 48, no. 3 (April 1970), p. 436.

34. Quoted in "The Week in Review," *New York Times*, 28 June 1970, p. 3. Subsequently the Japanese White Paper on Defense indicated that while the Japanese government will for the present refrain from manufacturing or possessing nuclear weapons, it would "not be impossible [under the Constitution] to possess small nuclear weapons, the capability of which is within the minimum limits required for self-defence." See the Notes on the White Paper in *Survival*, XIII, no. 1 (January 1971), p. 5.

35. Robert E. Osgood, "The Reappraisal of Limited War," *Problems of Modern Strategy, Part One*, Adelphi Paper no. 54 (London: Institute for Strategic Studies, February 1969), p. 46.

Chapter 7: Arms Control and Strategic Power

1. State of the Union Message, *New York Times*, 9 January 1964, p. 16.

2. These criteria for planning American force postures were set forth by Secretary of Defense Melvin R. Laird in U.S. Congress, Senate, Committee on Foreign Relations, Subcommittee on Arms Control, International Law and Organization, *Hearings, ABM, MIRV, SALT, and the Nuclear Arms Race*, 91st Cong., 2d sess., 1970, p. 308 (hereafter cited as *Hearings on ABM, MIRV, SALT, and the Nuclear Arms Race*).

3. "Foreign Policy for the 1970's: A New Strategy for Peace," *New York Times*, 19 February 1970, p. 24M.

4. Ibid., p. 17M.

5. Ibid., p. 25M.

6. *Hearings on ABM, MIRV, SALT, and the Nuclear Arms Race*, p. 289.

7. For a recent discussion of this concept, see Donald G. Brennan, "The Case for Missile Defense," *Foreign Affairs*, 47, no. 3 (April 1969), pp. 432–48.

8. For further and fuller discussions see Donald G. Brennan, ed., *Arms Control, Disarmament, and National Security* (New York: George Braziller, 1961); Thomas C. Schelling and Morton H. Halperin, *Strategy and Arms Control* (New York: Twentieth Century Fund, 1961); Hedley Bull, *The Control of the Arms Race*, 2d ed. (New York: Frederick A. Praeger, 1965).

9. See, for example, Hedley Bull's discussion of this point in "The Scope for

Soviet-American Agreement," *Soviet-American Relations and World Order: Arms Limitations and Policy,* Adelphi Paper no. 65 (London: Institute for Strategic Studies, February 1970), pp. 11–14.

10. *Washington Post,* 21 May 1970, p. 1.

11. *New York Times,* 25 July 1970, p. 7.

12. J. I. Coffey, "An Over-all Freeze on Strategic Forces," *Disarmament,* no. 11 (September 1966), pp. 5–7, 21.

13. Press conference of 30 January 1970, reported in *Washington Post,* 31 January 1970, p. A10. In his 1971 report to the Congress, Mr. Nixon again indicated that the Chinese capability to threaten major American population centers was a factor justifying a continuation of the Safeguard ABM program. See *United States Foreign Policy for the 1970's: Building for Peace,* 25 February 1971, mimeographed, pp. 135–36.

14. See the testimony to this effect of Dr. John S. Foster, Jr., Director of Defense Research and Engineering, in U.S. Congress, House, Subcommittee on National Security Policy and Scientific Developments, *Hearings, Diplomatic and Strategic Impact of Multiple Warhead Missiles,* 91st Cong., 1st sess., 1969, p. 248.

15. Leon Gouré, *Notes on the Second Edition of Marshal V. D. Sokolovskii's "Military Strategy,"* Memorandum RM-3972-PR (Santa Monica, Calif.: RAND Corporation, February 1965), p. 93.

16. Mr. Nixon explicitly rejected the Soviet proposal to limit only ABMs, arguing that "the strategic balance would be endangered if we limited defensive forces alone and left the offensive threat to our strategic forces unconstrained" (*United States Foreign Policy for the 1970's: Building for Peace,* p. 151).

17. See the testimony to this effect of Dr. John S. Foster, Jr., Director of Defense Research and Engineering, reported in *New York Times,* 5 June 1970, p. 10.

18. An outline of, and justification for, such a system will be found in *Hearings on ABM, MIRV, SALT and the Nuclear Arms Race,* pp. 534–54.

19. Ibid., p. 308.

20. *Washington Post,* 29 March 1971, p. 1.

21. *New York Times,* 29 January 1971, p. 3.

22. U.S. Congress, Senate, Committee on Foreign Relations, *Hearings, Intelligence and the ABM,* 91st Cong., 1st sess., 1969, esp. pp. 48–62.

23. For a European view of the effects see Wilhelm Grewe (West German Ambassador to NATO), "The Effect of Strategic Agreements on European-American Relations," *Soviet American Relations and World Order: Arms Limitations and Policy,* Adelphi Paper no. 65 (London: Institute for Strategic Studies, February 1970), p. 21.

24. Ibid., p. 19.

25. See the testimony of Dr. Thomas W. Wolfe, U.S. Congress, Senate, Committee on Armed Services, Subcommittee on Strategic Arms Limitation Talks, *Hearings, the Limitation of Strategic Arms,* 91st Cong., 2d sess., 1970, pt. 2, pp. 63–64.

26. See, for instance, the talk on "China and SALT," by Professor Harry G. Gelber, reprinted in *Survival,* XII, no. 4 (April 1970), esp. pp. 123–25.

27. Telecast of 30 July 1970, reported in the *New York Times,* 2 August 1970, p. E-13.

28. *Washington Post,* 11 July 1970, p. 1.

29. Alice L. Hsieh, *China's Nuclear Strategy and a U.S. Anti-China ABM,*

statement before the Subcommittee on Arms Control, International Law and Organization of the Senate Foreign Relations Committee, 9 April 1970, Internal Note N-711 (R) (Washington, D.C.: Institute for Defense Analyses, 1970), p. 19.

30. A. Doak Barnett, "Communist China and U.S. Arms Policy." *Foreign Affairs*, 48, no. 3 (April 1970), p. 433.

31. United Nations document A/7016/Addition 1, 10 June 1968.

32. Michael Stewart, "Britain, Europe and the Alliance," *Foreign Affairs*, 48, no. 4 (July 1970), p. 653.

33. Interview with West German Defense Minister Helmut Schmidt in *Die Welt*, 16 February 1970, p. 1, quoted in Lothar Ruehl, "The Impact of Strategic Arms Control Upon European Security and Defence Systems," paper presented at the Joint Conference on Strategic Arms and U.S.-West European Relations, Talloires, France, 17–19 June 1970, mimeographed, p. 6.

34. Grewe, "The Effect of Strategic Agreements on European-American Relations," in *Soviet-American Relations and World Order: Arms Limitations and Policy*, p. 22.

35. State of the Union Message, *New York Times*, 11 January 1967, p. 16.

Chapter 8: Power and Security in the Nuclear Age

1. V. Kulish and S. Fedorenko, "On the Current Debate in the U.S. on Strategic Arms," *World Economic and International Relations*, no. 3 (March 1970), pp. 41–49, translated by Nadia Derkach, 10 July 1970, mimeographed, p. 12.

2. Ralph K. White, "The Genuineness of Soviet Elite Fear of U.S. Aggression," in *Weapons System Decisions*, ed. Davis B. Bobrow (New York: Frederick A. Praeger, 1969), p. 227.

3. U.S. Congress, Senate, Committee on Foreign Relations, Subcommittee on International Organization and Disarmament Affairs, *Hearings, Strategic and Foreign Policy Implications of ABM Systems*, 1969, pt. I, pp. 134–35.

4. See *United States Foreign Policy for the 1970's: Building for Peace*, 25 February 1971, mimeographed, pp. 129, 131–32.

5. Marshall Shulman, *Beyond the Cold War* (New Haven, Conn.: Yale University Press, 1966), p. 54.

6. Lin Piao, "Long Live the Victory of People's War," *Peking Review*, 36, no. 12 (3 September 1965), pp. 41–42, quoted in Ralph L. Powell, *Communist China's Military Doctrines*, Technical Paper RAC-TP-269 (McLean, Va.: Research Analysis Corporation, November 1967), p. 20. See also Arthur Huck, *The Security of China* (New York: Columbia University Press, 1970), pp. 48–51. Huck argues further that the article was intended more as "an attack on unorthodox tendencies" within China than as a blueprint for Chinese expansionism (p. 49).

7. Michael Stewart, former British Secretary of State for Foreign Affairs, "Britain, Europe and the Alliance," *Foreign Affairs*, 48, no. 4 (July 1970), p. 650.

8. Telecast of 30 July 1970, quoted in *New York Times*, 2 August 1970, p. E-13.

9. U.S. Congress, Joint Economic Committee, Subcommittee on Economy in Government, *Hearings, the Military Budget and National Economic Priorities*, 91st Cong., 1st sess., pt. I, pp. 178–79. The figures cited were derived from

Dr. William W. Kaufmann's table "Sample Post-Vietnam Defense Budgets (in 1972 Prices)" by:

(1) Selecting for analysis the Postwar Baseline, Postwar "Superiority," and Streamlined Baseline budgets, in that order;

(2) Eliminating from Total Obligational Authority all monies for Airlift and Sealift (4), Guard and Reserve Forces (5), Support of Other Nations (10), and Retirement Pay and Pay Raise (11);

(3) Allocating other indirect costs such as those for Research and Development (6) and Central Supply and Maintenance (7) in proportion to expenditures for Strategic Nuclear Forces (1); and

(4) Reducing the figures for both direct and indirect costs by 10 percent to get them back into 1970 dollars.

Even though not all of the supporting Program Packages relate to Strategic Nuclear Forces in the same way, it is believed that the proportionate allocation of selected indirect costs provides a reasonable basis for estimating the overall expenditures for Strategic Nuclear Forces.

10. Interview with West German Defense Minister Helmut Schmidt in *Die Welt*, 16 February 1970, p. 7, quoted in Lothar Ruehl, "The Impact of Strategic Arms Control Upon European Security and Defense Systems," paper presented at the Joint Conference on Strategic Arms and U.S.–West European Relations, Talloires, France, 17–19 June 1970, mimeographed, p. 6.

11. Davis B. Bobrow, "Chinese Communist Response to Alternative U.S. Continental Defense Postures," in *Weapons System Decisions*, ed. Davis B. Bobrow (New York: Frederick A. Praeger, 1969), p. 171.

12. "Foreign Policy for the 1970's: A New Strategy for Peace," *New York Times*, 19 February 1970, p. 24M.

Glossary

Words in italic type are defined elsewhere in glossary.

ABM (antiballistic missile). Either (1) a missile designed to intercept and neutralize an incoming enemy *warhead* or (2) a system of radars, computers, and missiles designed to defend some specified target or geographic area against an enemy *ballistic missile* attack

Active defense. Defense utilizing aircraft, missiles, submarines, and/or ships to intercept attacking enemy aircraft, missiles, or missile-submarines

AMM (antimissile missile). An *antiballistic missile;* more specifically, an interceptor such as *Galosh* or *Spartan*

ASM (air-to-surface missile). Any missile fired from an aircraft against a target on the ground

Assured destruction capability. The ability to inflict on an adversary some level of damage (usually that which supposedly would be unacceptable to him) under all foreseeable circumstances

Assured destruction forces. The bombers, missiles, and missile-submarines required to inflict the requisite level of damage

---

Although terminology is more or less in the public domain, the author wishes to note that he drew heavily upon the glossary in *ABM: An Evaluation of the Decision to Deploy an Antiballistic Missile System,* eds. Abram Chayes and Jerome B. Wiesner (New York: Signet Books, 1969), pp. 217–26, and to a lesser extent upon that by Herbert Scoville, Jr., in *Toward a Strategic Arms Limitation Agreement* (New York: Carnegie Endowment for International Peace, 1970), pp. 44–47. Since these drawings were selective and additions and changes were made, the author is wholly responsible both for inaccuracies and for gaps.

ASW (antisubmarine warfare). The detection, identification, tracking, and destruction of hostile submarines

AWACS (airborne warning and control system). A system using large aircraft carrying radars, computers, and communication facilities to control engagements between fighter-interceptor planes and enemy bombers

B-52. A large American intercontinental subsonic bomber. (For details as to range, bomb load, etc., see appendix table 1)

B-58. A large American intercontinental supersonic bomber, now out of service

Ballistic missile. A missile that, after initial launch, moves freely along most of its trajectory under the influence of gravity alone

Bear [Tu-20]. A Soviet four-engine turboprop intercontinental strategic bomber. (For details as to range, bomb load, etc., see appendix table 2)

Bison [Mya-4]. A Soviet four-engine turbojet intercontinental strategic bomber. (For details, see appendix table 2)

Blackout. The effect of a nuclear explosion in space, which reflects, refracts, or absorbs radar rays

Blast. The pressure pulse (shock wave) in air initiated by the expansion of the hot gases produced by an explosion

BMD (ballistic missile defenses). A synonym for an *antiballistic missile* system

BMEWS (ballistic missile early warning system). A U.S. electronic defense network, based in Greenland, Scotland, and Alaska, established in the early 1960s to give early warning of incoming transpolar missiles

Bus. Reentry vehicle capable of limited postboost phase, which enables it to maneuver so as to sequentially dispense multiple warheads

CEP (circular error probable). A measure of the accuracy of missile attacks on point targets. It is the radius of a circle around the target within which half of the attacking missiles will fall

Chaff. Bits of metal or other material dispersed around an incoming *warhead* to confuse radar by reflecting multiple signals

Command and control system. The mechanisms for authorizing and directing the operations of the armed forces or some component thereof, such as the *Strategic Air Command*

Cost-exchange ratio. The ratio of the cost of a defensive system to the cost of the offensive force needed to overcome it

Counterforce attack (or strike). An attack in which weapons are aimed at opposing strategic launch vehicles—missiles or bombers—while they are still on the ground. (The term is also used to describe an attack against enemy forces at any time during a nuclear exchange)

Counterforce capability. The ability to destroy an enemy's strategic offensive forces through attacks on missiles and bombers before these can be launched

Countervalue attack (or strike). An attack in which weapons are aimed at civilian targets, such as industrial facilities and centers of population

Cruise missile. A missile powered by rocket or jet engines which flies like an airplane along most of its trajectory

Damage-limiting. A term describing the measures employed to reduce damage to a country from a nuclear attack by an enemy. These measures include *counterforce attacks* against adversary forces, *active defense,* and *passive defense*

Decoy. A *penetration aid* designed to complicate the problem of defending against a missile attack. A decoy or decoys might be detached from a *warhead* to increase the number of targets with which a defender must contend

Defensive forces. *See* Strategic forces

Delivery system. The collection of components—aircraft, missiles, or submarines, and their supporting equipment—which gets a weapon to its target

Depressed trajectory. A *ballistic missile* trajectory lower than a *minimum-energy trajectory;* in other words, a trajectory flatter than that normally used to fly missiles from one place to another

Discrimination. The art of distinguishing *decoys* and other *penetration aids* from nuclear *warheads*

ECM (electromagnetic countermeasures). Measures to baffle or delude radar and other electromagnetic devices for detecting or identifying incoming bombers or missiles

Endoatmospheric interception. Interception of enemy *warheads* after they enter the earth's atmosphere, i.e., below 150,000 feet

Endoatmospheric interceptor. An *antimissile missile* designed to operate effectively only within the earth's atmosphere, i.e., below 150,000 feet. It destroys or deflects incoming *reentry vehicles* by blast

Exhaustion. Attacking a given target with a larger number of *reentry vehicles* than the defender has interceptors, so that even if the defensive system works perfectly, some RVs will reach the target

Exoatmospheric interception. Interception of enemy *warheads* before they reenter the earth's atmosphere, i.e., above 150,000 feet

Exoatmospheric interceptor. An *antimissile missile* designed to operate effectively outside the earth's atmosphere, i.e., above 150,000 feet. It damages the incoming *reentry vehicle* or induces malfunctions by concentrated X rays or neutron flux

FB-111. Bomber version of the F-111 (TFX). (For details, see appendix table 1)

FBM. *See* SLM

Fireball. The luminous sphere of hot gases produced by a nuclear explosion

Fire storm. A phenomenon occurring in very large fires where the updraft produced by the fire causes winds to blow in toward the fire from all directions. In a fire storm, virtually all the combustible material within the area covered by the fire is burned

First strike. The launching of an initial nuclear attack—before the opponent attacked has used any strategic nuclear weapons

FOBS (fractional orbital bombardment system). A system involving the delivery of nuclear weapons from low-altitude orbital trajectories, thereby making detection by conventional long-range radars more difficult. The *payload* delivered by a given propulsion system is generally smaller than with an *ICBM*, and the accuracy is generally poorer

Footprint. Either (1) the area protected by one battery of *antimissile missiles* or (2) the pattern in which incoming *warheads* fall, associated primarily with *MRV* systems

Galosh. The NATO code for the Soviet exoatmospheric missile which is emplaced around Moscow. (For details, see appendix table 5)

Hardening. The protection of military facilities against damage from nuclear explosions. Land-based missiles are usually hardened by installation in underground silos with protective covers

Hard-point defense. *See* Terminal defense

ICBM (intercontinental ballistic missile). A long-range (6,000 to 8,000 mile) multistage rocket capable of delivering nuclear *warheads*

Interceptor missile. Surface-based missile used as part of either an air or an *antiballistic missile* defense system. Interceptors are divided into two classes: those designed for *exoatmospheric interception,* such as *Spartan,* and those designed for terminal or *endoatmospheric interception,* such as *Sprint* or Hawk

Ionization. The breakup of air or other substances into electrons and positively charged ions. Ionized substances conduct electricity and therefore reflect, refract, or absorb radar signals

IRBM (intermediate-range ballistic missile). A *ballistic missile* with a range of roughly 2,000 to 4,000 nautical miles. The United States has scrapped its Thor and Jupiter IRBMs, but the Soviets still carry them in inventory

KT (Kiloton). A unit of explosive force equal to 1,000 tons of TNT. *See also* Yield

Minimum-energy trajectory. The particular elliptical path followed by a *ballistic missile* for which the fuel needed to deliver a given *payload* at a given target is a minimum

Minuteman. The basic U.S. *ICBM* presently in deployment. (For details, see appendix table 1)

MIRV (multiple independently-targetable reentry vehicle). A system in which a *Bus* carries several separate *warheads,* with guidance systems which permit each of them to be delivered against separate targets. MIRVs will be incorporated in the U.S. *Minuteman* III and *Poseidon* missiles and could be placed on the SS-9 and other Soviet *ICBMs*

MRBM (medium-range ballistic missile). A *ballistic missile* with a range of about 1,500 nautical miles. The United States has never developed MRBMs, but the Soviets have deployed about 300 such missiles. (For details, see appendix table 3)

MRV (multiple reentry vehicle). A system of multiple *warheads* carried by one *reentry vehicle* or *Bus,* which are not independently targeted but are dispersed over a general target area. The U.S. *Polaris* A-3 carries MRVs and the Soviets have tested them

MSR (missile site radar). Part of the *Safeguard ABM* system. Performs surveillance and detection, target track, missile track, and command functions for the *Sprint* and *Spartan* missiles

MT (Megaton). A unit of explosive force equal to 1,000,000 tons of TNT. *See also* Yield

Neutron kill. The destruction of a nuclear *warhead* by neutrons from a nuclear-tipped *antimissile missile*

Nth power. The generic term for a country capable of "going nuclear" through the independent development of nuclear weapons or the acquisition of such weapons from an existing nuclear power

Offensive forces. *See* Strategic forces

Overpressure. The pressure in excess of ambient air pressure produced by a nuclear explosion, measured in pounds per square inch

Over-the-horizon radar. A long-range *ballistic missile* warning system that uses radar waves which are reflected back and forth between the earth's surface and the ionosphere and can therefore propagate over the horizon

PAR (perimeter acquisition radar). A long-range radar of the *Sentinel* and *Safeguard ABM* systems. Used for surveillance and tracking of incoming *warheads*

Passive defense. Defense of population or military facilities by protective shelters, *hardening*, dispersal, mobility, etc.

Payload. The useful weight which can be launched by a missile delivery system against an enemy target. This payload can either be in the form of a nuclear *warhead* or of *penetration aids* to overcome defenses

Penetration aids. Devices to aid the entry of aircraft or missiles through enemy *active defenses*. Penetration aids for missiles include *decoys, chaff,* and electronic jammers

Phased-array radars. Radars in which the beam is steered electronically and which therefore do not involve moving parts. They have an advantage over the older, mechanically steered radars in that they can handle many targets simultaneously and can be changed quickly from one target to another

Polaris. U.S. nuclear-powered, missile-launching submarine, carrying sixteen missiles. The term also refers to the missiles, of which there have been three versions. (For details, see appendix table 1)

Poseidon.   A new U.S. submarine-launched missile. Poseidon missiles have better accuracy, longer range, and higher *payload* than *Polaris* and will probably carry *MIRV*s. (For details, see appendix table 1)

Preemptive attack.   *First strike* against an adversary's offensive forces, population, or industry in anticipation of a possible attack by him

Radar cross section.   The effective reflecting area of an object observed with radar

RV (reentry vehicle).   That part of a missile which is designed to reenter the earth's atmosphere and at least part of which (the *warhead)* is to reach the earth's surface without burning up

SABMIS   (sea-based antiballistic missile system).   Defensive missiles mounted on surface vessels to intercept enemy *warheads* in mid flight, before the land-based defensive system can reach them, so as to destroy an enemy missile before it scatters a number of separate warheads and *decoys*

SAC (Strategic Air Command).   The U.S. force of intercontinental bombers and land-based missiles

Safeguard.   The modification of the *Sentinel ABM* system announced by President Nixon on March 14, 1969. It differs mainly in that it cannot be as readily converted into a "thick" or "extensive" system capable of protecting cities against large-scale attacks

SAGE (semiautomatic ground environment).   A U.S. command and control system designed to provide instantaneous information by computer for air defense operations

SALT (Strategic Arms Limitation Talks).   The name given to the series of discussions on the control of *strategic nuclear forces* which began in 1970 at Vienna and are (as of 1971) still continuing

SAM (surface-to-air missile).   A missile launched from the earth's surface to intercept a target in the air

Saturation.   Attacking a given target with a larger number of *reentry vehicles* than the system can handle simultaneously, so that some RVs get through to the target

SCAD (subsonic cruise armed decoy).   A relatively long-range bomber-launched cruise missile now under development by the United States

Second strike.   The launching of a retaliatory attack, following the initial use of nuclear weapons by an opponent

Second-strike capability.   The capability to deliver nuclear weapons on an enemy after absorbing a *first strike*

Sentinel.   An American *ABM* system capable of protecting cities against small-scale attacks and potentially expandable into a "thick" system offering protection against larger attacks. *See* Safeguard

Shoot-look-shoot missile control system.   A system whereby the impact areas of nuclear *warheads* are determined (presumably by satellite monitoring) and subsequent missiles are launched only against those targets not hit the first time. The aim is to increase the efficiency of counterforce operations, albeit at the cost of some delay in sorting out enemy missile sites

SLM (submarine-launched missile).   A missile mounted on long-range submarines, which can be utilized to attack either tactical targets such as ships, harbor defenses, etc., or strategic targets such as bomber bases. Divided into:
    SLBM—Submarine-launched ballistic missile (sometimes called fleet ballistic missile or FBM), and
    SLCM—submarine-launched cruise missile

Soft facilities.   Missile sites, command and control centers, or other facilities that have not been provided with protective shielding against nearby nuclear explosions

Spartan.   A long-range exoatmospheric *antimissile missile* which is a part of the U.S. *ABM* system. (For further details, see appendix table 4)

Sprint.   A short-range endoatmospheric *antimissile missile* which is a part of the U.S. *ABM* system. (For further details, see appendix table 4)

SRAM (short-range attack missile).   An *air-to-surface* missile scheduled to be deployed in fiscal year 1970 by the United States

SS-9.   A large Soviet liquid-fueled *ICBM*. (For details, see appendix table 2)

SS-11.   The liquid-fueled missile that comprises more than half of the Soviet *ICBM* force. (For details, see appendix table 2)

SS-13.   The latest Soviet *ICBM* and the first to employ solid fuel. In range, *payload,* and accuracy it is considered roughly equivalent to the American *Minuteman* I. (For further details, see appendix table 2)

SSN.   Nuclear-powered submarine

Strategic alert.   A status of heightened readiness for a strategic attack prompted by international political developments

Strategic forces (or strategic nuclear forces).   Includes offensive forces (long-range bombers, *IRBMs*, missile-launching submarines, etc.) capable of delivering nuclear weapons against military targets, industrial sites, and population centers; and defensive forces (fighter-interceptors, *surface-to-air missiles*, etc.) designed to defend against such attacks

Tallinn.   A defensive *SAM* system deployed by the USSR, which takes its name from the fact that some of the facilities were located near Tallinn, Estonia. The prevailing view in the U.S. intelligence community today is that the Tallinn system is an antiaircraft system with no significant capability to shoot down *antiballistic missiles*

Terminal defenses (also known as hard-point defenses).   Defenses designed to intercept a missile during the final part of its trajectory. The missiles are deployed to defend one point and cannot defend other points some distance away

Titan II.   A liquid-fueled U.S. *ICBM* carrying a *warhead* of several *megatons*. (For details, see appendix table 1)

ULMS (underwater long-range missile system).   A possible future U.S. missile system which would provide U.S. nuclear submarines with long-range missiles, supplementing or replacing the present medium-range *Polaris* and the projected *Poseidon* missiles

VRBM (variable-range ballistic missile).   A Soviet missile whose trajectory (and hence range) can be adjusted to strike at either midrange or distant targets

Warhead.   Either (1) that part of a *reentry vehicle* containing the nuclear explosives, fuzes, etc., or (2) a synonym for any *reentry vehicle*, bomb, or other device, as in "deliverable warheads"

X-ray kill.   The process by which X rays, generated by the explosion of a nuclear *warhead* on an exoatmospheric *ABM*, destroy or neutralize *reentry vehicles* at great distances

Yield.   The total effective energy produced in a nuclear explosion. Usually expressed as an equivalent tonnage of TNT *(kilotons or megatons)*

Index

211